D0897742

THE

CREEK WAR

OF

1813 AND 1814

Southern Historical Publications No. 15

THE

CREEK WAR

OF

1813 AND 1814

BY

H. S. HALBERT AND T. H. BALL

Edited, with Introduction and Notes,

BY

FRANK L. OWSLEY, JR.

UNIVERSITY OF ALABAMA PRESS
UNIVERSITY, ALABAMA

E
83,813
H15
1969

Copyright © 1969 by University of Alabama Press
Standard Book Number: 8173-5220-1
Library of Congress Catalog Card Number: 74-92656
Manufactured in the United States of America

24552

TABLE OF CONTENTS.

STRAND B.A. 4.50 1970/71

EDITOR'S ACKNOWLEDGMENTS.

THE editor wishes to express appreciation to Auburn University for providing him with the free time and financial assistance necessary to complete this project. He also wishes to express his thanks to his wife, Mrs. Dorothy Owsley, and to Mrs. James B. Sellers and Mrs. Marsha Williams for their clerical help. In addition he extends thanks to Milo Howard and his staff at the Department of Archives and History, Montgomery, Alabama, for their aid and suggestions, and to Dr. Malcolm C. McMillan for his good advice.

EDITOR'S INTRODUCTION.

The Creek War of 1813 and 1814 is by far the most detailed and probably the most accurate of the older works dealing with the Creek War. In writing this account Henry Sale Halbert and Timothy Horton Ball relied heavily upon the manuscripts and reminiscences of contemporaries. In addition they made good use of Albert J. Pickett's *History of Alabama,* J. F. H. Claiborne's *Mississippi as a Province, Territory, and State,* and A. B. Meek's unpublished "History of Alabama," which were the best secondary accounts available at the time.[1] Their use of manuscripts and reminiscences is probably their most valuable contribution to modern scholarship, since much of the material they preserved would have been lost otherwise. The authors' great familiarity with the area of South Alabama and Mississippi during the early period makes their volume necessary reading for anyone wishing to study the history of the region. They have managed to preserve an authenticity of the location and an understanding of the participants in the war that it would not be possible to recreate today.

The most valuable portions of this work are those dealing with the causes of the war and with its early stages in the Mississippi Territory. The rather cursory treatment of Andrew Jackson's campaigns and the activities of the Georgia armies is the major weakness, and because of it the book is not an adequate account of the entire war. The authors justified this shortcoming on the ground that this phase of the war was well covered in the plethora of biographies of Andrew Jackson—a statement more accurate today than at the time their volume was published.[2] Unfortunately, no author has given adequate coverage to the actions of the Georgia armies in the war, and it therefore remains for future historians to complete the work in that area, and to relate the action of the Tennessee, Georgia, and Mississippi Territorial armies in the final defeat of the Creek nation. It also remains for future historians to relate the Creek War to the larger War of 1812, of which it became a part.

In common with nearly all writers who have dealt with this conflict, Halbert and Ball had to rely on American sources for their research, for they did not have the advantage of access to the numerous British and Spanish records that bear on the subject. The abundant manuscript materials pertaining to the Creek War that are available in the British Museum, the National Library of Scotland, the British Public Record Office, and in the Archivo General de Indias in Seville have not been explored by American authors writing about the conflict, but future scholars who wish to see the Creek War in its true perspective and to prove or disprove the many speculations about it will find it necessary to research those foreign archives.

An unusual feature of Halbert and Ball's work is their largely successful effort to present the Indians' viewpoint and to explain why the usually friendly Creeks went to war and the Choctaws and Chickasaws did not. It is in this area that the authors have done some of their best work, especially in their account of the reactions of the Choctaws to the persuasion of Tecumseh and others who would have led them to the warpath. This emphasis should interest all students of the Indian wars. The Creeks' grievances are well described—their loss of land to the white man and their rejection of the cultural changes that were being imposed upon them by the white man's influence. Certainly Halbert and Ball have captured most of the facts as well as the feelings of both the Indians and whites.

Source material for the Creek War as the Indians saw it is quite rare, of course, owing to the total absence of any written records. It is usually possible to gain some idea of the Indians' feelings from the correspondence of their agents, but the letters of the Creeks' agent, Benjamin Hawkins, are sparse and poorly informed during the critical period when the war turned from a Creek civil war to hostilities against the white man. Hawkins was one of the ablest of Indian agents, and he carried on perhaps the most voluminous correspondence of any of them, but he was seriously ill during the crucial period when the sentiment for war was growing and was unable to travel among the Creeks to observe their activities at first hand.[3] His illness· was significant not only because he could not report adequately the activities of the Indians at the outset of the war, but also because there is good reason to believe that if he had been well and active he might have been able to prevent the war entirely or at least to limit its spread somewhat.

Despite friendship for the Indians, the authors did not attempt to gloss over the Indian atrocities. Neither did they condone the campaign of extermination that Jackson and some other American generals carried out. In deploring the atrocities of both whites and Indians, Halbert and Ball achieved a balance and impartiality most unusual in accounts of Indian wars, especially those written late in the nineteenth century.

In presenting their narrative as they did, the authors managed to depict quite graphically the horrors of Indian war and to show how the hatreds generated by such conflicts made peace between white and Indian extremely difficult of attainment.

The relative scarcity of material relating to the Indian side of the conflict has made it very hard to find information that can be compared or contrasted with the material offered in this book. The editor was fortunate in locating a manuscript account of the war's first stages that proved to be of invaluable assistance in evaluating the work of Halbert and Ball. This manuscript, "History of the Creek Nation," was written by George Stiggins, a literate half-breed.[4] Although Stiggins served on the side of the white man, he was well acquainted with a number of hostile Indians, and was therefore able to provide information not available in any other source.[5] Since the Stiggins manuscript was not used by Halbert and Ball, a comparison is especially useful. The significant fact, one that becomes apparent very quickly, is that the two accounts are very similar. They differ on a few points, but in the main the differences are in matters of detail. Their similarity obviously strengthens the claim of both accounts to accuracy.

The authors of *The Creek War* were both well-educated men who lived for many years in the area about which they wrote. Henry Sale Halbert was born in Pickens County, Alabama, on January 14, 1837, of parents who had come there from South Carolina.[6] He was raised in Lowndes County, Mississippi, and received the fine education usually provided for the son of a large planter.[7] In Halbert's case, this included attendance at good academies and, in 1857, an M.A. degree from Union University in Tennessee. He then served as a soldier with Texas state troops on the frontier. Most of this military service, which lasted from April 2 to October 14, 1860, involved actions against the Indians. At the start of the Civil War, Halbert enlisted as a private in the Confederate Army and served in the 6th Texas Cavalry throughout the war. He was severely wounded at New Hope, Georgia, on May 16, 1864, and did not return to duty until a few months before the war's end.

From 1866 to 1872 Halbert taught at Waco University, an institution that later merged with Baylor University, and from 1872 until 1884 he was an instructor at a number of different academies in Texas, Alabama, and Mississippi. But probably the most significant experience in his teaching career—and one that prepared him to do this book—was the educational work that he did among the Choctaw Indians of Mississippi from 1884 through 1899. It was during this period that Halbert obtained the intimate knowledge of Indians that was to inform most of his writing. Some idea of how vast his knowledge of Indians was can be obtained from his papers in the Alabama Department of Archives and History in Montgomery. During his lifetime Halbert was recognized as one of the nation's leading authorities on the Choctaws, and his knowledge of the Creeks was almost as good.

In addition to writing numerous short articles for the *American Antiquarian, The American Anthropologist, The Transactions of the Mississippi Historical Society, The Transactions of the Alabama Historical Society,* and various Baptist papers, Halbert also served as co-editor (with Dr. John R. Swanton) of Bulletin 46,

Bureau of American Ethnology, which is an edition of Cyrus Byington's dictionary of the Choctaw language.[8] It was during the period of his work with the Choctaws that Halbert made his contribution to *The Creek War,* the work that must be counted his most significant endeavor. In addition, he wrote a history of the Choctaw Indians which was never published.

Halbert's scholarly activity cannot be fully assessed in terms of his own publications, since he was quite willing to help other historians and ethnologists in their work. Thus, for example, he supplied a large amount of information concerning the Creek War and the Choctaw Indians to the famous frontier historian Lyman Draper, and there are numerous Halbert letters in the Draper Collection.[9]

During the last twelve years of his life Halbert was a clerk in the State Department of Archives and History at Montgomery, Alabama. Still a bachelor, he died of tuberculosis on May 9, 1916.[10]

The other author, Timothy Horton Ball, was born at Agawam, Hampden County, Massachusetts, on February 16, 1826. He came from a fairly well-to-do New England family and received a good education, including baccalaureate and master's degrees from Franklin College (in 1850 and 1853, respectively), and a divinity degree from Newton Theological Institution (in 1863). As a teacher and Baptist preacher Ball lived in a number of places, but his many years' residence in Clarke County, Alabama were of some special significance, for it was during those years that he wrote *A Glance into the Great Southwest or Clarke County Alabama, and its Surroundings from 1540 to 1877* and, still more importantly, obtained much of the material he would later use in *The Creek War.*[11] Ball, like Halbert, was an extremely active collector of all manner of historical information. During his Clarke County years he was reputed to have the largest library in the county, the contents of which he generously shared with the area's young students. He had the reputation of spending much of his time walking through the region and of passing many hours in conversation with old settlers. He kept careful notes of the settlers' reminiscences, pressing them for details and constantly cross-checking the facts one against the other for accuracy. In this way Ball collected large quantities of primary historical data.[12] The similarity of information found in his earlier *History of Clarke County* shows that he made a significant contribution to the factual material contained in his joint effort with Halbert.[13]

Ball was an extremely prolific writer, and sixteen different titles by him are listed by the Library of Congress. Some of these are short pamphlets, to be sure, but many are books of 300 to 500 pages. The range of interests covered by these publications is quite wide, including poetry, music, county and regional histories, genealogy, and numerous religious subjects.[14] In addition to those catalogued by the Library of Congress, the titles of several other works by Ball are listed in Thomas M. Owen's *Dictionary of Alabama Biography*. He married Martha Caroline Creighton of Clarke County, Alabama, and they had two children. Ball died November 8, 1913, at Crown Point, Indiana.[15]

The editor has been unable to discover precisely how Halbert and Ball became acquainted or how they went about writing *The Creek War*. However, they were both active Baptists and both extremely interested in work with the Indians, and it is possible that they became acquainted as a result of one or the other of these common concerns. As for their respective contributions to *The Creek War,* one must again rely largely on conjecture, but it is fair to suppose that both men furnished in about equal parts the information used in the volume. Ball was almost certainly the editor of the book, however, and very likely wrote and organized most, if not all, of the final version; he was, after all, an extremely prolific writer whereas Halbert never published a book-length work of his own. At all events, the final product is a very useful study of white and Indian conflict and remains, after seventy-five years, the best history of the Creek War to be published to date.

Auburn, Alabama   FRANK LAWRENCE OWSLEY, JR.
June 1, 1969

FOOTNOTES

[1]Albert J. Pickett, *History of Alabama, and Incidentally of Georgia and Mississippi from the Earliest Period,* 2 vols. (Charleston, 1851); J. F. H. Claiborne, *Mississippi, as a Province, Territory, and State, with Biographical Notices of Eminent Citizens* (Jackson, 1880); A. B. Meek, "History of Alabama," unpublished manuscript in Alabama Department of Archives and History, Montgomery, Alabama.

[2]Henry S. Halbert and Timothy H. Ball, *The Creek War of 1813 and 1814* (Chicago, 1895) pp. 13–14.

[3]See Hawkins letters to the Secretary of War, Letters to the Secretary of War, Record Group 107, National Archives, Washington, D.C.; Collected letters of Benjamin Hawkins, Georgia Department of Archives and History, Atlanta, Georgia.

[4]George Stiggins, "History of the Creek Nation," Georgia, Alabama, and South Carolina Papers, MSS I–V, Lyman Draper Manuscript Collection, State Historical Society of Wisconsin, Madison, Wisconsin.

[5]J. Pierce to Harry Toulmin, Jul. 13, 1813, enclosure in Willie Blount to the Secretary of War, Aug. 18, 1813, Letters to the Secretary of War, Record Group 107.

[6]Thomas M. Owen, *History of Alabama and Dictonary of Alabama Biography*, 4 vols. (Chicago, 1921), vol. 3, p. 723.

[7]Mobile *Register*, May 11, 1916.

[8]Owen, *History of Alabama*, vol. 3, pp. 723–24.

[9]A number of Halbert letters are located in the Tecumseh Papers, 4YY, Draper Manuscript Collection, State Historical Society of Wisconsin.

[10]Owen, *History of Alabama*, vol. 3, pp. 723–24; Mobile *Register*, May 11, 1816.

[11]Owen, *History of Alabama*, vol. 3, pp. 84–85.

[12]Montgomery *Advertiser*, Mar. 16, 1941.

[13]Timothy H. Ball, *A Glance into the Great South-Eas., or, Clarke County, and its Surroundings From 1540 to 1877* (Grove Hill, Alabama, 1882).

[14]William Warner Bishop *et al.*, eds., *The Association of Research Libraries, A Catalog of Books Represented by Library of Congress Printed Cards, Issued to July 31, 1942*, 164 vols. (Ann Arbor, Michigan, 1942–1946), vol. 9, pp. 60–61.

[15]Owen, *History of Alabama*, vol. 3, p. 85.

THE

CREEK WAR

OF

1813 AND 1814

T. H. BALL,

Historical Secretary of the Old Settlers' Association of Lake County, Indiana;

Honorary member of Lake County Teachers' Association;

Active Member of Indiana Academy of Science;

Corresponding Member of Wisconsin State Historical Society;

Honorary Member of Trinity Historical Society of Texas.

Author of

Lake County, 1834–1872,
Lake of the Red Cedars,
Clarke County, Alabama,
Notes on Luke's Gospel
Poems and Hymns
Annie B., &c., &c.

H. S. HALBERT,

Member of Mississippi State Historical Society;

Member of Alabama State Historical Society;

Contributor to American Antiquarian;

Contributor to Alabama Historical Reporter.

THE

CREEK WAR

OF

1813 AND 1814.

BY

H. S. HALBERT AND T. H. BALL.

———

CHICAGO, ILLINOIS:
DONOHUE & HENNEBERRY.

MONTGOMERY, ALABAMA:
WHITE, WOODRUFF, & FOWLER.

1895.

COPYRIGHT, 1895,

BY

H. S. HALBERT AND T. H BALL.

DONOHUE & HENNEBERRY,
PRINTERS AND BINDERS,
CHICAGO.

PREFACE

WHEN this work was commenced, several years ago, it was not expected that it would become in size what it has grown to be. It was then expected only to give facts in regard to the Creek war as connected with the white settlers in what is now South Alabama, giving especially a fuller account of the attack on Fort Sinquefield with other gathered reminiscences and traditions. But when large libraries were examined and many historical works were consulted, and so little that was really reliable could be found in regard to that border war, and its real beginning seeming to be altogether unknown to Northern writers, it was thought best to make thorough research and to prepare a somewhat voluminous work for the sake of those, or for the use of those, who, in years to come, in the North as well as in the South, might justly be expected to be interested in a work as full, and, in some respects, as minute in details, as this.

If, therefore, any readers should think that some of the chapters, as those in regard to Tecumseh and Fort Mims, are more full than was needful, or that, in some others, too many personal, biographical incidents and sketches or notes are given, let them please bear in mind that the work is designed for more than one class of readers; let the more critical charitably trust that there will be some readers interested in the minute details and the apparent

digressions; and let all who may read rest assured
that the authors have, with the idea of different
classes of readers before their minds, endeavored
faithfully to obtain and impartially to present historic truth.

November 19, 1894.

———————

Well may the inhabitants of Alabama, especially,
say in regard to the Red men,

> "Though 'mid the forests where they roved,
>   There rings no hunter's shout,
> Yet their names are on our waters,
>   And we may not wash them out;"

for well, of the Indian tongue, as speaking in the
flowing waters, does an Alabama poet say,

> " 'Tis heard where CHATTAHOOCHEE pours
>   His yellow tide along;
> It sounds on TALLAPOOSA's shores,
>   And COOSA swells the song;
> Where lordly ALABAMA sweeps,
>   The symphony remains;
> And young CAHAWBA proudly keeps
>   The echo of its strains;
> Where TUSCALOOSA's waters glide,
>   From stream and town 'tis heard,
> And dark TOMBECKBEE's winding tide
>   Repeats the olden word;
> Afar, where Nature brightly wreathed
>   Fit Edens for the free,
> Along TUSCUMBIA's bank 'tis breathed,
>   By stately TENNESSEE;
> And south, where, from CONECUH's springs,
>   ESCAMBIA's waters steal,
> The ancient melody still rings,—
>   From TENSAW and MOBILE."

CONTENTS.

INTRODUCTION.

THIS work proposes to give as accurate an account as can now be obtained from written and printed records, from traditions, and from personal observation, of that portion of American history known as the Creek War of 1813 and 1814.

Of these Creek Indians says BREWER, author of a history of Alabama: "In 1813 and 1814 they waged the bloodiest war against the whites anywhere recorded in the annals of the United States."

Says MEEK, one of Alabama's talented orators and poets: "Time as it passed on and filled these solitudes with settlers, at last brought the most sanguinary era in Alabama history."

And PICKETT, recognized as Alabama's leading historian, says: "Everything foreboded the extermination of the Americans in Alabama, who were the most isolated and defenseless people imaginable."

The reader who comes to our "Conclusion" may be disposed to change BREWER's statement; but he will not question the statements of PICKETT and MEEK.

But this work does not propose to give in full that part of the conflict waged in the Indian country which broke the power of the fierce Muscogees; but rather that part which has not been as yet so fully given, connected with the white settlers in what is now South Alabama. This portion of our

American history, as connected with Indian border warfare, the authors of this work believe will be given more accurately and fully than has ever been done before. They propose to do justice to the Indians and justice to the whites.

For this portion of history they hope to make this work an authority. And for this they suggest the possession of some special fitness:

H. S. Halbert is a member of the State Historical Societies of Alabama and Mississippi. He was born in Alabama, and was, in a great measure, educated by the late Dr. J. H. Eaton, of Murfreesboro, Tennessee. He spent a portion of his early manhood in Indian campaigns on the western frontier, where he became familiar with the sight of the wild warrior with his bow and quiver, his paint and feathers; and there he conceived an abiding interest in the strange history and destiny of the American Indians. He has also been not a little among the civilized tribes of the Indian Territory. After four years of service in the Confederate army, he was for a number of years engaged in teaching in Texas, Mississippi, and Alabama. While pursuing his profession in the two latter states he devoted much of his leisure to historical researches. He visited the homes and interviewed some surviving soldiers and contemporaries of the Creek war of 1813 and noted down their varied recollections, thereby collecting much new material for the history of that war. He was especially fortunate in securing from these aged survivors a full account of the attack on Fort Sinquefield, of which only a meagre sketch is recorded in the histories of Meek and Pickett.

For a number of years past he has been engaged in educational work among the Choctaws of Mississippi, with whose language, customs, and traditions he is familiar. From the immediate descendants of some of Pushmataha's warriors he has been enabled to rescue from oblivion a number of incidents in the career of that noted Mingo, and many facts in regard to Tecumseh's Southern visit. He has, in short, been interested largely for years in studies and investigations connected with the Southern Indians, and has visited in person and examined with care the Burnt Corn and Holy Ground battlefields. The Alabama Historical Reporter for January, 1885, said: "Mr. H. S. Halbert is now doing more than any man in the South, perhaps, in collecting everything connected with the Southern Indians in the shape of history, tradition, romance, legend, etc."

T. H. Ball had an early home in the state of Georgia, before 1833, not far from the Savannah River, and learned some of the customs and ways of the South; but in 1837, when eleven years of age, his home was transferred to the then almost untenanted solitudes of Northwestern Indiana (where the great prairie region of the West joined the woodland growth that extended to the Atlantic) and to the banks of a beautiful lake in the region then but lately occupied by the Pottawatomie Indians, some thirty-six miles from the old Fort Dearborn of Lake Michigan, some seventy-two miles from the Tippecanoe battle ground. He gained in those years of boyhood some knowledge of the Indians—Indians that had been associated with French missionaries and with fur traders—as he saw them in their wigwams, on their ponies, in their large birch-bark canoes, and when returning from the chase, and took a deep interest in Indian history and in pioneer and hunter life. His young footsteps followed the wild game and his rifle secured it where his almost immediate predecessors had been Indian hunters.

From 1851 to 1855 he resided as a teacher in Clarke county, Alabama, and was there again no small part of the time in 1859 and 1860, and from 1874 to 1883. With the region around the old Fort Sinquefield he became thoroughly familiar, examined carefully the location of Fort Madison and Fort Glass, saw the location of Fort White, and became well acquainted with all that early center of white settlement and of once crowded stockades.

Eggleston relies much upon Meek for localities and for facts in Clarke county, saying that he was familiar with that region. But neither Meek, nor even Pickett, seems to have had any personal knowledge of that fifteen hundred square miles of area now constituting Clarke county, Alabama. No other writer on this portion of history, has, so far as appears, been on the very ground of these forts and so has had a personal knowledge of the geography and topography of this region. Knowledge thus gained, and applied in some portions of this history, is what is meant by "personal observation" in the first sentence of this "Introduction." And not only did this writer have an opportunity to examine these localities well, but he was an inmate for several months in the home of Major Austill of the Canoe Fight, then residing near the old Fort Carney, was well acquainted with Isham Kimbell, Esq., a survivor of the

Kimbell-James massacre, and with others who as men and women or as children were in the different forts, and who passed through the trying scenes of the summer and fall of 1813.

In a valuable history of Indiana, by DeWitt C. Goodrich and Professor Charles R. Tuttle, a table is given, with names and dates, of "Sixteen American Wars." Among these are named King Philip's 1677, Tecumseh's 1811, First Seminole 1817, Black Hawk's 1832, Second Seminole 1845; but of the Creek War no mention is made. Did the writers forget that war? Or did they consider it of no importance?

That the Creek war should be better known at the South than in the North is natural; and that there, at least, it should be considered quite as deserving of a name and place among American Wars as Black Hawk's War or 'es Tecumseh's, is also natural. But surely the time has come, especially now, since that gathering of the millions on Lake Michigan's shore at the Columbian Exposition, the great World's Fair of 1893, when those who read and study our history in all parts of the land should be restricted to no localities and influenced by no prejudices in looking at our various conflicts with the Indian tribes.

The youth of the South should know something of the Pequods and the Narragansetts and of King Philip and of Black Hawk and of Pontiac, as should those of the North of Weatherford and of Big Warrior, and of Choctaws, Seminoles, and Muscogees.

Of the authors of this history it may be noticed that one was born in New England and the other in the South; that one was with the Confederates in that war that opened in 1861, and the other was, in the years of that strife in New England and Indiana, graduating at the Newton Theological Institution in 1863, standing constantly under "the stars and stripes;" that both have spent years in the South and have many friends there; and that both, as true Americans, and as interested in all facts connected with the aboriginees of this country, having devoted years of life to teaching, have here united their efforts to prepare for those who are now and who are yet to be, in the East and the West, in the North Central States and in the South, a readable, a full, an accurate account of that truly "bloody" Creek War. These statements are made as suggesting that the writers of this volume, both as free as any who can easily be found from local and educational prejudices and favoritisms, each having pursued his own line of research, are not without some special qualifications for the work which they have undertaken.

H. S. H.

T. H. B.

THE CREEK WAR.

CHAPTER I.

THE CHOCTAW—MUSCOGEE TRIBES.

THE Creek War of 1813 and 1814 is remarkable from the fact that all the branches of what ethnologists style the Choctaw-Muscogee stock of Indians were involved therein and took a part, on one side or the other, of that bloody conflict. As these tribes acted a prominent part in the early history of the Gulf States, a brief notice of their topographic location and ethnic affinites may, perhaps, be of interest to the general reader.

From incontrovertible linguistic evidence, it is certain that the habitat of the tribes composing the Choctaw—Muscogee family was much the same in the days of De Soto, in 1540, as it was in more recent historical times. If the Creeks, or any or all their congeners, ever migrated from Mexico, it must have been centuries before the advent of the Spanish invader. Whatever may be thought of Le Clerc Milfort's migration legend, the fact stands that De Soto found towns bearing Muscogee names in Alabama. Dr. A. S. Gatschet, the distinguished Indianologist, after a thorough study of the dialects of the Choctaw—Muscogee tribes, has subdivided the family into four branches.

The first and most prominent of these branches is the Creeks or Muscogees proper, whose settlements were upon the Coosa, the Tallapoosa, and the Chattahoochee. During the entire existence of the Creek Confederacy in Alabama, those living on the Coosa and Tallapoosa bore the appellation of Upper Creeks, whilst those on the Chattahoochee were known as Lower Creeks. The Seminoles of Florida are only a body of seceded Muscogees.

The second branch is the Hitchitees, whose towns were on the Chattahoochee, and who, living nearer the Lower Creeks, were assigned to that political division of the Creek Confederacy. The Mickasukees of Leon county, Florida, are an off-shoot of the Hitchitees and speak the same language. The Apalachees, who were a numerous and powerful people in Florida in the days of De Narvaez and De Soto, spoke a language closely related to that of the Hitchitees. The last remnant of the Apalachees were living in Louisiana, in 1830, numbering forty six souls—perhaps, now, all extinct.

The third branch is the Alibamos and Coshattees, (less correct form Coosawdas,) whose homes were mostly situated on the Alabama River, just below the confluence of the Coosa and Tallapoosa. Politically, these two tribes belonged to the Upper Creeks. When the French abandoned Fort Toulouse, in 1763, many of the Alibamos followed them across the Mississippi into Louisiana. These seceders eventually settled in Polk county, Texas, where they have a settlement to this day. Towards the close of the eighteenth century, many of the Coshattees also emigrated west and finally settled near the Alibamos. The language of both tribes is substantially the same. The Alibamos that remained in their native seats occupied, at the outbreak of the war of 1813, six villages, viz: Wetumka, situated on the Coosa, Muklasa, on the Tallapoosa, Ecunchattee, now a part of the city of Montgomery, Towassa on the same side of the river, three miles below Ecunchattee, Pawoktee, two miles below Towassa, and Autaugee, four miles below Pawoktee, but on the north bank of the river and near the mouth of a creek of the same name. The language of the Alibamos approximates nearer to the Choctaw than to the Muscogee, and their tribal name is undoubtedly of Choctaw origin and signifies Vegetation-gatherers, i.e. *gatherers of vegetation* in clearing land for agricultural purposes. Alba, *vegetation,* amo, *gather.* From this tribe, the Alabama River received its name, and the state, from the river. Alibamo is the correct form of the word, having, as noted above, the prosaic signification of vegetation-gatherer ; for modern research has forever annihilated the romance of *Here we rest.* The Coshattees, the kinsfolk of the Alibamos, lived, in 1813, on the northern bank of the Alabama River, three miles below the confluence of the Coosa and Tallapoosa. The present American town of Coosauda occupies the site of the old Coshattee town.

The fourth or western branch of the Choctaw–Muscogee stock of Indians are the Choctaws and Chickasaws, whose homes were mostly in the present state of Mississippi, the Choctaws occupying the central and southern, and the Chickasaws, the northern part. Both tribes speak the same language. The country between the Tombigbee and the Black

Warrior, from time immemorial, had been disputed
territory between the Choctaws and the Creeks,
though Choctaw settlements, more or less tran-
sitory, always existed on the east side of the
Tombigbee.

There is no doubt but the territory of the Choctaws, in the days of De Soto, extended farther to the
east than in more recent times. The people of the
town of Mauvila, destroyed by De Soto, were of
Choctaw lineage, as is evidenced by the name of their
chief, Tascalusa, *Black Warrior*. Mauvila, too, may be
the Choctaw Moelih, a plural of action, signifying to
row, to *paddle*, to *scull*, and the inhabitants of the
town, as we may conjecture, may have received this
name, *the rowers*, in consequence of their riparian situation, which necessitated a constant use of boats in
navigating the river. Mobile, a French abbreviated
corruption of Mauvila, is called by the modern Choctaws, Mo-il-la, a form bearing a close resemblance to
both Mauvila and Moelih.* The people of the
province of Pafallaya were also Choctaws—a fact
attested by the name itself—Pafallaya, by elision
[1]   from Pashfallaya, the long-haired.

The Chickasaws, who occupied not only North
Mississippi, but also a part of Northwest Alabama,
were a more martial people than their Choctaw kindred. No enemy, white or red, ever defeated them
in battle. They made a fierce resistance to the in-
vasion of De Soto and their subsequent wars with
the French have added a luminous chapter to the
annals of the Southwest.

---

* In Moelih *oe* must not be considered a diphthong. Both vowels
must be separately and distinctly pronounced.   H. S. H.

But not all the peoples living within the territorial bounds of the Choctaw-Muscogee tribes were of kindred blood. Living within and forming a component part of the Creek Confederacy were some allophylic elements. The Uchees, who claim to be the most ancient inhabitants of the country and whose language has no affinity with any other American tongue, were, in the eighteenth century, incorporated into the Confederacy and enrolled as Lower Creeks. In like manner, among the Upper Creeks, [2] were enrolled many Shawnees, a people of the Algonquin stock. Sawanogee, on the Tallapoosa, was a Shawnee town, subject to the Creek laws. A remnant of the celebrated Natchez tribe also lived among the Upper Creeks, having a village on Tallahatchee Creek, a tributary of the Coosa.

Of the Choctaw-Muscogee tribes, the Creeks, or Muscogees proper, stood pre-eminent over all the others, not only for prowess in war, but for political sagacity. The beginning of their famous Confederacy is lost in the depths of antiquity. The Muscogees, it seems, having gained, in ancient times, a supremacy over the contiguous tribes, adopted the custom of receiving into a political system tribes that they had subjugated in war, or else, broken or fugitive tribes that applied to them for protection. A district was forthwith assigned to the new allies, who were allowed to retain the use of their own language and customs, but were required to furnish aid for the maintenance and defense of the Confederacy. Towards the close of the eighteenth century a tradition was current among the Creeks that the Alibamos were the first tribe received into the Confederacy, then the Coshattees, then the Natchez, and last, the Uchees and Shawnees.

When the French first came in contact with the Southern Indians, early in the eighteenth century the Creek Confederacy already had a vigorous existence. Its power continually strengthened, until, in the early years of the nineteenth century, it stood forth, able to confront, for near ten months, the trained armies of the Federal Government and to threaten even the very existence of the numerous American communities within the present states of Mississippi and Alabama.

CHAPTER II.

CAUSES OF THE CREEK WAR.

THE part of Alabama, with which, mainly, this work has to do, has had a peculiar history and also some peculiar inhabitants. It may be well to rehearse briefly this history.

Every well informed American knows that Spain at first claimed and afterwards held Florida by " right of discovery," and its northern boundary was undefined ; that Georgia, as the last of the thirteen colonies, was settled by the English in 1733; and that the French came down the Mississippi as early as 1682, and claimed from the Great Lakes to the Gulf. In 1763 France ceded to Great Britain nearly all her claims east of the Mississippi and Spain ceded Florida to Great Britain.* The English divided Florida into two provinces, calling one East and the other West Florida. The latter extended as far north as latitude 32° 28′, which was the southern boundary of the English province called Illinois. As early as 1700-1699—the French commencing settlements on Mobile Bay, claimed what is now Alabama, and they held it for sixty-four years. They made

---

* The year 1763, the young reader will remember, marked the close of the French and Indian war by the treaty of Paris.

some settlements up the Mobile and Tensaw rivers.
In 1777 Anglo-Saxon or American settlements commenced along these rivers and up the Tombigbee.
In 1783 West Florida went again into the possession of Spain, and the Spanish officials did not retire
south of latitude 31° until 1799. During the War
of the Revolution, and so long as Spanish rule continued, this river region attracted settlers from the
Carolinas who were not satisfied with American
independence. But after 1800, following the royalists or tories, came also the loyal and true American
pioneers. The flags of three nations therefore, of
France, of England, and of Spain, had waved over
the waters of these rivers before the stars and stripes,
in 1799 were here unfurled.

Before proceeding further in the history we may
look at some of the peculiar inhabitants.

Of this whole south-eastern portion of the country a characteristic feature was, in the latter part of
the eighteenth century, the residence of white traders in every large Indian town, and at points well
adapted for commerce and for intrigue. At Fort
Toulouse on the Coosa river, established by the
French in 1714, Captain Marchand was at one time
commander. He was killed there in 1722. He had
taken as a wife a Muscogee or Creek maiden of the
Clan of the Wind, called the most powerful clan of
the Creek nation. He had a beautiful daughter
called Sehoy Marchand.

There came from a wealthy home in Scotland a
youth of sixteen to see the wonders of this land.
His name was Lachlan McGillivray. He landed in
Carolina, joined the Indian traders about 1735, saw

at length the young Sehoy Marchand, "cheerfu
in countenance, bewitching in looks, and graceful in
form," then herself about sixteen years of age, married her, some say about 1745, when he had gained
some property, spent nearly fifty years as Indian
trader and Georgia royalist in the American wilds,
left his Indian children and his plantations, when
the British left Savannah, about 1782, and returned
to his native land, taking with him "a vast amount
of money and movable effects." But of his Indian
children, part Indian, part Scotch, part French, one,
Alexander McGillivray, became noted, wealthy, and
powerful. He was well educated at Charleston.
He returned to the Indian country, took control of
the Creek nation, received from the British the rank
and pay of a British colonel in the War of the Revolution, in 1784 went to Pensacola and made a
treaty with Spain as being "Emperor" of the Creeks
and Seminoles, in 1790 at New York made a treaty
with the American government receiving the rank
of brigadier general with a salary of twelve hundred dollars a year, and afterwards was appointed
by Spain Superintendent-General of the Creek nation with a salary of two thousand dollars a year,
which was increased in July, 1792, to thirty-five
hundred. He was at the same time a member of a
wealthy commercial house. He died in Pensacola
February 17, 1793. One of his sisters, the beautiful
and talented Sophia McGillivray, married Benjamin
Durant, who was of Huguenot descent, who came
from South Carolina and as early as 1786 was
settled on the Alabama River. Another Indian
trader, Charles Weatherford, some say from Scot-

land, some say from England, married a half sister
of Alexander McGillivray, the daughter of a chief
of pure Indian blood, who had been formerly married to Colonel Tate, at one time a British officer at
Fort Toulouse.   We find here therefore the names
of Tate, Durant, Weatherford, and McGillivray, as
members of connected families of mixed blood,
talented, wealthy, influential, with whom, as individuals, in the Creek-War history we shall become
further acquainted.   A number of other noted
border men there were who need not here be named.
But one more name should not be omitted.

General Le Clerc Milfort, a well educated
Frenchman, was among the Muscogees from 1776
to 1796, and he also married a sister of Alexander
McGillivray, who was sometimes called Colonel
and in later life General McGillivray.   Milfort was
for some time a noted war chief among these Indians.
He returned to France and published at Paris in
1802 a work known as "Gen. Milfort's Creek
Indians."   It does not appear that he left among
the Indians any descendants

Mention has already been made of the settlement of this part of the early West Florida, which
became a part of the Mississippi Territory as that
was organized in 1798 as far south as the thirty-first
parallel of north latitude and extending north, as
has been stated, to latitude 32° 28′.*   Spanish and
British plantations had been along these rivers
where indigo was largely cultivated, Spanish grants
of land had been made to settlers, and French,

---

* Or from the mouth of the Yazoo River due east to the Chat-
ahoochee.

Spanish, and British royalists had all become, in some sort, Americans.

In 1799, May 5th, Lieutenant McLeary, for the United States, took possession of the old Fort St. Stephens on the Tombigbee River, the Spanish garrison marching out and descending the river below latitude 31⁰, the boundary line, this parallel, then having been but recently surveyed. In July of that year Fort Stoddart* was established, three miles below the union of the Alabama and Tombigbee rivers, five by water, and about six above the Spanish line. Here was built a stockade with one bastion. Already, in Spanish times, quite a settlement had been made on Lake Tensaw, just east of the Alabama and the Cut Off and Nannahubba Island, largely by tories, where was opened "the first American school" in what became Alabama, John Pierce teacher, probably in 1799. Says Pickett: "There the high-blood descendants of Lachlan McGillivray—the Taits, Weatherfords, and Durants—the aristocratic Linders, the wealthy Mims, and the children of many others first learned to read. The pupils were strangely mixed in blood, and their color was of every hue."†

These early white settlements, including those of mixed blood, were on lands which the Indians had ceded to the British and Spanish authorities, and which, when Washington county was formed in June, 1800, belonged to the United States. Says Judge

---

*Written at first Stoddert.

† Captain John Linder was a native of Switzerland. He had been in Charleston as a British surveyor. He was aided by General McGillivray to settle with his family and a large number of colored servants at Tensaw Lake in the time of the Revolution.

Meek: "The various treaties of the French, British, and Spanish with the Indians made this region the resort of the first emigrants. The experiences of this backwoods life, for more than twenty years, were quite as singular and wonderful as those of Boone and Kenton in Kentucky, or Sevier and Robertson in Tennessee."

These settlements, taking Judge Meek's quotation from the American State Papers, were " thinly scattered along the western banks of the Mobile and Tombigbee for more than seventy miles, and extending nearly seventy-five miles upon the eastern borders of the Mobile and Alabama." For some time there was no actual civil government ; there were no magistrates, no ministers, no marriage ceremonies. The young people were accustomed to marry themselves, that is they paired off, like birds, and lived together as husband and wife. Instead of weddings they had what were called pairings.

The reader may begin to think that the rehearsal of the history of this region with the notices of the peculiar inhabitants is not very brief ; but surely the young reader, at least, will not object to this note, in which we will take a glance at a home where a very different scene will appear by and by. I quote :—(The authority is Pickett, but not his words.)

" An instance is recorded of one couple who observed a little more form than the others. It was Christmas night of 1800. Daniel Johnson and Miss Elizabeth Linder, at Lake Tensaw, were acknowledged lovers. He was poor and she an heiress, so her parents objected, even in those wilds, to the 'pairing.' A large party were that night assem-

bled at the house of Samuel Mims, and among these
were the two lovers, enjoying the dance, the music,
the festivities. During the evening a few young
people, Johnson and Miss Linder among them,
secretly left the house, embarked on board of some
canoes, paddled down the lake and down the
Alabama, and arrived at Fort Stoddart an hour before the dawn of day. Captàin Shaumburg, a
merry-hearted German, in command of the fort
was called upon to perform the marriage ceremony.
In vain he declared his ignorance of such ceremonies
and his want of authority. He was told that he was
placed there by the Federal Government to protect
the people and to regulate their affairs, and that
this little affair needed his sanction.

" At length the captain yielded to their solicita-
tions, and having the two lovers placed before him
proclaimed : ' I, Captain Shaumburg, of the
second regiment of the United States army, and
commandant of Fort Stoddart, do hereby pronounce
you man and wife. Go home, behave yourselves;
multiply, and replenish the Tensaw country.' They
re-entered their canoes, returned to the Tensaw
Boat Yard, and the whole settlement pronounced
them to be ' the best married people they had
known in a long time.' "

In 1801 the inhabitants were estimated at seven
hundred and fifty, (five hundred being whites), in
these river settlements. In 1802 a trading house was
established at St. Stephens. There were American
settlers now between the rivers, and new ones on the
west, from Georgia and the Carolinas, from Tennessee and Kentucky.* Settlers came in rapidly until

---

* By a supplementary act of Congress in 1804 there was
added to the Mississippi Territory all the " tract of country "
south of the State of Tennessee between Georgia on the east and
Louisiana on the west. *From Mississippi Statutes in the library
of Colonel J. W. Portis of Suggsville, Clarke county, Alabama.*

1812, when it became evident that trouble with the
Indians was near.   In 1810 the population of Washington county was, whites 733, and blacks 517. Of
Baldwin, formed in December, 1809, the population
was, whites 667, and blacks 760. In the north, bordering on Tennessee, there was then one county
only, Madison. In December of 1812 Clarke county
was formed by act of the territorial legislature, being the fourth county in what became Alabama.   It
may readily be seen that these river settlements were
well called "completely insulated." South of them, between latitude 31° and the Bay, between the Perdido
River and the Mississippi, were the Spaniards; on the
east, between them and Georgia, were the Creeks ;
on the west, between them and the Natchez and the
Yazoo settlements, were the Choctaws; and on the
north were the Chickasaws and Creeks between
them and the nearest settlements in the bend of the
Tennessee River.   The reader will see therefore
why this history is largely of the Creek War in
South Alabama, although no Alabama state or territory existed then; for in what became South Alabama, then a part of the large Mississippi Territory,
were then living the white settlers, about two
thousand in number, with nearly two thousand
blacks, who were deeply interested in this war, to
whom it was indeed a matter of life or death.

And now we can more intelligently and with
larger interest, having looked at some of these inhabitants, examine the CAUSES of this Creek War. It
was considered at first, a war upon the whites ; it
became, at length, and mainly, a war, almost of extermination, against the Indians.

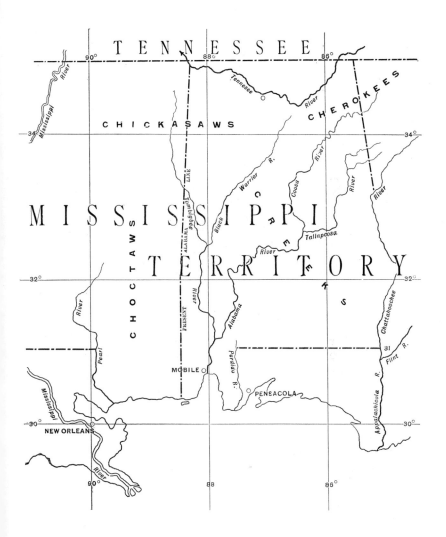

The opening paragraph of the fifty-third chapter of Ramsay's History of the United States, published in 1818, contains statements so just and appropriate that they are repeated as an introductory paragraph here.

"In treating of the causes and conduct of a war, maintained by a savage against a civilized nation, we are aware that the greatest caution ought to be observed, lest an undue degree of moral or physical superiority be ascribed to the latter. Between the contradictory narratives of enlightened nations, differing, as they often do, in the most minnte, as well as in the most important statements, the truth may generally be found. When, however, the art of recording and perpetuating events, is possessed only by one party, it is natural that misrepresentation should occur, and the annalist to whom one source of information only is open, finds it difficult to delineate the principal features of such hostilities without deserving the charge of partiality. Passion, prejudice, the love of gain, and contempt for the rude and uninformed people by whom they are surrounded, operate strongly to incite the frontier inhabitants of the Republic to hostilities, and to exaggerate the merit and importance of their triumphs over these undisciplined tribes. On the other hand, causes no less powerful, have long kept the greater part of the Indian people in a state of virtual warfare with the United States.

"The influence of feelings, common to all mankind in a similar situation, the desire of revenge, and the hope of re-possessing those happier seats, from which their ancestors were driven, added to the sense of their diminution, through the power and arts of their civilized neighbors, had, previously to the war of the United States with Great Britain, produced a spirit of irritation and animosity, which that event soon kindled into a flame."

That the Creek Indians should have been ready for war when opportunity offered is by no means surprising. That the Indians did not all unite and sweep off the white settlers from all the Alabama portion of the Mississippi Territory, is almost remarkable. From the time of the Spanish discoveries the tread of the white man on American soil has usually meant aggression. The white man crowds. He wants the choicest lands; he wants, in fact, the whole. The Indian is hospitable for a time; he yields; and then he tries to fight his way back.

In 1621 Edward Winslow of Plymouth wrote to a friend in London,

"We have found the Indians very faithful to their covenant of peace with us, very loving and ready to pleasure us. We often go to them, and they come to us.

"We entertain them pleasantly and familiarly in our cabins, and they, as friendly, bestow their venison on us."

But as settlements advanced a change came. Martyn writes for 1637, as introducing his account of the Pequod troubles,

"But now this old epoch was buried; a new one dawned. The Indians surveyed the in-coming paleface tide which seemed always to flow and never to ebb. They asked each other: 'Where will this end?'" And the Pequod war—the extermination of the Pequods, resulted. Often history repeats itself.

The Indians known in this history as the CREEKS, then occupying western Georgia and what is now eastern and central Alabama, a region watered by the Chattahoochee, Coosa, Tallapoosa, Cahawba, and Alabama rivers, had seen the growth of the settlements eastward of them in

Georgia. They knew something of the white settle-- ment in Tennessee. And since the year 1800 they had seen a brisk migration of white families from Georgia and the Carolinas, directly through their country, to the Mississippi Territory. They knew that white families were living east of the Tombig- bee river, between that and the Alabama river, in what is now the county of Clarke, and that some even settled east of the Alabama. They themselves claimed west of the Alabama to the water shed line, and this line bounded Clarke county on the east when it was set off from Washington county, December 10, 1812. They had claimed also to the Tombigbee River, although the Choctaws claimed to the water- shed ; and when in 1802 a treaty was made with the Choctaws and a tract of land was ceded by them to the United States, a Creek chief, the Mad Wolf is reported to have said : "The people of Tombigbee have put over their cattle in the Fork, on the Aliba- mo hunting grounds, and have gone a great way on our lands. I want them put back. We all know they are Americans."

These Alibamo Indians were the nearest of the Creek tribes and would naturally claim to the Tom- bigbee river. They would at once feel the encroach- ment of these white settlers. Thirty chiefs and warriors of the Creek nation were in Washington in the fall of 1805, and, through the influences brought to bear upon them there, they had granted the right "of using a horse path through their country." The chiefs agreed even to build bridges across the streams or to have ferry boats and to open houses of enter- tainment for travellers. In this same year the Choc

taws ceded five million acres of their land to the
United States, including that which the Creeks
claimed west of the water shed.   Instead of fighting
with the Choctaws for this strip of land it was agreed
to leave the question of ownership to be decided by
an Indian game of ball.   One game was played by
men and the Choctaws won the game.   The Creeks
were dissatisfied.   The Choctaws then proposed that
the women of each side should play.   To this the
Creeks agreed, and the Choctaw women won the
game and held the land.   This boundary line was
surveyed in 1808, Creeks and Choctaws assisting in
the work.   Starting from what was afterwards
called Hal's Lake, the line was to cross no water ;
and the corner post was driven near the north line
of Clarke county, the locality being called the Choctaw corner.   Not far away a village is now situated
called Choctaw Corner.

In 1811 Lieutenant Luckett with a party of
soldiers cut out a road, called the "Federal Road,"
through the Creek country, from a point on the
Chattahoochee River to Mims' Ferry on the Alabama,
and this road was soon, in the language of those who
knew the facts of that migration, "filled from one
end to the other" with parties of white families
bound for the river and the western settlements.

The "horse path" was now a government
wagon road, and the Creek Indians could not fail
to see that the whites were beginning to build up
a large and permanent settlement on their very
borders.   It was evident that they would encroach
more and more upon the Alibamo hunting grounds.
Choice hunting grounds these were between the two

rivers, even as late as 1850. This wagon road of 1811 and this stream of migration passing through the Creek nation awakened in many of the Creek warriors strong discontent. While efforts had been made to introduce civilization among them, and with some success, yet many were restless amid the restraints which were increasing around them. The Spaniards also disliked these river settlements, and they excited still more the discontent of the Creek warriors. As Pensacola was at this time the great place of trade for the Indians and for these white settlers, it was very easy for those Spanish traders to learn the growth of the settlements and to arouse hostility in the minds of the Indians. Pensacola, to some extent, was responsible for the Creek War. But perhaps the most active agent in stirring [3] up strife, outside of the Creek nation, was the noted Indian chief, Tecumseh, well called great, who came like a blast from the North, endeavoring to lead the Southern tribes to join his great confederacy. As he will be fully mentioned in other chapters two sentences only in regard to him will be given here.

"Brave, sagacious, and enterprising, he left no means untried to retard at least, if he could not prevent, the approaching extermination of his tribe."

"He visited, in person, all the tribes west of the Mississippi, and on Lakes Superior, Huron, and Erie, exciting them to hostilities by the appeals of religion and interest."

There is also another fact to be considered here. Alexander McGillivray who has been already mentioned, born at Little Tallassee, four miles above the

present Wetumpka, in 1746,—Drake says, about 1739
—commencing his public life as early as 1766, had
held a very firm control over these Indians. Brewer
speaks of him as the controlling mind in that region,
the most distinguished native then born, and at the
head of the Muscogee confederacy, which was more
compact and formidable at that time than at any
other known period of its history. Brewer further
says, that he wielded an influence over his people
"not felt since the days of Tuskaloosa. He was a
diplomatist and scholar among a nation of savages."

Pickett speaks of him as possessing the most
marked ability of any man born or reared on Alabama soil. He was now dead ; and there was no
one to take his place as a recognized head of the
nation. In that year after his death, 1793, such
was the commotion among Indians, Spaniards, and
Americans, (and some very bad Americans were
among the Indians), that Pickett wrote, "It appeared
that the evil one himself was stalking through this
wild region." Native Indian chiefs were now again
coming forward to exercise their rights of government, such as Big Warrior, as Menawa, and others;
while leaders of mixed blood were also exerting their
influence. There was no head. The United States
Agent, Colonel Benjamin Hawkins, residing for
some time among them, was not their ruler, and it
is not strange that a conflict broke out among themselves. Some of them continued on friendly terms
with the whites, but others became very hostile.

From these statements it appears that the great
exciting cause of this war was, the large and
growing settlement of white pioneers along the

Tombigbee and the Alabama rivers. Encroachments upon the Indian hunting grounds and rights
were of necessity made. The great wagon road
was an encroachment ; the presence of so many
white families with their cattle and hogs and horses
was an encroachment. It needed not Tecumseh's
stirring words to assure them that they must before
long give up their Indian life, cultivate the ground,
and accept the white man's civilization; or they
must migrate ; or they must break up this settlement
of sturdy frontier families on their western borders.
Their proposed attempt thus to do, encouraged by
the Spaniards, by Tecumseh and the British, brought
on the disastrous Creek War.   [4]

CHAPTER III.

TECUMSEH AMONG THE CHICKASAWS AND CHOCTAWS.

IN the summer of 1811, the celebrated Shawnee chief, Tecumseh, at the head of twenty armed and mounted warriors, visited the Southern Indians. His object was to induce these tribes to join the Indian Confederacy which he was forming to act in concert with the British troops in the war then [5] impending with the United States. In company with Tecumseh was his kinsman, Seekaboo, who was to act the role of prophet and interpreter in the Southern councils.

Seekaboo was, probably, born in the Creek nation, had certainly once lived there, and in early life had emigrated north with some Shawnees. He was, at the time of Tecumseh's visit to the South, about forty years of age, a brave warrior, an eloquent orator, and gifted linguist, speaking English, Shawnee, Choctaw, and Muscogee, by which attainments he exercised great influence in the Indian councils. Seekaboo was related to Tecumseh in this manner : His mother's mother was a sister of the mother of Tecumseh. His father was a half-breed, the offspring of a white man with a Creek woman.

Save one meager incident, both history and tradition are silent as to the details of Tecumseh's visit

to the Chickasaws, what places he visited and how
long he tarried among them, only that his mission
was in vain. The tradition that has been handed
down is that in the upper part of the Chickasaw
nation, Tecumseh and his warriors came to the house
of George Colbert. He made known to Colbert the
object of his visit, and that he wished the Chickasaws to join the confederacy, and that at the proper
time all the tribes were to go to war against the
Americans, and he wished Colbert to use his influence with his people in effecting this object. Colbert, in reply, told Tecumseh that the Chickasaws
were at peace with the whites and wished to remain
so: and that he certainly would not use his influence
towards involving them in any war. Tecumseh, seeing that Colbert would give no countenance to his
designs, took his departure.   [6]

On leaving the Chickasaw nation, as a tradition
runs, Tecumseh crossed the Oktibbeha Creek, the
Choctaw and Chickasaw boundary, some three miles
southwest of the present site of West Point, Mississippi, near Dick's old ferry, and there taking the
Six Towns' trail, which led southerly, he camped, his
first night in the Choctaw nation, in a grove on a
hill, in the southwestern part of Lowndes County,
about two miles from the Noxubee County line
and about two hundred yards from that of Oktibbeha.
This place is now occupied by the residence of
the late Allen Brooks. The next morning, Tecumseh continued his southward march in the Six Towns'
trail, which crossed Noxubee River, about six hundred yards above Bugg's ferry, and about seven
miles beyond, he arrived at the residence of Mingo

Moshulitubbee, the present Mashulaville, in Noxubee County.

Tecumseh remained at Moshulitubbee's house for several days, and a number of Choctaw mingoes and warriors came to see him. It seems that no regular council was held here, and Tecumseh made known the object of his visit, but it was received with no favor by the Choctaws present.

Tecumseh and his Shawnees then went to the village of a noted warrior, named Hoentubbee, Moshulitubbee sending a warrior with him as a guide. The village of Hoentubbee was situated near the present residence of Elias Roundtree, in the north-western part of Kemper County, some six hundred yards north of Ben Dick Creek and about two miles from the Neshoba County line. Hoentubbee, in after years, in speaking of Tecumseh and his warriors, stated that all were armed, dressed, and painted alike. Their arms were rifles, with tomahawks and scalping knives in their belts. Their dress was a buckskin hunting shirt, a cloth flap, with buckskin leggins and moccasins profusely fringed and beaded. All wore garters below the knees. Their hair was plaited in a long cue of three plaits hanging down between the shoulders, while each temple was closely shaven. The heads of all, except Tecumseh, were adorned with plumes of hawk and eagle feathers. Tecumseh wore, depending from the crown of his head, two long crane feathers, one white, the other dyed a brilliant red. According to Indian symbol-ism, the white feather was an emblem of peace,—peace among the various Indian tribes. The red feather was a war emblem,—war to their enemies,

the Americans. They wore silver bands on each
arm, one around the wrist, one above and one below
the elbow, and a few wore silver gorgets suspended
from their necks. Around the forehead of each,
encircling the head, was a red flannel band about
three inches wide, and over this a silver band. Semicircular streaks of red war-paint were drawn under
each eye, extending outward on the cheek bone. A
small red spot was painted on each temple, and a
large round red spot on the centre of the breast.

Tecumseh remained a number of days at the village of Hoentubbee, and at his request, many of the
noted Choctaws came there to meet him in council
and listen to his talk. Among those present, were
Pushmataha and Moshulitubbee, mingoes, respectively, of the southeastern and northeastern districts.
The Shawnees first danced their national dance, and
after this the council convened near Hoentubbee's
house. Tecumseh arose and through Seekaboo
made a long talk. He spoke much of the bad conduct of the white people, how they were seizing the
Indians' lands and reducing them to poverty, and
he urged the Choctaws to join him in a general war
against the oppressors. He urged, too, upon the
Choctaws the duty of living at peace with the other
Indian tribes ; and that all the tribes ought to quit
their inter-tribal wars and unite in a general confederacy; that by this means they could keep their
lands and preserve their nationalities. Tecumseh
also spoke of the impending war with Great Britain,
and that the Choctaws must unite with the other
tribes and all declare themselves allies of Great
Britain. If we are to credit one of our Choctaw

informants, Tecumseh also, in this talk, as well as in subsequent talks, spoke very earnestly against the Indian custom of killing women and children in war. This custom they should renounce, and henceforth, in all wars, the lives of women and children should be spared.

Such are some of the traditions of Tecumseh's talk, and among these, his reprobation of a barbarous war custom of his race is creditable to his humanity. Some of this talk was, by no means, displeasing to the Choctaws. They approved of the idea of the different tribes renouncing their intertribal wars and living at peace with each other. And they by no means objected to his advice that all Indians should renounce the custom of killing women and children in war; but they were suspicious and wary of his proposal to declare themselves allies of Great Britain. Their relations with the Americans had ever been harmonious, and they disliked any proposal that would sever those ties of peace.

Pushmataha replied to Tecumseh, and in his talk told his people not to think of going to war; that the Choctaws had never shed the blood of white men in war;* that they had ever been at peace with them and must continue so; that there was no cause of war with the white people, and that a war with them would end in the ruin of their nation; that the white people were the friends of the Choc-

---

[7]　　* It is true that the Choctaws fought against the Spaniards at Mauvila and Cabusto. But it must not be supposed that Pushmataha knew anything about these, to him, prehistoric matters.

　　　　　　　　　　　　　　　　　　　　H. S. H.

taws, and they must not make enemies of them by
taking the talk of Tecumseh.

The council dissolved and Tecumseh's talk was all
in vain. Not one Choctaw was disposed to take his [8]
talk. During his stay at this village, which was
several days, Tecumseh seems to have conceived a
warm regard for Hoentubbee. Before his departure,
he presented the latter a silver ornament or gorget,
which Hoentubbee kept for a long time until it was
destroyed by the burning of his house many years
afterwards. An aged son of Hoentubbee, still
living, states that Tecumseh also gave his father a
written or printed paper or parchment, to which a
red seal or stamp was affixed. The nature of this
document must be left entirely to conjecture. As
Tecumseh was connected with the British authorities,
could this have been a paper authorizing the holder,
in case he should join the hostiles, to draw military
supplies from the Spaniards at Pensacola?

Tecumseh and his warriors, after leaving Hoentubbee's village, next went to Yazoo, situated in
Neshoba County, about eleven miles south of east
of Philadelphia, now known as Yazoo Old Town.
The mingo of this place was named Tanampo
Eshubbee. The Shawnees remained here three or
four days, in which they danced their national dance,
and another council was held and another talk was
made by Tecumseh with reply by Pushmataha,—
both of the same nature and with the same result
as at the village of Hoentubbee.

Tecumseh and his warriors then went to Mokalusha. This was one of the most noted and popu-
lous towns of the Choctaws. It was situated upon

a plateau on the headwaters of Talasha Creek,
about twelve miles southeast of Philadelphia. The
houses of the town, with the small fields interspersed,
covered an area three miles long, north and south,
and a mile and a half wide, east and west. During
the farming season, the boys of the town kept the
horses and cattle herded out on the range beyond the suburbs, to prevent their depredating on
the crops, which were mostly cultivated by the
women, while the men generally spent their time
in hunting. Such was the division of labor in
Mokalusha. Mokalusha is a corruption of Imoklasha,
which signifies "Their people are there." About
1824, this ancient town was, in a great measure
abandoned on account of the ravages of the small
pox.

The Shawnees remained about a week at Mokalusha, and the same Choctaw mingoes came hither
who had attended the former councils. After the
Shawnees had danced their national dance, a council convened on a hill situated about the centre
of the eastern edge of the town. This hill is now
occupied by the residence of the late Colonel James
Wilson. Tecumseh here through Seekaboo made
his talk, to which Pushmataha again replied. The
Shawnee chief a third time failed to make any impression on the Choctaws.

After this council, the Shawnees, travelling
down the east side of Talasha Creek, went to Chunky
Town, which was situated on the west side of
Chunky Creek, half a mile below the confluence of
Talasha and Chunky creeks, and about five miles
above Hickory Station. It is stated that Pushma-

taha and the other mingoes, from some cause, did not follow Tecumseh to Chunky. In Tecumseh's day, and down to the treaty of Dancing Rabbit, in 1830, the long peninsular strip of country, into which Tecumseh entered after leaving Mokalusha, and which lies between Talasha and Tallihatta creeks and thence continuing southward to the confluence of Tallihatta and Chunky creeks, was under the jurisdiction of a mingo named Iskifa Chito, Big Axe. His residence was on the west bank of Tallihatta, near which spot is now Day's mill. This peninsula is still known by the old Choctaws as Iskifa Chito in Yakni, Big Axe's Country.

Pierre Juzan, a noted French Indian countryman, at this time was living at Chunky Town. He had settled among the Choctaws in early life, and had married a Choctaw woman, a niece of Pushmataha, and raised an Indian family. He spoke English, French, and Choctaw with equal fluency. Juzan had several trading houses among the Choctaws, one being at Coosha Town, situated three or four miles southeast of old Daleville, on the right bank of Issuba in Kannia bok (Lost Horse Creek), and another at Chunky. His dwelling house at Chunky was on the west side of the creek and about two hundred yards from it. He had here an apple orchard,—a rare thing in an Indian country—the trees or scions for which he had brought from France. He also had another residence at Coosha. Juzan died about 1840, at Tuscahoma, on the Tombigbee. Some time after his death, his family, with the exception of a daughter, emigrated west.

On the day of their arrival at Chunky, Tecumseh

and Seekaboo called upon Juzan and had a long
interview with him, in the course of which they
endeavored to persuade him to use his influence with
the Choctaws to induce them to join the Indian
Confederacy. Juzan became greatly indignant and
spurned the Shawnees' proposition. He turned
away and would hold no further conversation with
them. It so happened that same day that Oklahoma, a noted mingo from Coosha, a nephew of
Pushmataha and brother of Juzan's wife, was in
Chunky with a number of his warriors. He was
soon informed by Juzan of the object of Tecumseh's
visit, whereupon he became greatly enraged and
forthwith ordered his warriors to mould bullets and
prepare to make battle against the Shawnees. He
also sent a messenger to Iskifa-Chito, to inform him
of the situation and to urge him to prepare for war
against the Shawnee intruders. Tecumseh, whose
object was to harmonize all Indians, saw the drift of
affairs, and wishing to avoid any hostile collision, he
summoned his warriors and quietly withdrew from
the place. The Choctaw traditions here vary.
According to one tradition, Tecumseh with all
his warriors then returned to Moshulitubbee's.
But according to another, the Shawnees after
withdrawing from Chunky, divided into two
parties, one party, under Tecumseh, returning
to Moshulitubbee's, whilst the other party,
under Seekaboo, went down south into the present
Jasper County among the Six Towns Indians, who
were considered the fiercest and most warlike of all
the Choctaws. Here some talks were made. Thence,
making a detour to the northeast, Seekaboo's party

went to Coosha.   Whether at this place they again
encountered the hostility of Oklahoma, we have no
information.   From Coosha, Seekabo went to Yahnubbee Town, situated on Yahnubbee Creek, eight
miles southwest of DeKalb. The present DeKalb and
Decatur road traverses the site of the old town.
Making but a short stay at Yahnubbee, Seekaboo
thence returned to Moshulitubbee's, where the two
Shawnee parties again re-united.

In some way that cannot now be ascertained, it
seems that by mutual agreement, there was to be a
final council of the Choctaws with Tecumseh, and
another residence of Moshulitubbee, situated in
Noxubee County, about five miles northeast of
Brooksville, was selected as the council ground.
In going to this council, Tecumseh with his warriors
travelled back the same route that he came until he
crossed Noxubee River.   There he left the Six
Towns trail and took another, which led northeast
and terminated at this second home of Moshulitubbee.   Here the Shawnees remained full two weeks,
and all the great mingoes and principal men of the
Choctaws came hither to hear the talk of the great
Tecumseh.   Of these, tradition has preserved the
names of Pushmataha, Moshulitubbee, Puckshenubbee, Mingo of the western district, Hoentubbee,
David Folsom, and John Pitchlyn.   [9]

A few words as to this locality, which is now
embraced in the Chester plantation of the late
Colonel Thomas G. Blewett. The house of Moshulitubbee stood upon the crest of a hill, about a quarter
of a mile westerly of the dwelling house of the
plantation.   About one hundred and twenty-five

yards west of the dwelling house, stood a large red oak, with broad spreading leafy branches. Under this tree the council took place. It was the intention of Colonel Blewett to have this tree preserved on account of its historic associations. But in 1855, without the Colonel's knowledge, and to his great regret, the overseer had it destroyed.

When the appointed time came and the Shawnees had finished their dance, the council convened under the oak, and Tecumseh, through Seekaboo, made his talk. From the best information now attainable, the ideas of Tecumseh's talk at this council were much the same as in the harangue at Hoentubbee's; in fact, his harangues everywhere among the Choctaws were substantially the same. As a patriot, though it may be, a misguided one, Tecumseh saw the necessity of the tribes uniting in a confederation, so as to preserve their lands and their nationalities. To effect this purpose, he urged that it was necessary for them, under the circumstances, to take the side of the British in the inevitable conflict. A born savage, though he was, the great Shawnee had an innate humanity that caused him to reprobate all unnecessary barbarity in war, and in every council, he told his wild Indian fellow countrymen to renounce the custom of slaying women and children in war. The expression in Tecumseh's speech at Tuckabatchee, recorded in Claiborne's Sam Dale— "Slay their women and children"—is an error, a mistake. At no period in life, in none of his war speeches, did Tecumseh ever give vent to such a sentiment.

This was Tecumseh's last talk to the Choctaws. The next day, Pushmataha made his reply. He

spoke of the long existing friendship of the white
people and the Choctaws, between whom no wars
had ever occurred, and the Choctaws could truly say
that they had never shed the blood of white men in
war. There was no war, or cause of war with white
people, and the Choctaws must not be led into any
war by Tecumseh. In closing his speech he turned
to the mingoes present and said that if any Choctaw
warrior should take the talk of Tecumseh and join
the hostiles, and should he not be killed in battle, he
must be put to death on his return home.

The other mingoes also made talks after Pushmataha, and all concurred in his opinion that if any
warrior should take the talk of Tecumseh, he must
be put to death. All the mingoes seemed willing to
follow the lead of Pushmataha, who from the very
beginning, had taken a stand against Tecumseh.
John Pitchlyn and David Folsom also used an active
influence against the Shawnees. The statement in   [10]
Claiborne's Mississippi that some of the Choctaw
mingoes were hostile or inclined to take Tecumseh's
talk is altogether erroneous. As to the hostility of
Hopaii Iskitini, Little Leader, it is sufficient to say
that he was a mere boy at that time, probably about
twelve years of age.

After all the speeches were made, the mingoes
held a private conference in regard to Tecumseh,
after which they informed him of their decision,
which was that if he did not leave their country
they would put him to death. They also commissioned David Folsom to take a band of warriors and
see Tecumseh safe across the Tombigbee. It is not
known how soon after Tecumseh obeyed this injunc-

tion. But both parties, Tecumseh and his Shawnees, and Folsom with his Choctaws, all mounted and equipped, in due time, marched towards the southeast and arrived at the Tombigbee, near the present little village of Memphis, in Pickens County, Alabama, where they camped. Hoentubbee was with Folsom's party, and also two or three white men. The next morning all went to work to make rafts to cross the river. The rafts were made by tying logs together with grape vines. The warriors seated themselves on the rafts, and while some would paddle, others would hold the horses by the bridle and make them swim in the rear. By sunset, a part of the Shawnees had launched their rafts and crossed over, Tecumseh among the number. Folsom remained with the other party on the western bank.

The ensuing night, it happened that a large party of marauding Creek warriors crossed the river below, came into Folsom's camp and stole several Choctaw and Shawnee horses. They took them several miles below, tied them in a swamp, then taking the back trail, they hid themselves in the cane, about two miles below Folsom's camp. The next morning, finding several of their horses missing, some of the Choctaws and Shawnees, part mounted and part afoot, went in search of them. They soon discovered the marauders' trail and were eagerly following it up when they came near the Muscogee ambuscade. Here, all at once, they received a galling fire from the wily foe, by which some were killed and some wounded. The remainder returned the fire, then fled, hotly pursued, back to the camp. In the retreat, a horse was shot in the shoulder.

His rider, a Shawnee, then leaped to the ground
and continued his flight afoot. Without further
casualty, the party arrived at the camp. The Muscogees took possession of a hill which stood to the
south of the camp, and now from hill-top to valley,
the fight began to rage, the Choctaw and the Shawnee pitted against the martial Muscogee. The
camp on the other side of the river heard the firing,
and Tecumseh's warrior spirit was aroused. All
crossed over to the relief of the beleauguered camp,
and the fight raged with greater fury. The smoke
of battle soon darkened the field, enveloping the
Muscogees on the hill and settling down on the
cane-brake which sheltered the Choctaws and the
Shawnees. The Creeks made several efforts to
drive their enemies from their cover. At one time
two daring warriors, making a flank movement, had
even penetrated to the Choctaws' rear, but were
there discovered and slain. All day, with rival
bravery, the warriors of Tecumseh and Folsom
fought the common foe. About sunset, encouraged
by Tecumseh, an assault was made up the hill, the
Muscogees were disloged and put to flight, and the
shouts of the victors resounded over the field. Both
sides had a considerable number killed and wounded,
Folsom, whilst standing behind a tree, in the act of
shooting at a warrior in his front, received a rifle
ball through the right shoulder from another hostile
warrior, who had taken a position in front of the
Choctaw right flank. Hoentubbee also received a
wound, though a slight one, being struck by a spent
ball. While fighting bravely against the enemy, a
rifle ball struck a large cane in his front and glanc-

ing struck the warior with considerable force on the
breast.   For a moment supposing himself smitten
with a mortal wound, Hoentubbee cried out with a
loud voice, "Sallishke!" "I am dead!" But he soon
realized that he was not so dead after all. This little
incident afforded much amusement to the Choctaw
warriors.   The Creeks, according to their national
custom, bore off from the field all their wounded,
and as many of their slain warriors as they could
with safety to themselves. But they were compelled
to abandon a few, whom the Choctaws plundered
and scalped without compunction.   The Shawnees
took no part in this act, perhaps, by the command
of Tecumseh, since the fight was a necessity forced
upon them.   The next morning, the victors buried
their dead, then all able to do so crossed the river,
Folsom, notwithstanding his wound, crossing over
with his people.   Folsom's mission was now accomplished. He had seen the Shawnees across the
Tombigbee, and they now separated, the Shawnees
continuing their course towards the domains of the
Muscogees and the Seminoles.

The Choctaw warriors now resolved not to re-cross
the Tombigbee until they had retaliated upon the
Muscogees for the loss of their horses and the death
of their warriors.   Folsom returning to Moshulitubbee's on account of his wound, the fierce braves
selected another leader, went over to the Black Warrior, and there wreaked their vengeance to the full.
They burned a number of the houses of the Muscogees, slew their warriors, and seized their horses.
By a strange freak of fortune, they recovered, in a
cane brake on the Black Warrior, the very same

Choctaw and Shawnee horses that had been captured on the Tombigbee. At last, enriched with booty and scalps, they recrossed the Tombigbee in triumph, thence went to the house of Mingo Achillitubbee, (in Neshoba County, half a mile northeast of the Bogue Chitto bridge), where they underwent those ceremonies of purification customary, in ancient times, among the Choctaws on their return home from the war path.

NOTES.

The above sketch of Tecumseh's visit to the Chickasaws and Choctaws has been worked out from original and authentic sources. The greater part of the information was received from Charley Hoentubbee, of Kemper County, a son of the warrior, Hoentubbee. In 1880, the writer had repeated conversations with Charley Hoentubbee, who related to him all the facts that he had ever heard from his father in regard to Tecumseh's visit to the Choctaws. He stated that he had often heard his father talk about this visit. Hoentubbee, the warrior, died in Kemper County, in 1860. In 1885, the writer also interviewed the aged Hemonubbee, of Neshoba County, in regard to Tecumseh. Hemonubbee stated that he was a boy about twelve years of age, when Tecumseh passed through the Choctaw Nation; that his father, Fillamotubbee, attended several of the councils; and in after years, he had often heard his father and other Choctaws converse about Tecumseh's visit. Hemonubbee's statements were substantially the same as Hoentubbee's, though not so much in detail. Neither Hoentubbee nor Hemonubbee, however, was very familiar with the incidents of Tecumseh's visit to Chunky. For these incidents, the writer is indebted to the late Mr. James Cassels of Newton

County and Jack Amos, a Choctaw, of the same
county. Both related the same identical facts, Mr.
Cassels receiving the information from Pierre Juzan,
and Amos, from Oklahoma. Amos is a nephew of
Oklahoma and grand nephew of Pushmataha, being
a grandson of Nahotima, a sister of Pushmataha. In
1877, Mr. G. W. Campbell, of Noxubee County, related to the writer some facts about Tecumseh's visit,
he receiving the information, in early life, from
Stonie Hadjo, one of Moshulitubbee's captains, who
died in Noxubee County, about 1838. Stonie Hadjo's
statements, as far as they went, agreed with those
of Hoentubbee and Hemonubbee. Mr. Campbell
and Hoentubbee, however, could not recollect the
name of Tecumseh's interpreter, Seekaboo, Mr. Campbell simply remembering Stonie Hadjo's statement
that he was a relative of Tecumseh's mother. But
Mr. Cassels, Jack Amos, and Hemonubbee remembered the name distinctly, Amos stating besides that
the Choctaws were astonished at Seekaboo's familiarity with their language. Hemonubbee gave the
precise relationship of Seekaboo to Tecumseh, which
fact, Seekaboo must have related to the Choctaws.
The Choctaws' informants all agree in stating that
Tecumseh and his warriors were mounted.

From a short biographical sketch of David Folsom, in the bibliography of the Muskhogean languages, the inference might possibly be drawn that
Folsom was too young to be a man of affairs in Tecumseh's day. In reply to this possible objection,
the writer will state that he has been informed by
an old citizen of Mississippi, who knew David Folsom well, that Folsom had grown children at the
time of the treaty of Dancing Rabbit, in 1830. This
would surely make Folsom old enough to be a man
of some influence among the Choctaws in 1811,
nineteen years before the treaty. The writer besides closely questioned Charley Hoentubbee on this
special point, and he stoutly contended that David

Folsom was the man that conducted the Shawnees across the Tombigbee.

The meager incident of Tecumseh's Chickasaw visit was received from the late Mr. W. G. Harris, of Winston County. Mr. Harris stated that in 1833 he spent a night at the house of George Colbert, on Shookatonche Creek, and that in their conversation Colbert related to him this incident.

The best documentary evidence has been followed in giving twenty as the number of Tecumseh's warriors, but Hoentubbee's tradition makes them much more numerous.

After sifting and comparing all the information given by the above parties in regard to Tecumseh's Southern visit, the writer is satisfied that all the statements which he has recorded in the above chapter are substantially correct.

The topographical matter is the result of personal observations.   H. S. H.

CHAPTER IV

TECUMSEH AMONG THE CREEKS.

THE visit of this noted chief to the Creek Indians
has been named as one of the causes leading to
the Creek War.

Some notice of this visit seems to be desirable in
this history, although not a part, strictly, of the war
record.

It is singular that there is so much discrepancy
among good and, in the main, reliable historians in
regard to the time of this visit; but as one pushes
researches onward with thoroughness in almost any
line of investigation he finds that, in regard to man,
it is more than easy to make mistakes. Some of
these mistakes can be, some of them cannot be, corrected.

Ramsay says, and he is an excellent and careful
historian, speaking of the Southern Indians : " In
the spring of the year 1812, they were visited by the
celebrated Tecumseh, whose designs appear to have
been of the most extensive nature. The bold and
enterprising genius of this chief led him to penetrate into the most remote quarters in the further-
ance of his great object. With an ardent, but savage, eloquence he endeavored to excite them to

resistance against what he represented as a flagrant oppression." *

Many writers since have evidently followed Ramsay or Alabama's leading historian, Pickett. In "Indian Wars of the United States * * From the Best Authorities," by William V. Moore, published by R. W. Pomeroy, 1841, under the heading "The Creek War," the first sentence is the following: "In the spring of 1812 the Southern Indians were visited by the celebrated Tecumseh, who, with an ardent but savage eloquence, urged them to take up arms against the whites." (Moore has again followed Ramsay in saying that in Fort Mims were three hundred persons and that only seventeen escaped.)

An effort was made, as will appear in the notes on this chapter, to obtain some documentary evidence from state papers at Washington. The officials of the War Department, finding no desired document, referred as competent authority to Lossing's "Field Book of the War of 1812." This was examined and the statements were found, page 745, that Tecumseh had visited the Southern Indians "as early as the spring of 1811," and that "in the autumn of 1812 * * * Tecumseh went again to the Gulf Region." Also that he took his brother, the Prophet, with him and about thirty men. He seems to rely largely for his authority on Pickett. He gives yet another date. Speaking of the year 1813, he says: "* * * that in the spring of that year Tecumseh (who was slain on the Thames a few

---

* See Ramsay's United States, published May 1, 1818, "Second Edition, Revised and Corrected," vol. 3, page 351.

months later) went among the Southern tribes, to
arouse them to wage war upon the white people."
Lossing's U. S. History for families and libraries,
page 427.

Lossing is a good, in the main no doubt, a reliable
historian, but made, as all are liable to do, some mistakes.

Parton says, in his " Life of Jackson," published
in 1870: "In the spring of 1811 Tecumseh, leaving
his affairs in the hands of the Prophet, as Moses did
in those of Aaron when he ascended the Mount,
went to the South preaching his crusade.   Far and
long he travelled, sowing the seeds of future wars."
He speaks of his being among the Seminoles, the
Creeks, the Cherokees, and the tribes of the Des
Moines; how " he held the war council, delivered his
impassioned TALK, and strode away." He adds:
"The fall of 1812 again found Tecumseh, accompanied by the Prophet and a retinue of thirty warriors, haranguing the Creeks in the midnight council,
and this time with prodigious effect.   Now he could
point to the successes of the British in the North;
now he could give certain promises of assistance
from the English and Spaniards in Florida; now he
spoke with the authority of a British agent and officer. "

Francis S. Drake, in his " Indian Tribes of the
United States," 2nd volume, 1884, also says: " In
the spring of 1811 Tecumseh, leaving his affairs in
the hands of his brother, the Prophet,"—he omits
the allusion to Moses—" went to the South preaching his crusade." And again he says: " The fall of
1812 again found Tecumseh, accompanied by the

Prophet and a retinue of thirty warriors, haranguing the Creeks in the midnight council, and this time with prodigious effect." It is needless to quote further. The words are the same as the words of Parton. Both Parton and Drake write the same words without any marks of quotation. Evidently some of the historians are too credulous, some too imaginative, and some are too careless.

Even Pickett says that Tecumseh went in the spring of 1812 and was south as late as October of that year.

Eggleston rather strangely says, for one who might be supposed to be very accurate, "A careful comparison of dates shows that Tecumseh started to the South in the spring of the year 1811, and returned to the North soon after the battle of Tippecanoe was fought."

McKenney wisely says, Tecumseh went South "about the year 1811." It is no wonder that one who looks over the various works in which Tecumseh and the Creek War are briefly treated should feel it prudent many times to say "about."

But researches continued for several months seem now to leave, on this one point, no further room for doubt.   [11]

In C. R. Tuttle's "History of the Border Wars of Two Centuries" there is a reference to Charles De Wolf Brownell's Indian Races of North and South America, in which Tecumseh's visit to the Creeks is placed in 1811. This year is certainly the correct date. The following statements will prove this and also show the month and the day.

It is well established in Indiana history that the movements of Tecumseh and his brother, called the Prophet, retarded the settlement of Indiana Territory in the year 1810. The sagacious Indian chief was then endeavoring to perfect what became known as "Tecumseh's Confederacy." August 12, 1810, Tecumseh with some seventy warriors visited General Harrison, then territorial governor, at Vincennes. The conference lasted till August 22nd. August 20th, Tecumseh delivered his celebrated speech, in which he gave to the white people the alternative of restoring to the Indians, whom he claimed to represent, their lands, or of meeting those Indians in battle. Before this date, in 1805, the Prophet, who was called Law-le-was-i-kaw, or the Loud Voice, had assumed the name Pems-quat-a-wah, or the Open Door, and in the spring of 1808 he had removed from Greenville, Ohio, to the Wabash valley of Indiana, where he established what was called the Prophet's Town, and in August of 1808 he had visited Governor Harrison at Vincennes. Early in 1811 the British agent for Indian affairs adopted measures to secure the support of as many Indians as possible in the war that even then seemed to be unavoidable. That these measures included conferences and arrangements with Tecumseh seems probable, although no certain evidence has been found.

July 27th, 1811, Tecumseh again visited Governor Harrison at Vincennes. He objected persistently to the treaties that had been made, wherein lands were said to be sold to the United States by single tribes of Indians. He claimed that one tribe could not sell lands belonging more or less, as he claimed, to all the tribes in common. (In 1807, at Chillicothe, he had occupied between three and four hours in the delivery of a speech which was said to have been "eloquent and masterly, and showed that he possessed thorough knowledge of all the treaties which had been made for years."* "He was at this time one of the most splendid specimens of his tribe—celebrated for their physical proportions and fine forms." He is described as having been " tall, athletic, and manly, dignified and graceful   *   *   * the *beau ideal* of an Indian chieftain.")

As he and General Harrison could come to no perfect agreement at their conference, Tecumseh then said that he was going to visit the Southern Indians and would return to the Prophet's Town, and that the next spring he would visit the President at Washington and settle all cause of difficulty.

With twenty warriors he started immediately for the South. He left Vincennes August 5, 1811, and went down the Wabash River.† Of his journey south of the Ohio, till he reached the Chickasaws, there seems to be no record. Governor Harrison wrote to the War Department early in August, 1811, " that Tecumseh said he would be back next spring, but I am told in three months he will return. For four years he has been in constant motion."

That Tecumseh was in Indiana Territory in

---

* See Brice's History of Fort Wayne, page 175. I place large confidence in local histories.—T. H. B.

† How the statement originated that he left Detroit with thirty men mounted on horses, I have not ascertained. It is surely not correct history. I infer rather that he left Vincennes in boats, for he " descended the Wabash." **T. H. B.**

July, 1811, is certain. That he left Vincennes in August is beyond question.* That either in August or early in September of 1811 he was among the Chickasaws is also very certain.

For confirmation of these statements see the following extracts from American State Papers, copied April 26, 1894:

[FROM INDIAN AFFAIRS.]

Extracts from letters addressed to the War Department.

" Dated at VINCENNES, August 6, 1811.

"Tecumseh did not set out till yesterday; he then descended the Wabash attended by twenty men, on his way to the southward. After having visited the Creeks and Choctaws he is to visit the Osages and return by the Missouri." [Page 300.]

"NASHVILLE, Sept. 10, 1811.

" As I passed through the Chickasaw nation a respectable man of the nation informed me that a deputation of eighteen Northern Indians and two Creeks were on their way to the Creek nation, but would not tell their business. * * * The party consisted of six Shawnees, six Kickapoos, and six of some tribe far in the Northwest, the name of which they refused to tell. * * * ."

" NASHVILLE, Sept. 9, 1811.

" There is in this place a very noted chief of the Chickasaws, a man of truth, who wishes the President should be informed that there is a combination of the Northern Indians, promoted by the English, to unite in falling on the frontier settlements, and are inviting the Southern tribes to join them." [Page 301.]

---

* See Dillon's Indiana, also History of Indiana by Goodrich and Tuttle.

In a former chapter we have seen this restless chieftain among the Choctaws and Chickasaws. It is claimed that he then went through to Florida and that he succeeded there in arousing the Seminoles to make war upon the whites and to take the side of the British when they should hear that the great conflict between them and the Americans had commenced. There is little knowledge in regard to his visit among the Seminoles, except these two bare facts, if facts these are. It is reported that he gave them a bundle of prepared sticks, painted red, each stick to represent a day, according to the number of days to elapse before he wished them to enter on the war path, one of which they were to throw away each day that there might be no mistake ; and this is said to have been the origin of the term "Red Sticks" as applied to the hostile Indians. But quite a differerent origin of that term is also given.

That Tecumseh went among the Seminoles at all is questionable when the chronology of his Southern tour is closely examined. It took a little time [12] for his party to reach the Chickasaws in whatever manner they travelled, in boats for a time, and then on foot or on horses, and certainly some stop however brief was made among them. Among the Choctaws, according to the time records in the preceding chapter, Tecumseh spent at least four weeks, and he was among the Creeks by common agreement of the authorities in October. Surely he had not much time to spend in Florida.

From Florida Tecumseh started northward and made his noted tour among the Creeks. And again we come among conflicting statements. But per-

haps we will reach historic truth. 1. Before Tecumseh's visit, according to the Reminiscences of
General Thomas Woodward, a white man came from
Pensacola and made a visit to the Creek chief
called Big Warrior, at Tuckabatchee. Woodward's
informer was Weatherford, himself a noted Indian
leader of mixed blood. The time of the interview
was April, 1814. They were, says General Woodward, beside a camp fire on the west bank of a
stream called the Pinchgong. Weatherford thought
the Pensacola man was Scotch. So he is sometimes
called " the Scotch emissary." He held many conferences with Big Warrior "through a negro
interpreter." Shortly after the disappearance of
this man the oldest son of Big Warrior, Tuskanea or
Tuskahenaha, " took a trip to the Wabash and visited several tribes." He brought back some Shawnee women whom General Woodward saw. Weatherford further related that not long after the return
of Tuskanea, Tecumseh with a prophet called Seekaboo and with other stranger Indians appeared at
the town of Tuckabatchee. " A talk was put out "
by Big Warrior. This Weatherford and another
Creek of mixed blood called Sam Moniac, the original name having been McNac,* attended. " No
white man was allowed to be present." Weatherford reports, through General Woodward: "Tecumseh stated the object of his mission ; that if it could
be effected the Creeks could recover all the country
that the whites had taken from them; and that the
British would protect them in their rights." To

---

*See Weatherford's letter in the notes to Chapter IX.

Tecumseh's speech Moniac objected. He said the talk was a bad one, and he said that Tecumseh " had better leave the nation." The interpreter was Seekaboo " who spoke English." Weatherford told the interpreter to tell Tecumseh that the whites and Indians were at peace, that the Creeks were doing well, that it would be bad policy for them to take either side if the Americans and English went to war, and if they did unite with either side they "had better join the Americans."

"After this talk Tecumseh left for home and prevailed on Seekaboo and one or two others to remain among the Creeks."*

2. Hodgson in " Letters from North America " says, that his host told him that he was then living with an Indian wife among the Creeks ; that he was present at the midnight convocation of the chiefs ; that Tecumseh made a most impressive speech. The year of this interview is not given.

3. In the " History of the Tribes of North America," a book in the Newberry library of Chicago, the writer says he obtained his information at Tuckhabatchee in 1827 ; that Tecumseh went to the lodge of Big Warrior, " explained his object, delivered his war-talk, presented a bundle of sticks, gave a piece of wampum and a hatchet, all which the Big Warrier took ;" and that then, perceiving the Creek chief would not unite with him in his plans, he declared that when he returned to De-

---

* See " Reminiscences of the Creek or Muscogee Indians," by General Thomas Woodward. These Reminiscences consist of letters published in a Montgomery paper in 1859 and 1860, afterward published in book form. The work, as an authority, will be again mentioned.

troit he would stamp his foot and shake the earth. These accounts do not seem to have been copied the one from the other, but to be three independent [13] accounts. They agree sufficiently to be truthful.

4. Two other accounts there are which are quite different from these. The one is by Pickett, (Albert James Pickett), published in 1851; the other is by J. F. H. Claiborne of Mississippi—his large work entitled " Mississippi, as a Province, Territory, and State," having been published in 1880.

These two accounts are very similar, very "graphic," very full.

Claiborne says, page 315, "entering the Creek terri. tory he harangued the warriors at Autauga and Coosanda and the Hickory Ground. Wherever he went crowds attended, painted for war, and dancing the war dance." He adds. "In October the annual grand council of the nation, in pursuance of immemorial usage, assembled at the ancient town of Tookabatcha.* These councils were always attended. ed by the United States Agent, by all the traders, by many strangers, and by the warriors and their families. On this occasion the fame of Tecumseh's visit, and his expected address, had assembled some five thousand persons at Tookabatcha." Claiborne describes the entrance of Tecumseh and his warriors into the town square† the second day, their dress, arms, bearing, the passing of Big Warrior's pipe, and their departure from the square to a large cabin provided for them, and at night their war dance.

'*Different writers give different orthography for the same names.
†All Indian towns had public squares. Villages had no squares.

Each morning a Shawnee warrior announced that his chief would speak at noon, and each noon the speech was put off till the next day, until Colonel Hawkins, the United States Agent, left the town. The next noon after the Agent's departure, amid imposing ceremonies, Tecumseh made his appearance and delivered his speech. The assembly continued till midnight. Claiborne gives as the year, 1811, and the month October. Pickett, a statement of whose account will be found in the notes on this chapter, gives the same month, but by some means has the year date 1812. Claiborne gives the speech of Tecumseh "compressed."

No reporter is named except "Captain Sam Dale," although "an intelligent witness" is referred to.

The speech as to its genuineness is much like the historic speech of John Adams, "Sink or swim," given by Webster, although unlike that in failing to give the sentiments of Tecumseh. There is no reasonable evidence that it contains the substance of the statements of Tecumseh. It commences by claiming that his party murdered whites as they came through their settlemeuts.

"No war-whoop was sounded, no track was made,"—by thirty men on horseback—"no fire was kindled, but see! there is blood on our war clubs!"

It urges the destruction of women and children, of which Tecumseh did not approve. It says: "Two mighty warriors across the seas will send us arms— at Detroit for us, at Pensacola for you," ten months before Detroit came into the possession of the English. And in closing this murderous, vengeful, bar-

barous, furious Tecumseh of imagination rather than
of fact is made to say, "Soon shall you see my arm
of fire stretched athwart the sky. You will know
that I am on the war-path. I will stamp my foot
and the very earth shall shake." Claiborne says, in
a note appended to this "compressed" speech, "The
British officers at Detroit had informed Tecumseh
that a comet would soon appear, and the earthquakes
of 1811 had commenced as he came through
Kentucky." This note is surprising in view of these
facts: that Tecumseh did not start south from
Detroit, but from Vincennes, and no evidence has
been found that in July of 1811 "British officers"
were in Detroit—what business had they, then, in
that American post?—and no evidence that Tecumseh at that time had met with British officers; that
he must have passed through Kentucky, and through
or across very little of it at most, in August, and
there is evidence that the first earthquake shocks
were felt at Louisville the last week in November;
and that the noted comet of 1811, the most remarkable one that appeared in the first half of
this century, was visible in September and ceased
to be seen when the earthquake shocks com-
[14] menced.

In confirmation of these statements about the
comet and earthquake are these extracts from an
address before the Maryland Historical Society by
Hon. J. B. Latrobe of Baltimore. He is describing
the voyage of the steamboat "New Orleans," the
first to descend the Mississippi. "It was midnight
on the first of October, 1811, that the 'New Orleans'
dropped anchor opposite the town."

This was Louisville. "There was a brilliant moon. It was as light as day almost, and no one on board had retired. The noise of the escaping steam, then heard for the first time * * roused the population"and "there were those who insisted that the comet of 1811 had fallen into the Ohio and produced the hub-bub!" For weeks the boat waited for rains and for water to pass the falls. The time is now "the last week in November." And J. B. Latrobe says, "The comet of 1811 had disappeared and was followed by the earthquakes of that year." Also C. J. Latrobe, in his "Rambler in North America," speaking of 1811 as "the *annus mirabilis* of the West" on account of the overflow of rivers, the "unprecedented sickness," the migration of "a countless multitude of squirrels," adds: "The splendid comet of that year long continued to shed its twilight over the forests, and, as the autumn drew to a close, the whole valley of the Mississippi, from the Missouri to the gulf, was shaken to its center by continued earthquakes."

Now, as the facts concerning the comet and the earthquakes, in these quotations from the two Latrobes, were known to Claiborne, for they are in his "Mississippi," his note is surprising as explaining Tecumseh's speech. Tecumseh never made that speech. [15] Aside from the absurdity of its close, it does not breathe the well established humane spirit of Tecumseh. In order to obtain scientific as well as literary evidence in regard to the appearance of that comet, a letter of inquiry was sent to the astronomer at Harvard University, and, with the accustomed courtesy of the professors there, he soon returned the following reply:

Harvard College
Observatory,

Cambridge, Mass., Nov. 26, 1894.

Dear Sir:—Your letter of November 20th is at
hand. The comet you mention was discovered on
March 26, 1811, and was visible to the naked eye in
April, but only with difficulty. Its orbit was soon
sufficiently determined to show that it would be
nearer, and therefore brighter, in autumn; and it is
possible that this knowledge may have reached Detroit as early as July. During most of the summer
the comet was too nearly in the same direction with
the sun to be seen at all, but it reappeared August
20th, and by August 26th was easily visible to the
naked eye; it continued to increase in brightness
during September, coming nearest to the earth on
October 15th. By December it had become very
faint. It could be seen in this country as well as in
Europe.

With that brilliant comet, its tail according to
Milne "132,000,000 miles long," shining over them
night after night all through September, and being
nearest the earth Octotober 15th, it is unreasonable
to suppose Tecumseh to have said to those Creek warriors, "Soon shall you see my arm of fire stretched
athwart the sky." Tecumseh had too much good
[16] sense to say that. Nor is it probable that he claimed
to be able to shake the earth. The Claiborne speech
is not given here, for it does no credit to Tecumseh.
It rests on no authority.

5. Leaving now these reports of Tecumseh among
the Creeks, this of Claiborne, and also the one by
Pickett which the reader will find in the notes, the
most satisfactory statements at last are those of
Dr. Ramsay.

He says, after mentioning Tecumseh's ardent but savage* eloquence, "He reminded them of the usurpation of their lands by the whites, and painted in glowing colors their spirit of encroachment, and the consequent diminution, and probable extinction, of the race of Indians; and contrasted their sedentary and unmanly occupations with the wild and fearless independence of their ancestors." This sounds like Tecumseh, and it does not appear that anything more accurate can now be obtained than was secured before the year 1818 by that noble son of Pennsylvania and South Carolina, Dr. David Ramsay.

A few statements may here be added to show that Tecumseh could not have returned again to the South, as some historians state, in 1812.

Instead of returning, as he proposed, to the Prophet's Town and in the spring of 1812 going to Washington to see the President and settle all difficulties, he found on his return to Indiana in December that the Prophet had gone contrary to his instructions, had fought and lost the battle of Tippecanoe November 7th, that the Prophet's famous town had been destroyed, that his great confederacy was breaking up, and he appeared in that same month of December, 1811, at Fort Wayne. He asked for ammunition. It was denied him. He said he would go to his British father. He "gave the war-whoop and went off." †

---

*A savage is not always cruel. When Proctor and Tecumseh were together as commanders of the British forces, Proctor was evidently the more cruel, bloody savage of the two.

†See Brice's History of Fort Wayne, page 202.

In the spring of 1812 the Indians commenced
active hostilities.   May 15, 1812, Tecumseh attended
a council at Mississinaway, thirty miles below Fort
Wayne.   In June he visited Fort Wayne, then went
to Malden.   In July he was at Malden with his
warriors ready for the war, and was in the summer
aiding General Brock in the region of Detroit.   In
August he led the Indians in the attack at Browns-
town, in the first action after the formal declaration
of the War of 1812.   August 16th, when Detroit
was captured, he was at the head of the Indians.   In
August of this year he was appointed a British
Brigadier General.   In September he began to
assemble his forces to reduce forts Wayne and
Harrison.   Tecumseh continued actively engaged in
the North, and in December of 1812, with six hundred warriors, he was near the Mississinaway towns.
It is quite certain that he was not far from the scene
of conflict when Frenchtown was taken January 22,
1813.   In April, 1813, he was at Fort Meigs.   The
siege continued till May 9th.*   He was again at
Fort Meigs at the second attack in July, when he
led " two thousand warriors."   He was associated
with General Brock and also with General Proctor,
and was killed October 5, 1813, at the battle of the
Thames, called also the battle of the Moravian towns.

It thus appears that Lossing, Parton, Drake, and
others must be mistaken who claim that Tecumseh

---

* Says Ramsay (vol. 3, p. 280): " The British force, including
regulars and militia, during the siege, was supposed to have
been upwards of one thousand.   Their Indian auxiliaries were
not fewer in amount.   Among them the celebrated Tecumseh
was particularly distinguished.   The American garrison seldom
exceeded twelve hundred, a very small portion of whom were
regulars."

visited the Southern Indians a second time, making
that visit in the fall of 1812 or in the spring of 1813.
It is true that the actual presence of Tecumseh in
the Indiana Territory has not been shown for the
months of October and November of 1812; but that
he could have been absent from the "seat of war,"
could have gone South and visited all those Southern
Indians, and returned, in those two months, is hardly
credible.

NOTES.

1. Mention has been made of an effort to obtain
documentary evidence of Tecumseh's visit from the
War Department. The following are extracts from
a letter from a valued friend residing in Washington City, Mrs. Bessie Boone Cheshire:

" WASHINGTON, D. C., Nov. 29, 1892.

"Your letter of 24th inst. duly received. It is a
source of much pleasure to be of use to you in the
work in which your are engaged. Though I fear
the resources at my command are not so great as you
may think. There is no documentary evidence of
Tecumseh's visit to the Creeks. In fact there are
now no documents of any of the older Indian wars.
* * * The officials to whom I went were disposed to be very helpful. However they told me
that no outside parties were ever allowed to examine
documents—this was when I asked the privilege of
examining the records—but that they would examine and give me any desired information. I was told
that "Lossing's Field Book of the War of 1812"
would furnish all that I had inquired for. And
when I told them it was not historical but documentary evidence that I wished, they told me there
was absolutely none; that if you sent or had sent

direct to the War Department for it they could only have referred you to Lossing, page 187.

" All this did not quite satisfy me, and having quite a near neighbor who is an officer in the Indian Bureau I went to him about it. He told me to address a letter to the Commissioner of Indian Affairs, enclose yours to me, and send it through the mail, and then it would receive attention and whatever they found would be sent to you direct from the office and would be official. This in a measure, relieved me as there was really nothing left for me to do.

" This neighbor tells me that my letter with yours came to the Commissioner and was placed in his hands with a note from Commissioner Morgan in which he says:

" 'Rev. T. H. Ball is a particular friend of mine and I shall esteem it as a personal favor if you will furnish him the desired information.' "

Under date of December 22d the letter states that the neighbor called that morning to say that the office had a man looking up such old records as remained.

2. In due course of time the following, through the hands of my friend, Mrs. Cheshire, a lady of culture, interested in historical research, came through the mail from Washington:

DEPARTMENT
OF THE
INTERIOR
OFFICE OF INDIAN AFFAIRS.

WASHINGTON, December 31, 1892.

Mrs. Bessie Boone Cheshire, 105 Eleventh St., S. E., City—

MADAM: I am in receipt of your letter of December 1, 1892, forwarding a letter from Rev. T. H. Ball, of Crown Point, Indiana, dated November 24, 1892, requesting definite information **from** the records of this office as to the fact, whether or not the noted Indian Chief, Tecumseh, visited the Creek Indians in 1811, or in 1812, or both years, as Historical writers differ as to the time of said visit; but he had satisfied himself that Tecumseh was South at the time of the battle of Tippecanoe in 1811, but wished to know authoritatively if he went South again in 1812, and refers to the fact that Col. Benjamin Hawkins at that time had charge of Indian affairs in Georgia, and felt sure that in the records at Washington, his report of ,Tecumseh's visit could be found, if made.

Rev. Mr. Ball gives as his reason for making this call for information, the fact that he, in company with a friend in Mississippi, is preparing a work on the "Creek War in South Alabama," and that it has fallen to his lot to write up the chapter "Tecumseh's visit to the Creek Indians," and must have some documentary evidence, State paper or official report that he was *surely* there in 1812.

In response to this request, I have caused the records of this office to be searched, but they fail to disclose any information on the subject. The papers on file in this office, of that period, are very meagre indeed; the files were kept in the War Department, and when the papers were transferred from that Department to this office in 1849, when the Interior Department was organized, and this office made a branch bureau thereof, but few of the records or files pertaining to such subjects were transferred, so that if this visit was officially reported by Col. Hawkins, it must yet remain in the custody of the War Department.

I would state however that reference is made in the American State Papers, of the visits of Tecumseh to the Southern Indians, and your attention is invited to Volume 1, Indian Affairs, p. 799, where in a letter from General Harrison, dated Vincennes, December 4, 1811, to Wm. Eustis, Secretary of War, he speaks of Tecumseh's tour to the Southward; and on page 800, in letters addressed to the War Department, mention is made in one from Vincennes dated August 6, 1811, that "Tecumseh did not set out till yesterday, he then descended the Wabash, attended by twenty men, on his way to the Southward. After having visited the Creeks and Choctaws, he is to visit the Osages and return by the Missouri."

In a letter from William Wells of Fort Wayne, dated March 1, 1812, to the Secretary of War, Mr. Eustis, he writes:

"In my letter of the 10th ultimo, I informed you that the Indian chief, Tecumseh, had arrived on the Wabash. I have now to state to you that it appears that he has determined to raise all the Indians he can, immediately, with an intention, no doubt, to attack our frontier. He has sent runners to raise the Indians on the Illinois and the Upper Mississippi, and I am told he has gone himself to hurry on the aid he was promised by the Cherokees and Creeks." Idem, p. 806.)

In an extract from General William Clark, of St. Louis, dated March 22, 1812, appears the following, viz:

"The Winnebagoes, part of the Kickapoos, and some of the Pottawatomies are yet friendly to the Prophet and may join him again in the spring. His brother, Tecumseh, returned from the Southern tribes in December last. He made great exertions to get the Shawnees and Delawares of this territory to join the Prophet's army, but without success." (Idem p. 807.)

The History of Alabama, by Albert James Pickett, published in 1851, in two volumes, at Charleston, by Walker & James, has a chapter on Tecumseh (Chapter xxxi., Vol. 2.) After stating that his father and mother were of the Shawnee family, were born and bred at Souvanogee (old Augusta)

upon the Tallapoosa, in Alabama, who removed to
the forest of Ohio, where Tecumseh was born in
1768, and referring to other visits to the Cherokees
and Creeks, it states that—

"After many conferences with the British, at
Detroit, Tecumseh, in the spring of 1812, left that
country with a party of thirty warriors mounted on
horses, and shaped his course to the south. Passing
through the Chickasaw and Choctaw Country, he
was unsuccessful in arraying these tribes against the
Americans. He went down to Florida and met
with complete success with the Seminoles. In the
month of October he came up to Alabama, crossed
that river at Autauga, when he, for the first time,
appealed to the Creeks in a long speech. Continuing
to Coosawda, he had by this time collected many
followers, who went with him to the Hickory
Ground. Having from their boyhood heard of his
feats in the buffalo chase, the bloody wars which he
had conducted, and of his fierce and transcendent
eloquence, the warriors flocked to see him. He went
to Tookabatcha, where Colonel Hawkins was then
holding his grand council with the Indians. * *
Tecumseh visited all the important Creek towns,
enlisting all whom he could on the side of England.
* * Tecumseh having made numerous proselytes.
once more (November) visited the Big Warrior at
Tookabatcha, whom he was particularly desirous to
enlist in his schemes, but whom he had hitherto en-
treated to no effect, although his house was his
headquarters. * * * The common Indians believed every word of Tecumseh's last speech, which
was intended solely to intimidate the Big Warrior,
and (in December) they began to count up the time
it would take the Shawnee chief to reach Detroit,
when he would stamp his foot, as he had declared."

It seems that he became very angry with Big
Warrior, and pointing his finger in his face, emphat-
ically said, "Your blood is white. * * You do

not believe the Great Spirit sent me. You shall
believe it. I will leave directly and go straight to
Detroit. When I get there I will stamp my foot
upon the ground and shake down every house in
Tookabatcha." It appears that a mighty rumbling
in the earth was heard soon after, which caused the
houses of Tookabatcha to reel and totter. The
people ran out, saying, "Tecumseh has got to Detroit! Tecumseh has got to Detroit! We feel the
shake of his foot!"

In relation to this visit of Tecumseh to Alabama
the author makes this note on page 246, Vol. 2:

"I have consulted General Ferdinand L. Claiborne's MS. papers and Drake's Life of Tecumseh;
I have also conversed with Lachau Durant, Mrs. Sophia McComb, Peter Raudon, James Moore, and
others, who were at Tookabatcha when Tecumseh
arrived there."

The letter of the Rev. Mr. Ball is returned here-
with.   Very respectfully
            T. J. MORGAN, Commissioner.

3. Among other efforts to arrive at facts in regard
to Tecumseh, I wrote to Hiram W. Beckwith, Esq ,
of Danville, Illinois, who owns "what is probably
the most valuable collection in the West on French-
American history," a library which he has been
twenty-five years collecting from dealers on both
sides of the Atlantic, and which, it is said, "contains
nearly every known book on the language, imple-
ments, and manners of the aboriginal inhabitants,
and their wars with the border settlers."

The Governor "appointed him one of the Trustees of the State Historical Library, and his asso-
ciates selected him as President of their board."

From him, in answer to my special questions, I
received the following statements, which, as he
presents the same conclusions which my investigations have reached, giving authorities to which I

have not had access, I think ought to be placed here, at the conclusion of this chapter. His letter is dated "Danville, Illinois, Dec. 16th, 1892." I omit the introduction:

"1st. On the 27th of July, 1811, 'Tecumseh, with about 320 or 330 men, women. and children, arrived at Vincennes.' [*Vide* 'Memoirs of Gen. Harrison,' by Moses Dawson, Cincinnati, 1824, page 182.] This was the Shawnee's *second* personal visit to Gov. Harrison, the first having been on August 12th, 1810."

"2d. 'A few days after' the conclusion of the conference of 1811, 'Tecumseh accompanied by twenty men went down the Wabash.' 'The day before he told Governor Harrison that after visiting the Creeks, Chickasaws, and Choctaws he would go to the Osages (in Missouri) and return by the Missouri river.' 'He had given out the following spring as the time for his return, but the Governor had information that he intended to be absent no more than three months.' [*Vide* same work, page 184.]

"Just how long he was in the South, or the exact time of his return, is a matter I am without any authority to refer you. He was certainly back again upon the upper Wabash late the same year, or at least very early in that of 1812.

"3d. His whereabouts in 1812 and thence on until his death, October 5th of the following year, can be so closely followed as to have given him no time whatever for any other visit to the Creeks or their neighbors. It will be recalled that the battle of Tippecanoe took place Nov. 7, 1811, 'during Tecumseh's absence.' Now, Little Turtle, the Miami chief, in his address to Gov. Harrison, dated at Fort Wayne, Indiana, January 25, 1812, referring to the results of that affair, says: 'All of the Prophet's followers have left him except two camps of his own tribe. Tecumseh has just joined him with only eight men.' [*Vide* 'Little Turtle to Gov. Harrison,' Mem. Gen. Harrison above, page 258.]

"Again, we find him at a grand council of several Indian nations, 'held at Massassinway (near its mouth) on the Wabash, May 16, 1812,' when he made two speeches. [*Vide* minutes of those proceedings, same volume, page 266.] On this occasion Tecumseh, alluding to the action of Nov. 7th, said: 'Governor Harrison made war on my people in my absence.' The next month, 'on the 17th of June, he came to Fort Wayne,' saying 'he was on his way to Malden' (now Amherstburg, Canada, near the mouth of the Detroit river), to receive from the British government twelve horse loads of ammunition for the use of his people at Tippecanoe.' He went on to Malden and was there a few days before Gen. Hull's army arrived at Detroit, and thereupon 'declared he would join the British against the United States.' [*Vide* 'Letter of Capt. Wm. Wells to Gov. Harrison, Fort Wayne, July 22, 1812, copied into the above volume, page 278.]

"'On the 12th of July, 1812, his brother, the Prophet, reached Fort Wayne with nearly a hundred Winnebagoes and Kickapoos,' and went into camp near by.

"A week later one of Tecumseh's messengers from the head of Lake Erie arrived at the Prophet's camp telling the latter 'to at once send their women and children towards the Mississippi, while the warriors should strike a heavy blow on Vincennes, and that he, Tecumseh, if he lived, would join him in the country of the Winnebagoes,' then in Wisconsin. After the landing of Gen. Hull at Sandwich to attack Malden, July 12, 'Tecumseh and a hundred of his Indians remained at the latter place with the British.' [*Vide* same letter.]

"Wm. S. Hatch, then Quarter Master in the American army, saw him on the streets of Detroit, Aug. 17th of the same year, and graphically describes his appearance and dress. He was then an officer in the British service,[*Vide* 'Hatche's Chapter

on the War of 1812,' page 114], and on the 9th of the
same month he had commanded the Indians in the
engagement against the Americans a few miles below
Detroit. [*Vide* 'History of the Late War' (of 1812)
by Capt. Robert McAffe, Lexington, Ky., 1816,
page 78].

'On the 18th of December, 1812, Col. Campbell,
attacked the Indian towns 'on the Mississiniway
river' and 'learning from a prisoner that Tecumseh
with six hundred warriors was but eighteen miles below him,' near the Wabash. 'did not think it prudent
to remain there any longer.' [Same volume, page
181 to 182.]

"Thus can we trace Tecumseh in 1812 and 1813
from place to place on the northwestern frontier in a
way that gives him no time to be absent from that
field of military operation.

"Truly yours,

"HIRAM W. BECKWITH."

The critical reader may notice that, as in the text
of this chapter, so here in this letter, the presence of
Tecumseh in the North has not been shown for the
month of October, 1812, when some claim he was
among the Creek Indians. But even granting that
his presence on the Indiana Territory or in Canada
for that month cannot be shown, I think enough has
been shown to justify Mr. Beckwith's statement, that
there was "no time," in the fall of 1812, when Tecumseh could have been absent sufficiently long,
"from that field of military operation," to make that
visit described by Parton and by Drake. Mr. Beckwith adds in a postscript:

"The authorities quoted are above all dispute.
They are also quite rare. Dawson and Capt. Mc-
Affe were on the Northern frontier in active service

from start to finish, and both had access to contemporaneous writings as well as an extended personal intercourse with the leading officers in all military movements of those memorable campaigns."

———————

The writer of the foregoing chapter had access to Choctaw traditions to enable him to trace Tecumseh's movements from place to place, almost from day to day; but the writer of this chapter has had no Creek traditions to aid him in making up the facts as recorded, but has been obliged to sift many statements to secure a few grains of unquestionable historic truth. And he is well aware that some critical readers may say, he has made a needless parade of the work performed; but he hopes many readers will appreciate it at whatever may be its true [17]   value.   **T. H. B.**

CHAPTER V.

THE WAR CLOUD GATHERING.

WAR was declared between the United States and Great Britain June 18, 1812. Into this war Tecumseh entered heartily in favor of the British and against the Americans, as we have already seen. We are now to look at the Creek Indians in this year of 1812.

The following are extracts from letters to the War Department, written by Colonel Benjamin Hawkins, and taken from Indian Affairs as published in American State Papers, commencing on page 304.

CREEK AGENCY, Feb. 3, 1812.

Our Indians are, many of them, occupied in spinning, weaving, making new settlements, or improving those heretofore made. I believe nine-tenths of the Lower Creeks have left their old towns and formed,or are forming settlements on the creeks and rivers where the lands are good and the range for stock good.

CREEK AGENCY, April 6, 1812.

On the 26th ult., Thomas Meredith, Sr., a respectable old man, travelling with his family to the Mississippi Territory,was murdered on the post road, at Kittome,a creek 150 miles from this. Sam Macnac, a half breed, of large property, who keeps entertainment on the road, at whose house Meredith is buried, calls it an accident.

Colonel Hawkins then details circumstances and gives evidence showing that it was a murder.

CREEK AGENCY, May 11, 1812.
I have just returned from the council of the Lower Creeks, and have time only, by this mail, to write you a short letter.

He then states (given here in an abridged form) that Charles Hicks,late United States interpreter for the Cherokees, by order of his chiefs, had sent a friendly letter to the Creeks, in which he said to them that if they joined the English in the coming war they would lose every foot of their land, but if they joined the Americans they would gain their friendship forever. To this the Creeks replied that they would not " interfere in the wars of white people."

CREEK AGENCY, May 25, 1812.
I was this day informed by Mr. Cornells, our interpreter for the Upper Creeks, that on the 23rd inst. a white man, William Lott, was murdered, eight miles this way from his home, by four Indians, without the least provocation.　　*　　*　　*
The chiefs will meet in one week and we shall see what can be done. We have a report also that two families have been killed in Tennessee.

CREEK AGENCY, July 28, 1812.
I have just time to inform you that the Indian who murdered Meredith was put to death on the 19th.

CREEK AGENCY Aug. 24, 1812.
Those charged with the murder on Duck River are not yet come at.

This massacre of the Tennessee families on Duck River and the treatment of Mrs. Crawley and children, aroused strong feelings against the Creeks among the people of Tennessee. The reader will find, when he comes to the treaty of peace, at the close of the war, that Duck River was charged up against the Creeks along with Fort Mims.

The Lower and Upper Creeks united their efforts in having justice dealt out to the murderers of William Lott. We come now to 1813, the year of actual strife.

By an act passed in Congress February 12, 1813, General James Wilkinson was authorized to proceed to Mobile, then held by the Spaniards, and to take possession. March 8th, Commander Shaw, with General Wilkinson and his troops on board his fleet, reached Dauphine Island; and after a few days the following communication was sent to the Spanish commandant by the American General:

BEFORE MOBILE, April 12.

SIR: The troops of the United States do not approach you as the enemies of Spain, but by order of the President they come to relieve the brave garrison which you so worthily command, from the occupancy of a post within the legitimate limits of the United States. I hope that you will peacefully retire from Fort Charlotte, and from the Mississippi Territory, to the eastern side of the Perdido river.

This request was in a few days complied with.*

General Wilkinson did not long remain at Mobile. He was ordered to Canada—in June he was passing through the "Creek Nation" on his way to the North—and Major General Thomas Flournoy, of Georgia, succeeded him in the command at Mobile, and of the Seventh military division.

---

*I have taken the above from Claiborne's "Mississippi," which in regard to official documents, I consider perfectly reliable..

T. H. B.

General Flournoy, June 28, 1813, ordered Brigadier General Ferdinand L. Claiborne, with his brigade of six hundred Mississippi volunteers, to march from Baton Rouge to Mount Vernon, in order to be ready there "to repel any attack that may be made on any part of the frontier of the Mississippi Territory, either from Indians, Spaniards, or English" Leaving Baton Rouge June 28th, this brigade reached Mount Vernon July 30th, 1813. "You will put yourself," General Flournoy's order continued, "in communication with Lieutenant Colonel Bowyer, who commands at Mobile and Mobile Point, who will give you the earliest information of any movement by the English or Spaniards. The defence of the town of Mobile will be your principal care."

While the open war was between the Americans and the British, it was quite well understood that on the southern frontier both the Spaniards and Indians were likely to aid the British as against the Americans. The Spaniards and British had by turns been the nominal holders of Florida.

Leaving now General Flournoy in command in the summer of 1813, and General Claiborne at Mount Vernon, we are ready to look at the uprising of a part of the Creek confederacy, or at what was called their civil war.

J. F. H. Claiborne, in his "Mississippi," gives a letter written by General Wilkinson, when on his way northward, to one of the prominent citizens of Washington county, Judge Toulmin, which is dated —a misprint or mistake is here corrected—"Sam Manacs, Creek Nation, June 25, 1813."

In this letter he says: "Your favor of the 22d reached me near this place, surrounded by dangers; but I am too far advanced to retreat. Indeed, I dare not turn my back on reports, and, therefore, shall proceed this evening [afternoon] to Catoma, and to-morrow to Doyle's, where I expect to see the Big Warrior, who has begged an interview with me. He has been intrenched against the war party a week or ten days and lives in fear of his life, as his antagonists are daily making converts and increasing in strength, with the avowed intention to destroy him and all who have been concerned in the execution of the murderers; after which, it is believed by all with whom I have conversed, they expect to intimidate the rest of the nation to join them, and then it is their intention to make war on the whites. This seems to be the general impression; but no one can tell or even guess where a blow will be struck." General Wilkinson then speaks of "one Joseph Francis," living on the road, who claimed to have "had a visit from the Lord," and who detailed the things revealed to him "in the manner most impressive on his barbarian auditors." General Wilkinson also wrote that he was assured that Francis with more than three hundred followers was at a camp on the Alabama about sixteen miles above the Big Swamp, and that it was reported that this party was about "to move down the river to break up the half-breed settlements and those of the citizens in the forks of the river."

He adds:

"I know not what stress to lay on these wild reports, but the whole road is deserted—the Indians are all assembled, and their villages ahead of me, many towns on the Alabama and Tallapoosa and Coosa, are deserted, and consternation and terror are in every countenance I meet. I have considered it proper you should receive this information, and, therefore, I send back Weatherford with this infor-

mation for your government, and will only observe,
that I think the volunteers should be called up to
your frontier, without a moment's delay."   General
Wilkinson was now on his way to his command in
Canada, and was travelling, the reader will notice,
over that "Government road" through the Creek
country.   One quotation more:

"I have about twenty armed men, and our caval-
cade consists of about forty persons. Our horses and
carriages are in good order. * * * Colonel
Hawkins is profoundly silent.   Alexander Cornels
has fled the country and I cannot hear of any
preparation to succor the Big Warrior."   The letter
is signed "James Wilkinson," and is addressed "Hon.
Judge Toulmin, Fort Stoddert."

It appears from this letter that open war among
the Creeks had not then commenced but might
break out any day. Weatherford was at that time
friendly. (Some suggest that the Weatherford
mentioned in the letter was not the noted William
but Jack Weatherford, but, if so, it will not affect
the statement as a fact, although affecting it as a
[18]   conclusion; for as a fact it rests on other evidence.)

The murderers referred to in this valuable letter
are no doubt those concerned in the murder of
Thomas Meredith and William, or as some call him,
Arthur, Lott. General Woodward says: "I have
often heard Sam Moniac say, that if Lott had not
been killed at the time he was, it was his belief that
the war could have been prevented."*

---

* The student of history finds King Philip's war originating
about as did the Creek war. 1. "It became evident to the
Indians that the spreading settlements were fast breaking up
their hunting grounds." 2. A converted Indian was found murdered. "The execution by the whites of three Indians, con-
victed of the murder, may be considered as the immediate cause
of the war." See Anderson's history of King Philip's War.

The following deposition copied from the Alabama Historical Reporter of June, 1880, is an interesting document which will show what plans some
of the chiefs had formed as early as July 11, 1813,
the time of the interview with Jim Boy or High
Head Jim to which Sam Moniac refers.

MISSISSIPPI TERRITORY, WASHINGTON DISTRICT.

*The Deposition of Samuel Manac, of lawful age,
a Warrior of the Creek Nation.*

About the last of October, thirty Northern
Indians came down with Tecumseh, who said he had
been sent by his brother, the prophet. They attended our council at the Tuccabache, and had a
talk for us. I was there for the space of two or
three days, but every day whilst I was there, Tecumseh refused to deliver his talk, and on being requested to give it, said that the sun had gone too far
that day. The day after I came away, he delivered
his talk. It was not till about Christmas that any
of our people began to dance the war dance. The
Muscogees have not been used to dance before war,
but after. At that time about forty of our people
began this Northern custom, and my brother-in-law,
Francis, who also pretends to be a prophet, was at
the head of them. Their number has very much increased since, and there are probably now more
than half of the Creek nation who have joined
them.

Being afraid of the consequences of a murder having been committed on the mail route, I had left my
home on the road, and had gone down to my plantation on the river. I stayed there some time. I went
to Pensacola with some steers, during which time,
my sister and brother, who have joined the war
party, came and got off a number of my horses and
other stock, and thirty-six of my negroes. About

one or two and twenty days ago, I went up to my
house on the road, and found some Indians camped
near it whom I tried to avoid, but could not. An
Indian came to me, who goes by the name of High-
Headed Jim, and whom I found had been appointed
to head a party sent from the Auttasee Town, on the
Tallapoosa, on a trip to Pensacola. He shook hands
with me, and immediately began to tremble and jerk
in every part of his frame, and the very calves of his
legs would be convulsed, and he would get entirely
out of breath with the agitation. This practice was
introduced in May or June last by the Prophet
Francis, who says that he was instructed by the
Spirit. High-Headed Jim asked what I meant to do.
I said that I should sell my property and buy
ammunition, and join them. He then told me that
they were going down to Pensacola to get ammunition,and that they had got a letter from a British General which would enable them to receive ammunition
from the Governor. That it had been given to the
Little Warrior, and saved by his Nephew when he
was killed, and sent down to Francis. High-Head
told me that when they went back with their supply,
another body of men would go down for another
supply of ammunition, and that ten men would go out
of each Town, and that they calculated on five horse
loads for every Town. He said that they were to
make a general attack on the American Settlements—
that the Indians on the waters of the Coosa and Tallapoosa, and on the Black Warrior, were to attack the
Settlements on the Tombigby and Alabama, particularly the Tensaw and Fork Settlements.—That the
Creek Indians, bordering on the Cherokees, were to
attack the people of Tennessee, and that the Seminoles and lower Creeks were to attack the Georgians.
—That the Choctaws also had joined them and were
to attack the Mississippi Settlements.—That the
attack was to be made at the same time in all places
where they got furnished with ammunition. I found,

from my sister, that they were treated very rigor-
ously by the Chiefs, and that many, particularly the
women among them, (two daughters of the late Gen.
McGillivray, who had been induced to join them to
save their property,) were very desirous to leave
them, but could not.

I found, from the talk of High-Head, that the war
was to be against the whites and not between Indians
themselves,—that all they wanted was to kill those
who had taken the talk of the whites, viz.: the Big
Warrior, Alex. Cornells, Capt. Isaac, Wm. McIntosh,
the Mad Dragon's son, the little Prince Spoko Kange
and Tallasee Thicksico.

They have destroyed a large quantity of my
cattle, and burnt my houses on my river plantation,
as well as those of James Cornells and Leonard
McGee.

(Signed,)   his
SAMUEL S. M. MANAC.
mark.

Sworn and subscribed before me, one of the U. S.
Judges for the Mississippi Territory, this 2d day of
August, 1813.   HARRY TOULMIN.

A true copy.

GEO. T. ROSS, Lt. Col. V.

This deposition, although sworn to by as friendly
and trusty a man as Sam Moniac, must not all be
taken as reliable history. The reader must not suppose the October mentioned to be in the year 1812,
as would be natural, but in 1811. In what year the
Christmas was can only be conjectured, so far as the
deposition is concerned. High Head Jim, whom
Dr. A. B. Clanton of Leaf, Mississippi, calls Tuskegee, and of whom he says: "In his person he was
the beau ideal of a hero," "beyond all comparison
the finest looking man" that he had chanced to see,

was evidently mistaken in some of his statements.
But the critical reader will find these out for himself. He can see what the River Settlements had
reason to expect. How fully any plan for such a
widespread extermination of the white settlers was
matured, it is impossible now to ascertain ; but they
were determined, evidently, to make an effort to
prevent their own extermination, and the Spanish
authorities at Pensacola had promised that, in the
event of their failure, they would transport them all
to the island of Cuba.

About this same time, probably in July, 1813,
Latecau, an Indian youth eighteen years of age,
claiming to be a prophet, and collecting eight others
as subordinate prophets, went to the old town of
Coosa and invited all the unbelievers or friendly
Indians to come and see the display of their magical
powers. Many assembled. The prophets commenced " the dance of the lakes," as taught by Tecumseh's warriors, then suddenly gave the war-
whoop, rushed upon three friendly chiefs and killed
them. The other chiefs immediately retired to their
own towns, assembled their warriors, returned to
Coosa, killed the nine prophets, and then went to
LittleOcfuskee and put to death some more of Tecumseh's deluded followers. Thus, it seems, the civil
war, so called, among the Creeks, began. The hostile
bands also commenced killing the cattle of the
friendly Indians, as Moniac testified, or driving them
off and selling them.

Another valuable letter, in this connection, is the
following from General Flournoy to General Claiborne. The date is August 25, 1813.

"SIR: Your letters and documents, by express, have been received. As I have already written you, and likewise Governor Holmes, very fully on Indian affairs, I will not now go into further details. A recent letter from Colonel Hawkins (a copy herein enclosed), will show the situation of the Creek Indians. They must finish their civil war before they go to war with us. And it is by no means certain that the war party will succeed in overpowering the party friendly to us."

Some time between the date of these two letters it is evident that Weatherford joined the war party, for before August closed we find him at Fort Mims, General Woodward places it in 1813, but does not name the month. And it may be here observed that Tecumseh seems to have had no influence over Weatherford. Woodward says that Sam Moniac and Weatherford, returning from a trip into the Mississippi Territory, where they had been "trading in beef cattle," found several chiefs assembled—it is said on Tallewassee Creek, a mile and a half from the Alabama River—and taking the "black drink."*

These chiefs told Weatherford and Moniac that they must join them or be put to death. The following are Woodward's own words: " Moniac boldly refused and mounted his horse.† Josiah Francis, his brother-in-law, seized his bridle. Moniac

---

* This drink, a kind of tea, was made from the leaves of the Ilex Cassine, or holly of the Gulf states, and used on various occasions.

See Wood's botany and see Gatschet.

† Whether the trading in beef cattle took place after Moniac made his deposition August 2, 1813, or whether it took place before he took his steers to Pensacola, or whether the two accounts are different versions of one transaction, I will leave for the consideration of those understanding the principles of "higher criticism."   T. H. B.

snatched a war club from his hand, gave him a severe
blow and put out, with a shower of rifle bullets following him.   Weatherford consented to remain.
He told them that he disapproved their course, and
that it would be their ruin, but that they were his
people, he was raised with them, and he would share
their fate."   General Woodward names among these
chiefs Hopie Tustanuggee, or Far Off Warrior, a
Tuskegee, their eldest or principal chief, "the one"
says Woodward, "looked upon as the General," and
who was killed at Fort Mims; Peter McQueen; Jim
Boy or High Head Jim; Josiah Francis or Hillis
Hadjo, "the new made prophet," probably the same
who is called Joseph by General Wilkinson; Seekaboo
the Shawnee prophet; and several others.   He says
that Weatherford offered some advice to these chiefs,
but they declined to follow his suggestions.   ·The
reasons which Weatherford assigned for joining the
war party, as detailed at some length by Woodward,
are very creditable to Weatherford's humanity.   He
thought he would thus be the means of preventing
not a little bloodshed. *

---

* Brewer in his "Alabama," "from 1540 to 1872," published
in 1872, a work designed to be "indispensable to the intelligent
Alabamian," says of General Woodward that he "had Indian
blood in his veins," was reared on the frontier and among the
Indians, coming into the Mississippi Territory from Georgia as
early as 1810; that he was an officer in the Florida war of 1817
and 1818, and was a brigadier general of militia. He says that
he was an interesting man and a "famous character" in the Tallapoosa region. Brewer further says that his volume of Indian
Reminiscences "attempts to confute many of the statements made
by Pickett, Meek, Coxe, and others," and that he has himself, in
his history, "in part adopted" them. I think that in saying
"confute" Brewer has used too strong a word here. It seems to
me that all Woodward designed to do was, to give what he believed to be facts, and thus to correct any errors into which Pickett
and Meek had been led.
   Wishing to learn still more in regard to Woodward's Remi-

There is surely truth in Drake's remark that "the process of fermenting a civil war was a long and doubtful one," so attached to the whites had the more intelligent chiefs become, although many of the Creeks may have believed, as did some of the Western tribes, that they were on the eve of a great revolution through which they would gain their lost ascendency in America. The pending struggle between Great Britain and the United States with Spanish Florida to help the British seemed to be a favorable time for the attempt to be made.

And so there came into what is known as

"THE WAR OF 1812,"

continuing until 1815, the side issue, the Southern conflict, like a stirring episode into some great epic,

"THE CREEK WAR OF 1813 AND 1814."

The main question at issue between the two factions of the Creek nation was, whether they should undertake the extermination of the white settlers on

---

niscences, I wrote to the present Secretary of State of Alabama, Hon. J. D. Barron, in regard to them, and in reply, in a letter dated Montgomery, May 19, 1894, he says that "in Woodward's letters   *   *   *   there is a great deal of useful and interesting information." "I give a great deal of credit to what he says, as I find a great deal of outside evidence to strengthen what he says."

I have given this lengthy note because General Woodward, who died in 1861, is an authority often referred to in parts of this work. His little book of reminiscences is now very rare. The copy used for this work came from the hands of that excellent student of history, the late Dr. Lyman C. Draper of Wisconsin.   [19]

General Thomas S. Woodward must certainly be regarded as a truthful man, and he had undoubted facilities for obtaining some valuable information. When he was not himself an eye-witness he may, like others, have been sometimes misled. But certainly by comparing, combining, and sifting statements, all designed to be true, we shall reach the probable facts. T. H. B.

their western borders. The Alibamos especially, says Pickett,—those joining these river settlers on the east, upon whose hunting grounds encroachments had already been made,—"were furious advocates of American extermination." Colonel Hawkins acknowledges that all the Alibamo towns, without exception, were hostile.

That war of extermination for which some of them had been preparing, was, as we shall soon see, precipitated upon them; and when they finally came into contact with American citizen soldiers they fought with a determination which some one has said, "has hardly a precedent in Indian contests." It is no wonder that they fought then, for the war became for them one for their homes, their hunting grounds, their burial places, their native land.

That Confederacy of Indians known as the Creek or Muscogee, occupied a broad territory extending from the Oconee River in Georgia to the Alabama River, and it included a number of tribes. In 1791 these tribes had fifty-two towns and some ten thousand members, including the women and children.* Their large division was into UpperCreeks and Lower Creeks. The map inserted here is sufficiently accurate to show the extent of the Muscogee lands.

It was, and still is, a well watered region. On Colton's map of the states of Georgia and Alabama there are laid down more than fifty water courses of

---

*Bancroft, as quoted by Lewis H. Morgan in Indian Migrations, estimates the Indians east of the Mississippi and south of the Great Lakes, at the beginning of the seventeenth century, at about one hundred and eighty thousand; and of those Bancroft assigns to the Cherokees twelve thousand; to the Chickasaws, Choctaws, and Muscogees fifty thousand.

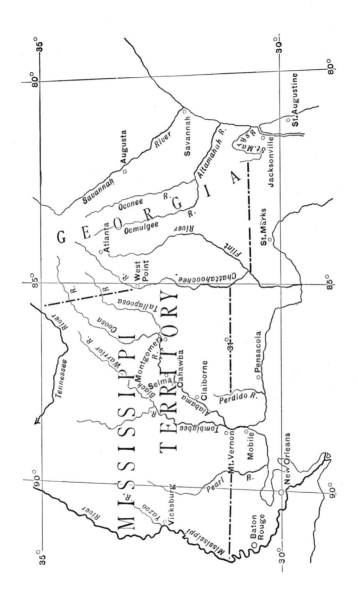

various sizes that one would cross in passing from the Altamaha to Claiborne on the Alabama.

This well known place is named, once Weatherford's Bluff, two hundred and fifty steps leading up from the landing to the top of the bluff, as it is almost directly south from Tuscaloosa on the Black Warrior, near which locality a Creek chief, by per. mission of the Choctaws, had established himself ; and this meridian line continued northward is sufficiently accurate to mark the boundary in the present North Alabama between the Chickasaws and Cherokees, and eastward of it, south of the Cherokee lands, will be indicated the Creek lands west of the Alabama on the Cahawba and on the upper Black Warrior. This meridian line, which would thus nearly mark the western limits of the Creeks in 1813, is thirty miles east of the St. Stephen's meridian. The Creeks once claimed, perhaps held, as far west as the Tombigbee.

Of the Upper Creek towns, according to Weatherford and General Woodward, they were nearly all hostile except the Natchez and Hillabee towns, and were controlled largely by Menawa, or, as the name is now written by his grandchildren, Monahwee (known as Ogillis Incha or Fat Englishman), who commanded the Indian warriors at Tohopeka, called in English, Horse Shoe. Also there should be excepted the Tookabatchees who adhered to Big Warrior and some of the Coshattees with their leader Captain Isaacs.

Gatschet, Migration Legend, Vol II, pages 189, 190, gives the following as the names of the hostile Upper Creek towns, his orthography not being adopted : Hoithlewahlee, Fooshatchee, Kolumee, Ekanhatkee, Sawanogee, Muklasa, Ochee-apofa, Oakchoyuchee, Pochus-hatchee, Pakan-talahassee, Wakokayee, Wewaka. These towns "made themselves red." So Gatschet translates itchatidshalgi. The Alibamo towns, which are counted among the Upper Creeks, have already been named as hostile.

The Lower Creeks, under the influence more largely of Colonel Hawkins, were, for the most part, friendly. Noted among these friendly Indians were General William McIntosh, a Creek chief of the tribe of the Cowetas, Mad Dragon's Son, and Timpony Barnard of the Uchees.

In the narration of events we left Weatherford with the war party on the east of the Alabama, surely, according to the letter of General Wilkinson, in July or August of 1813. And some of that party very soon proceeded to Pensacola, then the great mart of trade, to procure military supplies. On their return occurred the attack and defense known as the Battle of Burnt Corn, which will be detailed in another chapter

APPENDIX.

NOTE.—It seems fitting to append here some extracts, if lengthy, yet interesting and valuable, from the memoranda of Mr. George S. Gaines, originally published in the Alabama Historical Reporter. With some members of the Gaines family I have been personally acquainted, and these memoranda I am sure are reliable.   T. H. B.

"A Creek chief, known as O-ce-o-chee-mot-la, obtained permission of the Choctaws to make a settlement at the falls of the Black Warrior, so that the hunters of each tribe might have a resting place when visiting each other. This settlement had increased to many families before I took charge of the U. S. Choctaw trading house at St. Stephens (1805), and they traded with us. I was in the habit of extending a credit to the old chief of about a hundred dollars, which he always paid off at his next visit, but expected the same indulgence after he had finished bartering. During the spring and fall of every year he came down the river with a fleet of canoes to visit me. In the fall of 1811 he arrived with a large fleet manned by thirty or forty warriors, and having each canoe freighted with larger cargoes than usual of skins and furs, etc. At that time Tandy Walker, who had lived many years in the Creek nation as a "public blacksmith," sent by the government for the benefit of the Indians, resided in the neighborhood of St. Stephens. He learned their language and was a great favorite, and when O-ce-o-chee-mot-la came down to trade with me he acted as interpreter.

On the present occasion I noticed that the old chief was exceedingly anxious to make me believe that he was very much attached to me. He informed me that he had acted upon my advice in relation to building a good store house, and now brought with him several hundred dollars' worth of peltries, etc., to purchase a supply of goods for his store—that I had offered him credit several times before to the amount of several hundred dollars.

Next day, after this conversation, the Chief remarked he would make his debt an "old hundred" (one thousand) this time. I replied that the times were changed. The British government had a misunderstanding with the President which might end in a war, and it would be unwise in me to allow him to contract so large a debt and imprudent in him to do so. He remarked that his friend, Tandy Walker, who was a man of property, would be his security for one or two "old hundreds." While this conversation was progressing I noticed Walker was greatly troubled, and was endeavoring to appear calm. I reiterated I could only let him have the usual amount of credit under the existing circumstances. But the crafty Chief was not to be put off so readily, and entered into an ingenious argument to overcome my objections.

The sun went down and I told the chief that it was time to prepare for sleep, and we would "tell each other our dreams in the morning." Bidding me good night with assurances of affection and respect, he led his party off. In a few minutes Walker returned and leaning over the counter he whispered to me, " I told the chief I left my knife in the store so that I might come back and speak to you privately. Meet me at the Rock at midnight. Let no one know of this, for our lives depend upon secrecy." Before I could answer he was gone. At midnight I went cautiously to the " Hanging Rock," so called because it projected over the bluff of the river, near the old Spanish Fort. Walker was there, and he whispered, "let us go further in the thicket." He then informed me, still in a whisper, that the Creeks had determined to join the British in the war about to commence. The Chief of the Black Warrior settlement proposed to unite with him in obtaining all the goods they could probably get from me; and that Walker should take his family up to the Falls of the Warrior and enjoy half the profits of the business. " Before the time to pay for the goods there will be no one to demand it, for the trading house will be the first object to capture when the war begins," the chief had told him many times since proposing the scheme. He consented, fearing that if he did not the Indians would immediately attack the place, but took care to impress O-ce-o-chee-mot-la with the danger of offending me, as my brother was a war chief much loved by the President.

Walker remained with me only a few minutes, fearing his absence would be discovered by the Indians and that they might suspect the object of his mission, which would certainly, he assured me, result in the destruction of us all. The balance of that night was passed without sleep because of the uneasiness I felt. There were no troops in St. Stephens and but few men—not more than six or seven all told.

Next morning the chief and his warriors came to the store apparently in excellent spirits. He inquired what I had dreamed. I replied, " I dreamed there was a war. The English came over in their ships and engaged some of the northern tribes to assist them to fight, but the President's warriors soon drove the English back over the great waters, leaving the Indians who helped them to suffer alone." O-ce-o-chee-mot-la said, " I dreamed that my good friend sold me all I wanted, and when I reached home my people said, Mr. Gaines is a great man—he is a man of his word and our Chief, who has always told us this and how Mr. Gaines trusted him, is a man of but one talk !" I said to him, I was obliged to believe my dream, and it was useless to waste words in idle talk. After bartering his cargoes and obtaining his usual credit he departed with his fleet, and I never saw him again.

Rumors of the rapidly increasing bad feeling of the Creek Indians rendered the settlers on the Alabama and Tombigbee rivers very uneasy during the year of 1812, checking emigration to a great extent. In the fall of this year Tandy Walker called on me to inform me that he had just learned from a Creek Indian that a white woman had been brought from Tennessee as a prisoner to Tuscaloosa

by a party of Indians returning from a visit to the
Shawnees on the northern lakes. Mrs. Gaines, who
was present, said to Walker that he ought by all
means to endeavor to rescue the woman and bring
her down to the white settlement. Walker replied he
would try to effect her release, but it would be at
the risk of his life. He proposed to walk up to the
falls on pretense of paying a visit to his old friend
O-ce-o chee-mot-la and lull suspicion by declaring
his adherance to the cause of the hostile Indians.
He would then obtain a canoe, buy or steal the
woman and bring her down the river. He departed
immediately, returning in about two weeks with the
woman in a canoe. She was in a very feeble condition, her mind a good deal impaired by suffering,
and her limbs and feet were still wounded, caused by
the hardships she was forced to undergo after she
had been captured. Mrs. Gaines took charge of her
and after a week's tender nursing her mind appeared
to be restored.

Her name was Crawley. Her home was in a
new settlement near the mouth of the Tennessee
river. During the absence of her husband, a party
of Creek Indians rushed to her house and while they
stopped to murder two of her children who were
playing in the yard she concealed her two youngest
in a potato cellar under the floor. The Indians
broke open the door and dragged her out with the
intention of killing her, but concluded to take her to
their town. They compelled her to cook for them on
the march, but offered no other violence.

After her recovery, we sent Mrs. Crawley home
with a party of my friends who were going through
the wilderness to Tennessee * * * The Legislature of Tennessee voted thanks and an amount of
money to Tandy Walker for his agency in this affair.

I promptly communicated to the War Department the conduct of the chief O-ce-o-chee-mot-la on
his last visit to the Trading House ; also Mrs. Crawley's capture and rescue.

CHAPTER VI.

THE STOCKADES.

THE writers who have treated of the "Creek War" briefly are many. Those who have gone much into the details are few. And these few seem to have had influences bearing upon them which led them to take different views of the same facts or sometimes to disagree in regard to the facts. Claiborne, to whose large work reference has already been made, doubtless meant to be, as he says in his Introduction that he has striven to be " truthful and impartial ;" but it is difficult to read several things in his "Mississippi," without thinking that his strong feelings and sympathies and his love for that brilliant rhetoric, which he knew how to command, have un. duly colored some of his statements. He objects strongly to the view which Colonel Hawkins, the Government Agent among the Creeks, took of Tecumseh, as Claiborne himself gives that view, and of Colonel Hawkins' claim that there would not be much war if the Creeks were let alone. He says that General Flournoy was misled by Colonel Hawkins' representations concerning the degree of civilization attained by the Creeks and their peaceful disposition towards the whites. He makes this statement : " Even after the massacre at Fort Mims,

Colonel Hawkins reiterated these assurances, laid the blame of that affair on the Tombigbee people, and declared that the war would be ' a civil war among the Creeks and not on the whites,' if let alone."

Claiborne adds: " Unfortunately General Flournoy adopted these views and forbade any aggressive movement on the savages."

Pickett also speaks of Colonel Hawkins as having been "strangely benighted," not properly realizing the danger that existed.   It is not designed to suggest, here, who had the most accurate knowledge of the real state of affairs among the Creeks,—some of Brewer's statements will appear in other chapters, and the readers will have other facts before them on which to form their own opinions—but it is certain that the inhabitants of these river settlements, these pioneers along the Mobile and Tensaw and the Alabama and Tombigbee, saw a dark looking war cloud rising to the eastward, and that they felt it needful, and that it was needful, for them to do the best which they could do in preparing for self-defense.   They therefore erected as speedily as possible stockades, which they called, in the language of war, forts, in which they spent quite a little time in the summer and fall of 1813.   No dates have been found giving the exact time of the erection of the stockades in Clarke county, but it is evident that some were erected in July.

[20]

An enumeration and some description of these forts is the object of this chapter, including also some erected long before 1813.

1. Fort St. Stephens, established by the French, probably about 1714, held afterwards by the Span-

ish, who made there a settlement about 1786, given up by the Spaniards to the Americans in 1799, has been already mentioned. So far as the Creek Indians were concerned, this was considered an impregnable fortress. As this locality, the old St. Stephens, will be again more fully mentioned, it needs no further notice here, only the statement that it was on the west bank of the Tombigbee, on a high bluff, at the head of sloop navigation.

2. Fort Stoddart, as established by United States troops in July, 1799, has also been named, with its stockade and bastion. As this was for some years a government post, held by United States troops, and became a port of entry where the Court of Admiralty was held, it was of course a strong point. In 1804 Captain Schuyler of New York was commander here, with eighty men, Edmund P. Gaines was Lieutenant, and Lieutenant Reuben Chamberlain was paymaster. At Fort Stoddart duties were exacted on imports and exports.* Four miles west of Fort Stoddart was Mount Vernon.

3. Passing down the river, a strong fort was located at Mobile called Fort Charlotte. Another was also constructed here, Fort Bowyer.

4. Going now northward, on the east side of the Alabama, two miles below the " cut off," a quarter

---

*A beautiful, or at least an instructive and strong example of the effect of duties on articles reaching the consumer was shown here in 1807. In that year the Natchez planters in the western part of the Mississippi territory paid for Kentucky flour four dollars per barrel, and the same flour brought round by Mobile and there subjected to Spanish duties, and coming up the river past the Fort Stoddart port of entry, cost the Tombigbee planters sixteen dollars a barrel.

of a mile from the Tensaw Boat Yard, was the illfated Fort Mims. This was built in the summer of
1813 and will be again noticed. When the erection
of this stockade was commenced is uncertain, perhaps in July, and, according to Pickett, its last block
house was never finished.

This might be called No. 1 of the stockades
erected especially for protection against the Creeks,
but the former notation will be continued.

5. Fort Pierce was a small stockade some two
miles south-east of Fort Mims. It took its name
from two brothers, William Pierce and John Pierce,
who came from New England and made there their
home in Spanish times. William Pierce was a wea-
ver and John Pierce a teacher.

6. Crossing the Alabama and coming into the
new Clarke county, we reach Fort Glass, built some-
time in July at the home of Zachariah Glass by
himself and his neighbors, Nah-hee, called a Tory
Creek, an intelligent Indian, employed in the Creek
war as a scout, assisting, it is said, in the building.

7. Fort Madison was in the north-east corner of
section one, township six, range three east of the St.
Stephen's meridian, on the water-shed line, which
was then the eastern boundary of Clarke County.
As will be seen from the accompanying cut, it was
north of Fort Glass only two hundred and twenty-
five yards, and the two stockades constituted one
locality, being the center of the quite large Fort
Madison neighborhood. The first store in this
region was about due east from Fort Madison, on the
Alabama River, distant six miles, opened, probably,
in 1812; and one of the first grist mills was built

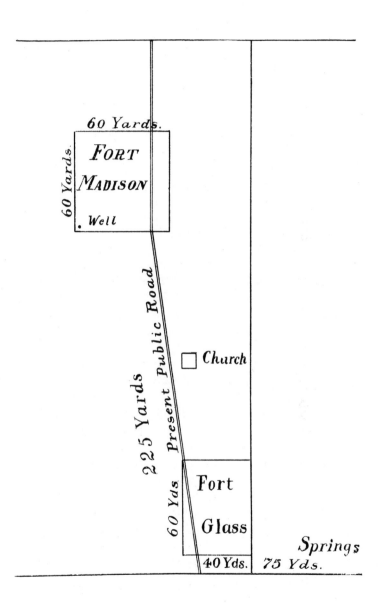

about the same time, perhaps about four miles north;
and in 1813 the first cotton gin in the vicinity was
erected some two miles north.   This was one of the
seven principal settlements in the then new Clarke
county and the region west of the Alabama.   As is
evident from the mention of the store and the mill
and the gin, and the plantations that were opened
around these, it was an important locality for these
settlers to hold.

Fort Madison contained not quite an acre of
ground, having been, as will be seen from the cut,
sixty yards square.   A trench three feet in depth
was dug around the outside and bodies of pine trees
cut about fifteen feet in length were placed perpen-
dicularily in the trench side by side, making thus a
wall of pine wood twelve feet in height.   Port
holes were cut at convenient distances so as to enable the inmates to look out, and in case of an attack
to fire upon the beseigers.   In about the same way
all these stockades of 1813 were constructed.   They
were lighted at night by means of the abundant
pitch pine placed upon scaffolds, covered with earth,
erected for the purpose.   Additional securities were
added at Fort Madison and an improved method of
lighting introduced, which will be by and by mentioned.   Within this enclosure, bearing the name of
the President of the United States, were the tents
and cabins of the settlers of that neighborhood, and,
after its erection, the date not certain, Fort Glass
was occupied by the soldiers.*

* From information gathered in Clarke county, in the region
occupied by several of these forts, it seems that when General
Claiborne reached Mount Vernon, July 30th, he immediately
ascertained what could then be learned about the Burnt Corn

8. Fort Sinquefield was about ten miles north of Fort Madison, on the western side of Bassett's Creek, a large stream of water for a creek, on section thirteen, township eight, range three east, a smaller stockade built very much in the same manner. As the map in this book will show, it was about five miles south-east from the present town of Grove Hill, formerly called Macon, the county seat of Clarke county. This fort stood on a table-land or height of ground extending for a mile north and south. Eastward is a gentle slope which terminates finally in the Bassett's Creek valley. Westward are deep valleys and narrow, between large, high ridges of land. No actual hill is within miles of this locality, yet the ascent from the valleys to the top of the ridges or table, might be called going up hill. The spring which supplied this stockake with water is south of west, in one of the deep valleys, distant two hundred and seventy-five yards.

Ninety feet distant from the once stockaded ground, in a north-west direction, are some graves. A few rods eastward of the fort ground is supposed to be an old burial place, although here the traces of the graves were not distinct in 1879. One of the principal highways of Clarke county runs directly by this locality, but, as it has been for many years a family home, no traces of the stockade outlines can

---

action, and in regard to the stockades around the residences of Glass, Lavier, Sinquefield, White, Easley, and Carney, which of course were then already erected; and that he sent Colonel Carson with two hundred mounted men to Fort Glass; and that after their arrival Fort Madison was immediately constructed. This fixes the date some time in August. It may be added here that General Claiborne also sent Captain Scott with a company of men to St. Stephens, to occupy the old Spanish block–house,

be found here which are still so distinct at forts Glass and Madison.

9. Fort White was a small stockade a short distance north-east of the present Grove Hill.

10. Landrum's Fort was eleven miles west from Fort Sinquefield; on section eighteen, township eight, range two east.

11. Mott's Fort was in the same neighborhood. These both were small.

12. Going now to the Tombigbee River and northward, Fort Easley was on section ten or eleven, township eleven, range one west, at what is now called Wood's Bluff. This fort was named, as were nearly all others, from a prominent settler in the neighborhood, and the bluff took its name from Major Wood, an officer in the Burnt Corn expedition. This stockade was on a small plateau containing about three acres. On the side next to the river the bluff is almost a perpendicular wall, there is "a bold spring of water flowing from its side," and the descent is quite abrupt from this plateau above and below the stockade ground, making this fort a naturally strong position.

General Claiborne visited this stockade about the last of August, having received a report that it would be attacked by the Indians. It is possible that some of the Creeks started this report to call attention away from the real fort which they designed to attack, that Fort Mims, which was fifty miles south and twelve miles east from Fort Easley.

13. Turner's Fort was some eight miles south and five west, in the west bend of the Tombigbee River, near the residence of Abner Turner. This fort was built of split pine logs doubled and con-

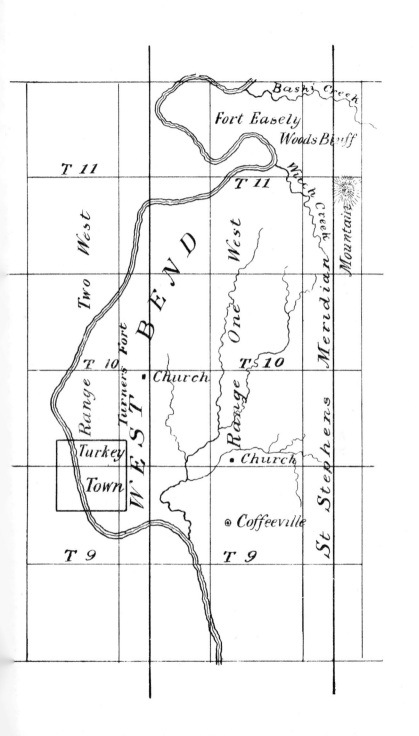

tained two or three block-houses. It was held by
the citizens of the neighborhood, thirteen men and
some boys forming the garrison that expected to
protect the women and children. Two or three miles
distant, on the river, was a Choctaw reservation
known as Turkey Town, called by the Choctaws
" Fakit Chipunta," Little Turkeys. In this stockade
were members of the Turner, Thornton, Pace, and
other families, early settlers in what became the
delightful West Bend neighborhood. Here for a
time resided Tandy Walker, who is mentioned
in the Gaines records, who was "a most experienced and daring backwoodsman ;" but in the summer of 1813 he was connected with the affairs at
Fort Madison.

The inmates of the two forts, Turner's and Eas-
leys', held religious services in their fort life. At
Fort Easley a camp-meeting was held, probably in
August, which some from the other stockade attended. The "love feast " on Sunday morning was
held outside the fort, but guards were stationed to
give warning if any attacking party of Indians appeared.*

14. Passing, now, down the river, on the west
side, five miles below Coffeeville, about a mile from
the river, was Cato's Fort.

---

* Among those attending this meeting from West Bend was
Mrs. Martha Pace, known in her later life as Aunt Patsy, born
about 1800, then a girl of thirteen, with whom I became acquainted in 1859, and who mentioned the incident of the " love
feast," when she was about eighty years of age, a very active,
even then, and noble hearted woman. In this West Bend neighborhood, at the home of Hon. Eli S. Thornton, among those who
were in the Turner fort and their descendants, I spent nearly two
years.—T. H. B.

15. Still further west, in Washington county, was Rankin's Fort, quite a large stockade, and the most western one of the River Group.

16. McGrew's Fort was in the corner of section one, township seven, range one west, about three miles north of Fort St. Stephens, in Clarke county, five miles north and eighteen west from Fort Madison. It is claimed that the area here enclosed with palisades was about two acres. Some of the posts were remaining in 1879, and around the fort locality was an old field. Here two brothers, William McGrew and John McGrew, British royalists then, refugees, probably, from the Atlantic coast, made an early settlement near the Tombigbee River. McGrew's Reserve, an old Spanish grant, is still a landmark in Clarke county. These brothers left the reputation of having been exemplary men, and of having become good Americans. How many families were in this fort is not known.

17. Six miles south from Jackson, at Gullet's Bluff, was Fort Carney, on the line of travel to Mount Vernon. This fort was built by Josiah Carney, who settled on the river in 1809.*

18. Three miles south of Fort Carney, near Oven Bluff, was Powell's Fort, where were about six families, including those of John McCaskey, James Powell, and John Powell.

---

* At this stockade an incident occurred illustrating the statement that skill, acquired through disobedience, may be useful. In one of the families was a girl about fourteen years of age who found the large water course attractive, but whose father, knowing nothing about the management of a boat, fearing no doubt for her safety, had forbidden her to go to the river. One day an alarm was given that the Indians were near, and the families hurriedly sought safety on the west side of the river. But how

19. Lavier's Fort, written sometimes by mistake or misprint Rivier's, was built, so far as has been ascertained, (the only authority is an aged colored man, Dick Embree), near the residence of Captain Lawson Lavier, who traded with the Choctaw Indians. It was built by himself and a few neighbors, but its locality is not known. Pickett names it, but no resident of Clarke County was found in 1877 who knew anything of it.

20. At Mount Vernon, to which as General Claiborne's headquarters we now come, and where was a United States arsenal, were two forts. An arsenal was maintained here until 1861, and since 1865 this has been held as a United States post, where a few officers and soldiers may always be found. Near the parade ground are some of those beautiful trees known as live oak, and the long leaf pine growth extends a long distance northward. The landing place on the river, known as Arsenal Wharf or Fort Stoddart, four miles distant, the early United States "port of entry," is distant from Mobile by the river channel forty-five miles, and five miles further north by the river brings one to the head of the Mobile River, the union of the Alabama and

should this family cross, when the father could neither paddle nor row? The daughter procured a boat, and, to the astonishment of her father, took them all rapidly over the river. And then the fact came out that she had slipped off secretly to the river when opportunities offered and by practice had learned to take a boat across that current. What her father said or did tradition has not preserved, but that girl, surely not generally disobedient nor wayward, grew up to womanhood, became Mrs. Blackwell, one of the highly respected women of Clarke county, and died near Jackson in the fall of 1879, eighty years of age. If disobedient she was at least, in her girlhood, a heroine, and in her womanhood we may be sure she did not encourage disobedience.

Tombigbee. The Mobile River, of the formation of which, judging from the school maps of Guyot and others, many must be ignorant, is fifty miles in length. Mount Vernon is distant now from Mobile by railroad only twenty-nine miles. As a place supposed to be very secure the two forts there, in the summer of 1813, are said to have been "packed." How many people were in these different stockades at any one time is not certain. But after the alarm caused by the massacre at Fort Mims there were at Forts Madison and Glass more than one thousand citizens and soldiers. At Fort Carney there were about four hundred. Rankin's Fort contained five hundred and thirty. How many hundred were at St. Stephens and at Mount Vernon is not known.

In these river settlements there were at that time, it has been already stated, about two thousand whites and two thousand blacks, taking for the basis of authority the United States census of 1810.

Besides these twenty or twenty-one forts, so called, which were in the line of the river settlements proper, two forts, named Roger's and Patton's, were constructed in what is now Wayne county, Mississippi, Patton's Fort at Winchester and Roger's Fort, six miles above. There was little use for these, however, and no real need, for the Creeks were not likely to cross the Tombigbee and go into the Choctaw territory. In fact families of Clarke county instead of trusting themselves in the stockades and enduring the inconveniences of thus living, for even a few weeks, crossed the Tombigbee and selected camping grounds far enough west to be, as they thought, out of danger. Among some such was the family of Mrs. Cathell, a widow with four sons and four daughters, having come into Clarke county from Georgia in 1812. Two of her sons went as soldiers against the Indians. She dreaded to have them leave her, saying that she had lost two brothers in the Revolutionary War and she felt sure these sons would fall in the coming conflict. And they did fall with so many others at Fort Mims. Disliking fort life for herself, as she had experienced it in her girlhood in the war of the Revolution, she with the other members of her family and ten or twelve other families crossed the river and went into camps.

NOTES.

1. Soon after the return of the Cathell family into Clarke County, one of the daughters, Jane Cathell, was married to Captain William R. Parker, and with her, eighty-four years of age in April, 1879, the writer of this chapter became acquainted. She had good use of her faculties, was intelligent and sprightly in mind, her eyes rather dim, but her hearing good.

She died suddenly in May, 1879, falling "lifeless to the floor, from the chair in which she was sitting."

2. That this fort life, although a necessity with many for a time, was to many mothers with their little children not pleasant, is evident from the statements of Mrs. Mary Cammack, with whom also this writer was acquainted. She was born in April, 1789, in South Carolina, was married in Kentucky in 1804, came into the Mississippi Territory in 1810, and when visited by the writer in August, 1874, then eighty-five years of age, was active, intelligent,

cheerful, and recounted with a ready recollection
the events of her earlier life.   In 1810, for some five
weeks, five hundred Choctaw Indians had camped
within sight of her husband's cabin, near the Clarke
county water-shed line.   She reported them as well
behaved, drinking no whiskey, not attempting to
steal or plunder.   Their chief was the noted Pushmataha.   But when the Indian troubles commenced
sixteen out of the seventeen of her husband's pack
horses were taken by the Creek Indians, and the family were all soon obliged to seek safety in Fort Madison.
But Mrs. Cammack expressly said, she did not think
the behavior of some of the white people in the fort
was equal to the conduct as she saw it of Pushma
taha's Choctaws.   The practices of some of them
she very much disliked.   And it is very evident,
however virtuous these pioneer settlers were, as they
had lately come from Georgia and the Carolinas,
from Tennessee and Kentucky, that life in a crowded
stockade, to sensitive mothers and little children,
could not be pleasant.

Mrs. Mary George Cammack, in 1813 twenty-
four years of age, then the mother of four children,
was a woman of more than ordinary physical and
mental endowments, as many of our pioneer women
were, and hers I consider to be first class testimony,
as an observing and unprejudiced woman, for all
facts within her range of knowledge connected with
the Creek Indian troubles of 1813.

3.   This note is for the lovers of curious facts.

Mrs. Cammack was the mother of thirteen children, and these facts appear in examining the years
in which they were born.   The first birth was in
1805, and then the births were in each odd year, or
every other year, until the year of the fort life, the
year of dangers and alarms.   As one illustration of
the alarms, fifteen Indians, before fighting had commenced, called one day at her home, and so startled
her that she took refuge in the home of a neighbor.

No child was born in 1813. Then beginning with December, 1814, the other children were all born in the even years, thus: 1805, 1807, 1809, 1811, —1814, 1816, 1818, 1820, 1822, 1824, 1826, 1828, 1830. What could be more regular in birth years?

A new England writer of note, some years ago, questioned the statement of a Sunday-school man in regard to families in the South having as many as eight and twelve children. Many of our questionings doubtless display our ignorance rather than our knowledge, for it is well known by those who have the means of knowing that many such large families were and still are in the South.

CHAPTER VII.

INTER-TRIBAL COUNCILS OF THE CREEKS AND THE CHOCTAWS.

THE Creek confederacy, in undertaking war against the Federal Government, was entering upon a conflict, that, for disparity of numbers and resources, never had a parallel in the annals of savage warfare. However little the ignorant and deluded warriors may have reflected over the magnitude of this undertaking, the wiser of their chiefs knew that the confederacy, even with British and Spanish aid, could not successfully cope with the Federal power, unless they secured the alliance of the powerful nation of the Choctaws on their western border. Many efforts were made to accomplish this object.

It was at some period in July that a council was held between the two nations, at or near the present town of Pushmataha, in Choctaw County, Alabama. The Choctaws were chiefly represented by Pushmataha, Moshulitubbee, and Huanna Mingo. It is not known what Creek chiefs represented the confederacy. During the conference there were regular communications between the Choctaws and the whites, then in the fort at Winchester. About midway between the two places, lived a citizen, a white man, named Robert McLaughlin. Every event occurring at the council was conveyed to McLaugh-

lin by a Choctaw messenger, and thence by
McLaughlin through a white messenger to the whites
at Winchester. The council lasted several days, the
Creeks urging the Choctaws to join them in war
against the whites, the Choctaws, on the contrary,
contending for peace and appealing to their national
tradition that they had never shed the blood of white
men in war and they must not begin it now. Pushmataha was the principal speaker on the part of the
Choctaws. It is said that he spoke the greater part
of two days endeavoring to dissuade the Creeks from
war. The council at last terminated with the Creeks
bent on war, and the Choctaws firmly resolved that
they would not co-operate with them in the impending conflict.

A tradition states that another attempt was likewise made by the Creeks to secure the alliance of at
least a portion of the Choctaw people by means of
a conference which Weatherford and another Muscogee chief, named Ochillie Hadjo, had with Mingo
Moshulitubbee. But it, too, resulted in failure. It
can not now be determined whether this conference
occurred before or after the inter-tribal council, of
which we have given some account above.

Both history and tradition agree that much
interest was manifested by the Choctaws in the war
impending with the Creek confederacy, and that
they were resolved to maintain their peaceful relations with the Americans. During this exciting
period, before the actual clash of arms had begun,
councils were held at various places in the Choctaw
nation, in which the most noted Mingoes made talks
expressing their sympathy for the American cause

and urging upon their warriors the duty of living at peace with the whites; and in every council was iterated the national tradition that the Choctaws had never shed the blood of white men in war.

No apprehension of Choctaw hostility was felt by the frontier people living along the Choctaw border, in the old counties of Wayne and Hancock. It is true that there were two forts built in Wayne county, Patton's Fort, at Winchester, and Roger's Fort, seven miles above. But the whites had taken temporary shelter in these forts, not on account of their Choctaw neighbors, with whom they lived daily in perfect concord, but from the fear of a possible inroad from the dreaded Creek warriors to the east of the Tombigbee.

But the case was somewhat different in the fork of the Tombigee and Alabama, where the people lived on the border of the Creek nation. Some solicitude prevailed there, for a brief period, among the new settlers in regard to Choctaw fidelity. The older settlers, however, who had been acquainted with the Choctaws for many years, did not share in this solicitude, but were confident that the Choctaw people would not deviate from that long-tried and unwavering friendship, which they had ever manifested toward the Americans.

Had the Choctaws united with the Creeks at the inception of the war of 1813, as has been truly said, in less than thirty days, the whole Southern frontier would have been drenched in blood; and the Federal Government, hampered, as it was with war elsewhere, would have been forced to put forth its mightiest effort to retain a hold upon the territory of the South-west. But the Choctaws, true to the old tradition, did not break their record as steadfast friends of the whites; nay, even more, for as the war progressed, hundreds of their warriors enlisted in the armies of Claiborne and Jackson. No lapse of time should ever permit the people of Mississippi and Alabama, the old historic South-west, to forget this action of the Choctaw people. The story of their fidelity to the American cause should never be permitted to pass into oblivion.

As a fitting close to this chapter, we quote from Claiborne's Mississippi the following eulogium upon this race of Southern red men: "Honesty on the part of the men and chastity of the women were characteristics of the Choctaw people, the real proprietors of the domain of Mississippi, whose traditions have been preserved in the names of our streams and our counties, which should ever remind us and our posterity, that, when we were but a feeble people, they fought for us the martial Muscogee; and when we had become numerous and opulent, in the darkest days of our history, when pressed to the earth by a superior adversary, when we had no reward to hold out, only our broken lances and shattered shields, they came to our aid and shared with us the doom of the vanquished. Mississippi, if she survives for a thousand years, as God grant she may, should never forget the brotherhood that binds her to this noble race, born under her own stars and skies."

NOTES.

The account of the international council of the Creeks and the Choctaws rests upon the authority of the late venerable Edmund Chapman of Newton County, Mississippi, who was an inmate of the fort at Winchester, at the time the council occurred.

The tradition in regard to Weatherford and Moshulitubbee was related to the writer in 1877, by the late Mr. G. W. Campbell of Noxubee County, Mississippi, he receiving the statement in early life from one of Moshulitubbee's noted captains, named Stonie Hadjo, who died in Noxubee County, about 1838.

The statement in regard to the attitude of the Choctaws towards the whites is based upon conversations and correspondence with several aged frontiersmen, now dead a number of years, who lived in Wayne and Jefferson counties during the Creek War. These informants, without exception, were unanimous in their statements, that nowhere along the Choctaw border, and at no time, were there the slightest manifestations of hostility towards the Americans. One of these informants was the late venerable Mr. Archibald McArthur, of Winston County, Mississippi, whose early life was passed among the Choctaws, and who was for several years connected with the Presbyterian Choctaw Mission at Emmaus. The statements of these trustworthy informants, who had every opportunity to know the real facts, are utterly at variance with the statements in Claiborne's Mississippi, page 396, in regard to the Choctaws, and that "the Chickasahay towns began to paint and to chant their war-songs." This sentence strikes us as a mere rhetorical flourish. We are compelled to accept the evidence of these old frontiersmen as conclusive.   H. S. H.

CHAPTER VIII.

THE BATTLE OF BURNT CORN.

From the letter of General James Wilkinson, much of which has been quoted in a preceding chapter, we learn that more than three hundred hostile Creeks, under the Prophet Francis, were camped, on the 25th of June, at the Holy Ground. General Wilkinson writes : " The last information received of their doings was on Wednesday [the 23d of June], by Ward's wife, who has been forced from him with her children. She reported that the party, thus encamped, were about to move down the river to break up the half-breed settlements, and those of the citizens in the fork of the rivers." While this was, no doubt, the real and ultimate design of the hostile Creeks, it was first necessary to put themselves on a thorough war footing by procuring supplies of arms and ammunition from Pensacola. With this object in view, at some period in the early part of July, a party of Creeks, comprising a portion, if not all, of the hostile camp at the Holy Ground, with many pack-horses, took up the line of march for Pensacola. This party was under the command of Peter McQueen, at the head of the Tallassee warriors, with Jim Boy, as principal war chief, commanding the Atossees,* and Josiah Francis, com-

---

*Pickett in his narrative has here evidently made a slip, writing Autaugas for Atossees.   H. S. H.

manding the Alibamos. Pickett gives the entire
force as amounting to three hundred and fifty warriors; Colonel Carson, in a letter to General Claiborne, estimates them at three hundred; but General
Woodward, in his Reminiscences, simply states that
[21] their numbers have been greatly overrated. "On
their way," writes Pickett, "they beat and drove
off every Indian that would not take the war-talk."
On their arrival at Burnt Corn Spring, situated at
the crossing of the Federal and the Pensacola roads,
they burned the house and corn-crib of James
Cornells, seized his wife and carried her with them
to Pensacola, where she was sold to Madame Ba-
ronne, a French lady, for a blanket. A man, named
Marlowe, living with Cornells, was also carried prisoner to Pensacola. Cornells, it seems, was absent
from home, at the time of this outrage. We hear of
him, soon afterwards, at Jackson, on the Tombigbee,
"mounted on a fast-flying grey horse," bringing to
the settlers the tidings of Creek hostilities.

The perilous condition of the southern frontier
at this period, the early part of July, is well por-
trayed in the following passages from Pickett: "The
inhabitants of the Tombigbee and the Tensaw had
constantly petitioned the Governor for an army to
repel the Creeks, whose attacks they hourly expected. But General Flournoy, who had succeeded
Wilkinson in command, refused to send any of the
regular or volunteer troops. The British fleet was
seen off the coast, from which supplies, arms, ammunition, and Indian emissaries, were sent to Pensacola and other Spanish ports in Florida. Everything foreboded the extermination of the Americans

in Alabama, who were the most isolated and defenceless people imaginable."

When Colonel Joseph Carson, commanding at Fort Stoddart, was informed that the above mentioned force of Creek warriors had gone to Pensacola, he despatched David Tate and William Pierce to the town to ascertain the intentions of the Creeks and whether Governor Manique would grant them a supply of ammunition. The information gained by [22] these spies and reported on their respective returns, all summed up, was that the Creeks, on their arrival in Pensacola, had called upon the Governor and presented him a letter from a British general in Canada. This letter had been given to Little Warrior when he was in Canada and at his death was saved by his nephew and afterwards given to Josiah Francis. The Creeks, whether right or wrong, supposed that this letter requested or authorized the Governor to supply them with ammunition. The Governor, in reply, assured them that it was merely a letter of recommendation, and at first refused to comply with their demands. He, however, appointed another meeting for them, and the Creeks, in the meanwhile, made every exertion to procure powder and lead by private purchase. According to Tate's information, which he received from some of the prisoners whom the Creeks had brought down with them, their language breathed out vengeance against the white people, and they dropped some hints of attacking the Tensaw settlers on their return. The Creeks finally succeeded in their negotiation with the Governor, who issued an order supplying them with three hundred pounds of

powder and a proportionate quantity of lead. To
obtain this large supply, McQueen handed the Governor a list of the towns ready to take up arms,
making four thousand eight hundred warriors. Even
this large amount of ammunition was not satisfactory to the Creeks; they demanded more, but it
seems that Manique yielded no further to their de.
mands. The Creeks now openly declared that they
were going to war against the Americans; that on
their return to the nation they would be joined by
seven hundred warriors at the Whet Stone Hill,*
where they would distribute their ammunition and
then return against the Tombigbee settlers. They
now held their war-dance, an action equivalent to a
[23] formal declaration of war.

Such was the information brought by the spies
from Pensacola, and their evidence clearly shows
that the disaffected section of the Creek Confederacy
was now committed to open war against the Americans. No other construction can be placed upon the
words and actions of the agents or reprsentatives of
this disaffected section,—the hostile party in Pensacola. We may conjecture that this party left Pensa.
cola about the twenty-fourth of July, but, as will be
noticed hereafter, it seems that it was only a part of
the force, mainly under the command of Jim Boy,
that took up the line of march, while the greater
party, from some cause, tarried a while longer in
Pensacola.

A slight incident here, perhaps, is worthy of being
placed on record to the credit of Jim Boy. While in

* The hill on which the present town of Lownsboro' is situated.

Pensacola the Creeks met with Zachariah McGirth a man well known in the Creek nation. Some of the Creeks wished to kill him. But Jim Boy interposed and said that the man or men that harmed McGirth should be put to death.

In the meanwhile, the inhabitants of the Tombigbee and the Tensaw were in a state of great alarm. Many had abandoned their farms and taken refuge in the forts situated along the Tombigbee and the Alabama. Judge Toulmin, writing from Fort Stoddart, the twenty-third of July, says, " The people have been fleeing all night." This brief sentence clearly reveals the alarm and anxiety pervading the Alabama frontier at this period

Upon the report of the spies from Pensacola relative to the action of Governor Manique and the Creeks, Colonel James Caller, of Washington County, the senior militia officer on the frontier, forthwith ordered out the militia. A force was soon embodied and enrolled under his command. Colonel Caller resolved to intercept the Creeks on their return and capture their ammunition. His command, at first, consisted of three small companies, two from St. Stephens, commanded respectively by Captains Baily Heard and Benjamin Smoot, and one company from Washington County, commanded by Captain David Cartwright. With this force Colonel Caller crossed the Tombigbee at St. Stephens, Sunday, July 25th; thence passing through the town of Jackson, he marched to Fort Glass, where he made a short halt. At this place he was reinforced by a company under Captain Sam Dale, with Lieutenant Walter G. Creagh as second in command. Another force had

also joined him in the expedition commanded by
William McGrew, Robert Callier, and William Brad.
berry.   The whole party were well mounted and
carried their own rifles and shot guns, of every size
and description.   Captain Dale carried a double
barrel shot gun—an unusual weapon in that day. An
eye-witness has described Colonel Caller at Fort
Glass as wearing a calico hunting shirt, a high bell-
crowned hat and top boots and riding a large fine
bay horse. Leaving Fort Glass, the party bivouacked
the ensuing night at Sizemore's ferry, on the west
bank of the Alabama River. The next morning they
crossed the river, the horses swimming by the side
of the canoes.   This occupied several hours.   They
now marched in a southeastern direction to the cow-
pens of David Tate, where a halt was made.   Here
Colonel Caller received another reinforcement, a
company from Tensaw and Little River, commanded
by the brave half-breed, Captain Dixon Bailey. The
whole force, composed of white men, half-breeds and
friendly Indians, now numbered one hundred and
eighty men, rank and file, in six small companies.
From the cow-pens they marched to the intersection
of the Wolf-trail and the Pensacola road, at or near
the site of the present village of Belleville, in Conecuh County, where they camped for the night.   The
next morning, the twenty-seventh of July the command was reorganized.   William McGrew was
chosen Lieutenant Colonel, and Zachariah Phillips,
McFarlan, Wood, and Jourdan were elected to the
rank of Major.   It is stated that this unusual number of field officers was made to satisfy military
aspirations.   The command now took up the line of

march down the Pensacola road, which here ran,
and still runs, parallel with Burnt Corn Creek.
About eleven o'clock the spies returned at a rapid
rate and reported that they had found the enemy
encamped near Burnt Corn Creek, a few miles in
their advance, and that they were busily engaged in
cooking and eating.   A consultation of the officers
immediately took place, and it was decided to take
the Creeks by surprise.   The troops were thrown
into three divisions, Captain Smoot in front of the
right, Captain Bailey in front of the centre, and
Captain Dale in front of the left.

As the descriptions of the Burnt Corn battle
ground given by Meek and Pickett are somewhat
vague and inaccurate, a more correct account of the
topograpy, gained from personal observation, is here
given to the reader.   Burnt Corn Creek, near which
the battle was fought, runs southward for several hundred yards, then making an abrupt bend, runs south-
eastward for half a mile or more. Right at the elbow of
the bend is the crossing of the old Pensacola road.
The low pine barren enclosed in this bend—not a
peninsula as called by Pickett—is enveloped by a
semicircular range of hills, which extends from the
creek bank on the south some half a mile below the
crossing, and terminates on the west at the bank,
some three hundred yards above the crossing.   This
western terminus is now locally known as the Bluff
Landing.   The Pensacola road from the crossing
runs northward some two hundred yards, then turning runs eastward half a mile, making a continuous
and gradual ascent up the slope of the hills, and
then again turns northward.   The spring, now

known as Cooper's Spring, is situated about half a
mile nearly east of the crossing, and about one hundred and fifty yards south of the road.   It gushes
forth at the base of a steep hill and is the fountain
head of a small reed-brake branch, which empties
into the creek about two hundred yards below the
crossing.   The hill, at the base of which the spring
is situated, is about the centre of the semicircular
range of hills which envelops the pine barren.
About sixty yards northwest of the spring, between
the spring and the road, is a comparatively level
spot of land, about an acre in extent.   This spot,
we conjecture, was the Creek camp, or at least
where the main body was encamped, as it is the
only place immediately near the spring suitable for
a camp.   The hill here rises steep and abruptly to
the northeast, and a hostile force could well approach and charge down this hill within close gunshot of the camp before being seen.   This locality,
famed as the battle ground of Burnt Corn is in
Escambia County, one-half a mile from the line of
Conecuh County, on the north.

As reported by the scouts, the Creek camp was near
the spring, and their pack-horses were grazing around
them.   No rumor of the foe's advance had reached
their ears; all were careless, off their guard and
enjoying themselves, for good cheer was in the
Muscogee camp.   Their martial spirits, as we may
well imagine, were not now stirred by thoughts of war
and bloodshed, but were concentrated on the more
peaceful delights of cooking and feasting, the pleas-
ures of the pot, the kettle, and the bowl.

The Burnt Corn battlefield was in the unorganized part of Mississippi Territory (in the Indian country proper), in the year 1813. Monroe county organized in 1815, included Burnt Corn. In 1818 the same locality was in Conecuh county, established that year. Now, it seems, it is in Escambia county, established in 1868, although Brewer, writing in 1872, still places the battle ground of Burnt Corn in Conecuh. (The following cut will give some idea of the locality).

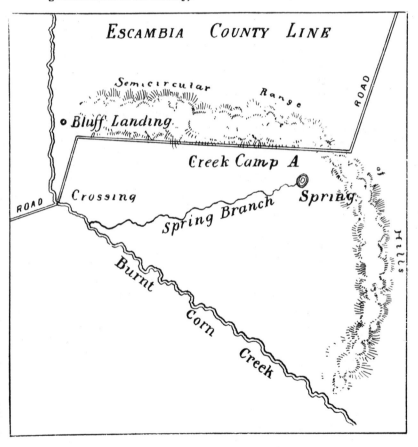

Colonel Caller's troops, as we may conjecture, must have turned to the left, off the road, perhaps near the Red Hollow, about a mile distant from the spring, and thence approached the Creek camp from the northeast and east, as from the nature of the country this was the only route they could have taken so as to surprise the Red Stick camp.* The troops moved cautiously and silently onward until they reached the rear of the hill that overlooked the Creek camp. Here, Pickett says, they dismounted; but Meek says the main body dismounted; yet neither Pickett nor Meek makes any statement as to the disposition of their horses— whether they were tied or were consigned to the care of a guard, or whether each trooper, as he dismounted, left his horse to shift for himself. From the fact that many of the horses fell into the hands of the enemy, one is led to the conjecture that no regular system was employed, but that every man did that which was right in his own eyes. After dismounting, the troops moved silently to the crest of the hill, whence they made a rapid charge down its slope and opened fire upon the Creek camp, as the red warriors stood, sat, or reclined in scattered groups over the ground. The Creeks, though startled by this sudden and unexpected onset, quickly sprang to arms, returned the fire, and for several minutes bravely withstood the charge of the whites, then gave way and retreated in wild confusion to the

---

* The hostile Creeks were often called "Red Sticks," because their war-clubs were invariably painted red. "Red Stick" was considered an honorable appellation, and as such it will occasionally be used in this work. "Red Stick War" is the name by which the War of 1813 is still known among the Creeks of the Indian Territory. 　　　　　　　　　　　　　　　H. S. H.

creek. Early in the fight a Creek woman and a
negro man were slain. It is stated that the latter,
who was busily engaged in cooking, had ample time
to make his escape, but being a slave and non-combatant, he doubtless apprehended no danger from
the whites. A portion of the troops pursued the
Indians to the creek—Meek says they even drove
them across the creek into a reed-brake beyond—
but we think this latter statement exceedingly doubtful. While these were performing this soldierly
duty, the more numerous party devoted their energies to capturing and leading off the pack-horses.
This led to a disastrous reverse. The Creeks in the
cane and reed-brakes soon saw the demoralization of
the greater part of the whites and the fewness of
the assailants confronting them. They rallied, and,
with guns, tomahawks and war clubs, rushed forth
from the swamp, and with the fiercest cries of vengeance charged upon their foes and drove them
headlong before them. Colonel Caller acted bravely,
but unable to restore order, he commanded the
troops to fall back to the hill so as to secure a
stronger position and there to renew the battle. The [24]
plundering party, misconstruing this order, and seeing the fighting portion of the troops falling back
before the enemy, were now seized with a panic, and
fled in wild confusion, still, however, notwithstanding their terror, driving their horses before them,
some even mounting their prizes so as to more
quickly escape from the fatal field. In vain did
Colonel Caller, Captain Bailey and other officers endeavor to rally them and pursuade them to make a
stand against the foe. Terror and avarice proved

more potent than pride and patriotism, and the panic-stricken throng surged to the rear. Only about eighty fighting men now remained, and these had taken a stand in the open woods at the foot of the hill. Commanded by Captains Dale, Bailey, and Smoot, they fought with laudable courage for an hour or more under the fire poured upon them by McQueen's warriors from the cover of the thick and sheltering reeds. The battle may now be briefly described as "a series of charges and retreats, irregular skirmishes and frequent close and violent encounters of indviduals and scattered squads." It was noticed that the Creek marksmanship was inferior to that of the Americans. It was in the fight at the foot of the hill that Captain Dale was wounded by a rifle ball, which struck him in the left side, glanced around and lodged near the back bone. The captain continued to fight as long as his strength permitted, and then threw aside his double barrel into the top of a fallen tree. This gun, we may here state, Dale recovered after the war from an Indian, at Fort Barancas. About the same time that Dale was wounded, Elijah Glass, a twin brother of David Glass, was slain. He was standing behind another soldier, who was in a stooping position, when a rifle ball struck him fatally in the upper part of the breast.

The battle now at last began to bear hard upon the Americans. Two-thirds of the command were in full retreat, and no alternative lay before the fighting portion but to abandon the field, which they did in the greatest disorder. Many of them had lost their horses, some of which had been appropriated by the fugitives, and others, in some manner, had fallen into the hands of the enemy, among these, the horses belonging to Colonel Caller and Major Wood. The troops now fled in all directions. Some succeeded in reaching and mounting their own horses; others mounted the first horses they came to; in some cases, in their eagerness to escape, two mounting the same horse; while others actually ran off afoot. It was a disgraceful rout.

"After all these had left the field," writes Pickett, "three young men were found, still fighting by themselves on one side of the peninsula, [bend,] and keeping at bay some savages who were concealed in the cane. They were Lieutenant Patrick May, a private named Ambrose Miles, and Lieutenant Girard W. Creagh. A warrior presented his tall form. May and the savage discharged their guns at each other. The Indian fell dead in the cane; his fire, however, had shattered the Lieutenant's piece near the lock. Resolving also to retreat, these intrepid men made a rapid rush for their horses, when Creagh, brought to the ground by the effects of a wound which he received in the hip, cried out 'Save me, Lieutenant, or I am gone'. May instantly raised him up, bore him off on his back, and placed him in the saddle, while Miles held the bridle reins. A rapid retreat saved their lives. Reaching the top of the hill, they saw Lieutenant Bradberry, bleeding with his wounds, and endeavoring to rally some of his men." This was the last effort made to stem the tide of disaster.

Two young men were slain in the battle, ———— Ballard and Elijah Glass, both it is believed, being

members of Dale's company. Ballard had fought
with great bravery. Just before the final retreat, he
was wounded in the hip. He was able to walk, but
not fast enough to reach his horse, which in the
meantime, had been appropriated by one of the fugitives. A few of the soldiers returned and succes-
sively made efforts to mount Ballard behind them
on their horses, but the Indians pressed them so
closely that this could not be done. Ballard told
them to leave him to his fate and not to risk their own
lives in attempting to save him. At last the Indians
reached him, and for some moments, he held them
at bay, fighting desperately with the butt of his
musket, but he was soon overpowered and slain.
Several Indians now sprang forward, scalped him
and began to beat him with their war clubs. Two
of the retreating soldiers, David Glass and Lenoir,
saw this. Glass was afoot, Lenoir mounted. "Is
your gun loaded," asked Glass of Lenoir. "Yes,"
was the reply. "Then shoot those Indians that are
beating that man yonder." Lenoir hesitating,
Glass quickly spoke, "Then lend me your gun."
Exchanging guns, Glass then advanced a few paces
and fired at two or three of the Indians whose heads
happened to be in a line, and at the discharge one of
them fell, as Glass supposed, slain or wounded. This
was the last shot fired in the battle of Burnt Corn,
which had lasted from about midday until about
three o'clock in the afternoon.

The Creeks pursued the whites nearly a mile in
the open woods and nothing but their inability
to overtake them saved the fugitives from a
general slaughter. Pickett writes: " The retreat

continued all night in the most irregular manner, and
the trail was lined from one end to the other with
small squads, and sometimes one man by himself.
The wounded travelled slowly, and often stopped to rest." Such was the result of the battle
of Burnt Corn, the first engagement in the long and
bloody Creek War. Most of the Creek pack-horses,
about two hundred pounds of powder and some lead
was all the success the Americans could claim from
this engagement. Their loss was two men killed,
Ballard and Glass. Fifteen were wounded, Captain
Sam. Dale, Lieutenant G. W. Creagh, Lieutenant
William Bradberry, shot in the calf of the leg; Arm-
strong, wounded in the thigh ; Jack Henry, wounded
in the knee ; Robert Lewis, Alexander Hollinger, William Baldwin, and seven others whose names have
not been preserved.

The Creek loss is not positively known. Colonel
Carson, in a letter to General Claiborne, written a
few days after the battle, states that from the best
information it was ten or twelve killed and eight or
nine wounded. [25]

As to the numbers engaged at Burnt Corn, we
know that the American force numbered one
hundred and eighty. General Woodward, in his
Reminiscences, states, on the authority of Jim Boy,
that the Creek force was two-thirds less. He writes.
" Jim Boy said that the war had not fairly broke
out, and that they never thought of being attacked ;
that he did not start [from Pensacola] with a
hundred men, and all of those he did start with were
not in the fight. I have heard Jim tell it often that
if the whites had not stopped to gather up the pack-

horses, and had pursued the Indians a little further, they, the Indians, would have quit and gone off. But the Indians discovered the very great confusion the whites were in searching for plunder, and they fired a few guns from the creek swamp, and a general stampede was the result. McGirth always corroborated Jim Boy's statement as to the number of Indians in the Burnt Corn battle."

The above, perhaps, may be regarded, in some measure, as the Creek version of Burnt Corn. If possession of the battlefield may be considered a claim to victory, then Burnt Corn may well be regarded a Creek victory

After the battle, a part of the Red Sticks retraced their steps to Pensacola for more military supplies, and a part returned to the nation. Their antagonists, Colonel Caller's troopers, were never reorganized after the battle. They returned home, in scattered bands, by various routes, and each man mustered himself out of service. About seventy of them on the retreat collected together at Sizemore's Ferry, where, for a while, they had much difficulty in making their horses swim the river. David Glass finally plunged into the stream and managed to turn the horses' heads towards the other shore. After the horses had all landed on the further bank, the men crossed over in canoes.

Colonel Caller and Major Wood, as we have related, both lost their horses at Burnt Corn. As the fugitives shifted, every man for himself, these two officers were left in the rear. They soon became bewildered and lost their way in the forest, and as they did not return with the other soldiers, their

friends became very apprehensive as to their safety.
" When General Claiborne arrived in the country, he
wrote to Bailey, Tate, and Moniac, urging them to
hunt for these unfortunate men. They were afterwards found, starved almost to death, and bereft of
their senses." When found, Colonel Caller had on
nothing but his shirt and drawers. After the war,
the Colonel, with some difficulty, recovered his fine
horse from the Creeks. But Major Wood was not
so fortunate.

Colonel J. F. H. Claiborne, in his "Life of Sam
Dale," writes : " Colonel Caller was long a conspic-
uous man in the politics of Mississippi Territory,
often representing Washington County in the legislature. No one who knew Caller and Wood intimately doubted their courage; but the disaster of
Burnt Corn brought down on them much scur-
rility. Major Wood, who was as sensitive as brave,
had not the fortitude to despise the scorn of the
world, and sought forgetfulness, as too many men
often do, in habitual intemperance."

The battle of Burnt Corn, on the whole, was
damaging to the prestige of American prowess. For
many years its participants had to endure the ridi-
cule of their neighbors and friends; for it was not
considered creditable to any one to claim that he had
been a soldier in the Burnt Corn battle.

It should here be stated that at the time of its
occurrence many of the citizens of Washington
County censured Colonel Caller severely for this
expedition and believed that he acted too hastily in
the matter. They believed that, while putting themselves on a war footing, it would have been better

to have made use of conciliatory measures towards the Creeks; that they thereby might have overruled them and perhaps averted hostilities. But this attack by Colonel Caller maddened them and converted numbers of hesitating and neutral warriors into deadly foes, and the massacre at Fort Mims was the result.

NOTES.

In writing the history of the Burnt Corn expedition, the writer has drawn his materials from the following sources: Pickett's History of Alabama, Meek's Romantic Passages of Southwestern History, General Thomas Woodward's Reminiscences of the Creek or Muscogee Indians, letters of Judge Toulmin and Colonel Carson, addressed to General Claiborne, published in the Alabama Historical Reporter of June, 1880, and a letter from Colonel Carson to General Claiborne, published in Claiborne's "Life of Sam Dale."

In addition to the above sources must be added conversations with the late Rev. Josiah Allen, of Jasper County, Mississippi, who, perhaps, was the last survivor of Capt. Sam Dale's company. Mr. Allen was not in the Burnt Corn expedition, but was intimately associated with many of the participants in the battle, from whom he derived a number of incidents and other minor facts, which have been incorporated in this narrative.

The description of the battle ground, as has been stated, is the result of personal observation.

H. S. H.

CHAPTER IX.

FORT MIMS.

INTRODUCTORY NOTE.—For the statements in this chapter different authorities have been consulted, as the writer has had access to the Chicago City Library, the Illinois State Historical Library, the Newberry Library of Chicago, and the State Library of Indiana, all containing a large number of valuable historic reference books in regard to the American Indians; the last containing a large and choice collection of works pertaining to these Indians.

Among many others there has been consulted — "Tuttle's Border Wars of Two Centuries," 608 pages, by Charles R. Tuttle, Chicago, 1874.

In the preface the author says, "There is not a single person interested in the history of the United States who has not felt the want of a reliable history of the Wars between his country and the Indians." Of his own work he says: "It has been compiled and written from the most reliable sources, and, it is confidently believed, will be found complete, authentic, and interesting." He expresses the opinion that it will be found to be the most accurate "and satisfactory history of the wars with the Indians * * * that has yet been written."

He gives to the Creek War the last three pages and nine lines of his large work, and relies for authority largely on Brownell.—I have examined the work of Charles De Wolf Brownell, pages 638, published 1856, called "The Indian Races of

North and South America," and find that he refers
to Samuel G. Drake, to Henry R. Schoolcraft, to
William V. Moore, James Adair, and to many other
writers.—Tuttle assigns to Fort Mims from Brownell one hundred and sixty officers and soldiers, and
says, "The rest of its occupants, to the number of
one hundred and fifteen, consisted of old men,
women, and children." He mentions no other attacks made by the Indians upon the whites, but says
something of Jackson's battles. So brief an account of the Creek War as Charles R. Tuttle gives,
however "authentic" it may be, can hardly be considered "satisfactory" by any one interested in the
history of the Southern Indians.

Samuel G. Drake, the father of Francis S. Drake,
who gives in two large volumes the results of the
life long researches of Henry R. Schoolcraft, gives
two hundred and seventy-five as the number in Fort
Mims, of which number, he says, one hundred and
sixty were soldiers, and "the rest old men, women,
and children." Numbers and statements corresponding so exactly as these do, show a common
origin for the statements of both Tuttle and Drake

F. S. Drake, in his large work, "Indian tribes of
the United States," follows Pickett in regard to the
number in the fort and the number of Indians making
the attack, and says, on what was then good authority, "Not a white woman or child escaped."

Trumbull in his "History of the Indian Wars,"
pages 320, published in 1846, gives an account of the
massacre at Fort Mims as detailed in a letter written
by Judge Toulmin and dated September 7, 1813.

This letter puts the number of Indians making
the attack as not over four hundred, and states that
in the fort were about twenty-four families, nearly
all of whom perished, not more than twenty-five or
thirty white men and "half-breeds" escaping. The
letter also says there were in the fort "about one
hundred negroes." Judge Harry Toulmin, a good

scholar, well versed in law, a native of England, for eight years Secretary of State of Kentucky, would be for many things good authority; but the date of this letter is against it as being reliable information in regard to Fort Mims. The letter is dated September 7th, and it was not until September 9th that troops from Mount Vernon reached Fort Mims to see what could be done for burying the dead. So early as the seventh the rumors that reached Judge Toulmin could not be expected to be accurate in regard to the Indians or the whites.

Samuel G. Drake, who has just been mentioned, goes to the other extreme, and assigns to Weatherford about fifteen hundred Indian warriors when attacking Fort Mims.

I take the liberty in this introductory note to refer to one of our school histories, Anderson's "Grammar School History of the United States," a work said to be "used in more than three hundred of the most important cities and towns in the United States," and commended as being "unusually accurate." In this children are taught in the recapitulation, page 131, "Creek War began by the Massacre at Fort Mims, Aug. 30th, 1813." "1814 the battle of Tohopeka ended the Creek War, March 27th."

The full text is, pages 120, 121, "In the spring of 1813, several months before the successes of Perry and Harrisson, the Southern Indians were visited by Tecumseh, and induced to take up arms against the whites. On the last day of August, fifteen hundred of their warriors surprised Fort Mims, and massacred nearly three hundred men, women, and children.

"This unprovoked attack"—all of our histories seem to omit any mention of Burnt Corn—"aroused the whole South, and volunteers assembled to avenge the deed of horror. Several battles were fought in quick succession, in every one of which the Indians were defeated. At length a thousand warriors made a final stand at Tohopeka, where they were defeated by General Jackson, on the 27th of March, 1814, with great slaughter. Their subjugation was complete."

Chateaubriand of France, speaking of ancient writers once said, "The historians are greater liars than the poets." The old historians had not the facilities we now have for securing a large degree of accuracy in their narrations; but surely some of the moderns do not avail themselves of the resources at hand.

From S. Putnam Waldo's "Memoirs of Andrew Jackson," published in 1818, the following extracts are taken : Speaking of Fort Mims, "Major Beasly commanded, and with a band that reminds the reader of the Spartan band of Leonidas at Thermopylæ, maintained a conflict with more than four times their force until they slew more than their own numbers."

Waldo himself quotes this : "Under the double influence of British gold and furious fanaticism, the savages fought in a manner scarcely to be credited." He calls the Creeks "The most warlike tribe of barbarians in the universe," and calls the Creek war "The most sanguinary war which savage vengeance, aided by British gold and Spanish perfidy, ever prosecuted."

He too, it seems, believes in the gold. We are left to conjecture whether Tecumseh brought that gold down from Detroit on his thirty horses, or whether it reached the Creeks through the Spanish traders at Pensacola, or whether the gold really went no further than to Tecumseh, as Claiborne asserts that when in 1811 Tecumseh visited the Southern tribes, "with a party of thirty warriors," he was "in British pay."

In Philo A. Goodwin's "Life of Jackson," 1832, are the following statements, and where he could have found authority for any one of them is singular. The first is, after mentioning the battle of

Tippecanoe, " Tecumseh fled to the Southern tribes upon the Alabama, early in 1812, to inspire the savages there to act in concert with their red brethren of the north."

The second is, " A complete concert was established between all the Southern tribes, and a general concert between them and the Northern ones."

And the third is, which has a bearing upon this and succeeding chapters, after saying that at Fort Mims about two hundred and sixty persons perished, " The panic caused at the other outposts or stations by this dreadful catastrophe can scarcely be described ; the wretched inhabitants, fearing a similar fate, abandoned their retreats of fancied security in the middle of the night, and effected their escape to Mobile after the endurance of every species of suffering." Surely, if we can get no more truth than this from our border war historians, we may as well leave them and turn to the poets.

As in regard to Tecumseh's visit to the Creeks, so in regard to the massacre at Fort Mims, the original authorities are few, very few ; and the main reliance for the statements of this chapter will be upon Alabama's own historian, Albert J. Pickett, including additional evidence which we have, individually, been able to gather. **T. H. B.**

After the battle of Burnt Corn, which did not terminate as the whites had hoped, as the settlers of this exposed and isolated River Region gathered more fully into their various stockades, the inhabitants on the Tensaw and along Little River, many of them being of mixed and of Creek blood, yet dreading the fury of the war party of the Creek nation, gathered around the residence of a settler named Samuel Mims, an old Indian countryman, one mile from the

Alabama River, two miles below the Cut Off, and one-fourth of a mile from the Tensaw boat-yard. Here, where before the Burnt Corn action many families had gathered, they had erected a stockade, nearly square, enclosing about an acre, built very much as was Fort Madison and the other stockades, entered through a large eastern and a western gate. In this enclosure were several buildings, the home of the Mims family being near the center. One of these buildings was known as Patrick's loom-house, and having some extra picketing attached to this, the inmates called it the bastion.

According to Pickett's researches, and no authority has been found of sufficient weight to set aside his statements, there were in this stockade in August, 1813, five hundred and fifty-three human beings, white settlers, some Spaniards, colored [26] people, and those of mixed Indian blood. Two hundred and sixty-five of this number were soldiers, and, in round numbers, one hundred were children. Of the soldiers there were seventy home militia, all probably being what General Woodward calls "half-breeds," under the command of Captain Dixon Bailey; sixteen men had been sent from Mount Vernon or Fort Stoddart under Lieutenant Osborn to help defend this exposed stockade; and soon after one hundred and seventy-five Mississippi volunteers were sent under the command of Major Daniel Beasley. He of course took the command of the fort. General Claiborne, commanding at Mount Vernon, came himself to Fort Mims August 7th to inspect this stockade. He instructed Major Beasley "to strengthen the pickets and to build one or two

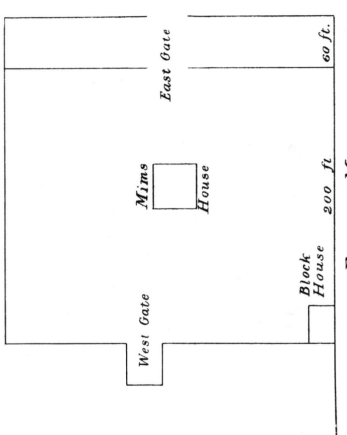

FORT MIMS.

East Gate

West Gate

Mims House

Block House

200 ft

60 ft.

additional blockhouses." To this Lieutenant William
R. Chambliss testified, and added, "And I further
certify that Major Beasley received a letter, one or
two days before the attack on Fort Mims, from General Claiborne (who was on his way to Fort Easley)
advising him of the reported movements of the
enemy."

And who were these called in military language,
"the enemy"? After that unfortunate action at
Burnt Corn, members of that war party returned to
Pensacola, obtained more military supplies, and
came again, more cautiously, back to their own
towns and hunting grounds. A large war force was
soon collected from the towns, says Pickett, of
Hoithlewale, Fooshatche, Cooloome, Ecunhutke,
Souvanoga, Mooklousa, Alabama, Oakchoicoochie,
Pockuschatche, Ochebofa, Puckuntallahasse, Wew-
ococ, and Wocescoie, and went south from the Tallapoosa River towards the Tensaw settlement.* The
leaders of this band of warriors gathered from so
many hostile towns were, a Tuskegee chief, Far Off
Warrior, Peter McQueen, High Head Jim, and with
them as an influential leader but not a real chief,
the noted William Weatherford, of truly mixed
blood, the renowned Red Eagle. He was acquainted
with the Tensaw settlers, had met with the young
people in their dancing parties, but had for some
reasons joined the war party, and was now one of
the recognized leaders of the savage warriors. The

---

*"Five of these towns were on the Tallapoosa, six on the Coosa,
and two on the Alabama. The last six of these towns were situated on the Coosa, Sawanogee—Pickett's Souvanoga—was a
Shawnee town. Alabama and Muklosa, on the Alabama River,
were Alibamo towns. The remainder were genuine Muscogee
towns."

Indian army halted for a time at a plantation not many miles from Fort Mims. Some negroes were taken prisoners and permitted by Weatherford to escape; he had learned that a military officer was in command at the fort; and if the testimony of Weatherford's friends is reliable, he expected the fort to be prepared to resist the assault.

There was truly an officer of the Mississippi Volunteers in command, as has been stated, Major Daniel Beasley, but that he was unfit to command at such a post in time of danger is evident. Claiborne himself says of him that "although often warned he turned a deaf ear to all idea of danger." Judge Meek speaks of him as "unflinchingly brave," but also as being "vain, rash, inexperienced, and over-confident." He adds: "In vain did several of the most experienced and cautious of the backwoodsmen give warning of the impending danger; in vain even did a hostile warrior the very evening before, apprise some of his relatives in the fortress of the intended attack; in vain did two negroes declare that they had seen twenty warriors painted for battle, in the vicinity of the fort. Major Beasley would listen to no remonstrance, but steadily refused to keep the gate of the fortress shut, and permitted the inmates to wander unrestrained along the banks of the lake." It might be added, in vain did his superior officer, General Claiborne, send to him urging him to be prepared for an attack from the Indians. Of the two negroes mentioned above by Meek, Pickett says that one of them "belonging to John Randon, was tied up and severely flogged for alarming the garrison with what Major Beasley deemed a sheer fabrication. Fletcher, the owner of the other, refused to permit him to be punished, because he believed his statement, which so incensed the major that he ordered Fletcher with his large family to depart from the fort by ten o'clock the next day."

It is to be hoped that a man so unfit to command will seldom have five hundred lives committed to his care. The Indians were now near. They remembered the dinner hour at Burnt Corn, and they arranged to make the attack at noon, August 30, 1813. On that day "the sun rose, beautiful and with a dewy coolness, over the forests of needle-leaved pines that extended off to the east, and concealed beneath their high and shafted arcades the grimly painted and fast approaching warriors of Weatherford and McQueen. In the fort all was confidence and hilarity."

In the words of Pickett, "The inmates had become inactive, free from alarm, and abandoned themselves to fun and frolic."

It is well attested that the day before, which was Sunday, a fresh supply of whiskey had been brought into the stockade, of which more than one had made too free use. The noon hour of Monday was drawing near. Meek says that "Major Beasley with a party of his officers was engaged in a game of cards." Pickett says that "the soldiers were repos- ng on the ground, some of the settlers were playing cards, the girls and young men were dancing, while a hundred thoughtless and happy children sported from door to door and from tent to tent." Major Beasley had been instructed by General Claiborne **to** send out scouts frequently, to be prepared for an

attack, and this was his preparation, with the fort
gate open and, as was afterwards discovered, blocked
open with sand.   On the 29th of August, the very
day before, an express message arrived from General Claiborne, sent out from Fort Madison, warning
Major Beasley of danger and "enjoining the utmost
circumspection."   And on the morning of August
30th Major Beasley wrote to General Claiborne.

> MIMS BLOCK HOUSE, August 30, 1813.
>
> SIR: I send enclosed the morning reports of my
> command.   " I have improved the fort at this place
> and made it much stronger than when you were
> here.   *   *   *   There was a false alarm
> yesterday." He mentions the report brought in by
> the two negroes and says, "But the alarm has proved
> to be false."

False, it is evident, simply because he chose to
call it so. Two hours later, as the bearer of the
letter had not left the stockade, Major Beasley wrote
a second note assuring General Claiborne of his
"ability to maintain the fort against any number of
Indians."   And now a solitary horseman from the
north is rapidly approaching.   General Woodward
says that Jim Cornells left Fort Mims in the morning of August 30th and rode some miles up the
river.   Before noon he returned on a fast trot,
halted at the fort gate, and shouted to Major Beasley
that the Indians were coming.   He replied to Cornells that he had seen only a gang of red cattle, to
which Cornells answered that the gang of red cattle would give him a terrible kick before night.
Woodward does not hesitate to say, in plain words,
on the authority of eye witnesses whom he knew
well, "Major Beasley was drunk."   Others at the

gate then took sides with Major Beasley, and said Cornells, a man whose testimony that commanding officer was in duty and honor bound to respect, was no better than Fletcher's negro who was then tied up to be whipped. Major Beasley now ordered Cornells to be arrested, but the intrepid scout wheeled his horse and started for Fort Pierce, telling the people at the gate once more that the Indians were coming, and that if they would prepare to defend themselves he would stay and help fight, but if not, then he would take care of himsslf. Receiving no encouragement from them he rode rapidly away. It would seem that on that day more than one man was no better than drunk.

Surely no where else in American history can an example be found where a fort was so poorly guarded, where a massacre was so needless.

"The hour of twelve o'clock arrived, and the drum beat the officers and soldiers of the garrison to dinner." The Indians had waited for this signal, and now "one thousand Creek warriors" rushed for the open gate, reached it, struck down Major Beasley (who at last, when it was too late, believed there was danger and tried to shut the sand-barred gate), and commenced at once their work of carnage. One of their leaders was William Weatherford, already mentioned, in whose veins Scotch, French, and Indian blood was mingled, and who rushed in on foot at the head of his Indians, for the time apparently as savage as they. A prophet decked with his [27] feathers was among the leaders, who was imme_ diately killed by Captain Dixon Bailey.

The carnage that followed was dreadful. Among the Mississippi volunteers that came to defend Fort Mims were two captains ànd their companies— Captain Middleton and Captain Jack. These, with most of their men, must have fallen in the early part of the assault.*

The following sentences are taken from "Clarke and Its Surroundings " :

" The officers bravely endeavored to drive the Indians from the gateway, but bravery was now of no avail. Officers and soldiers fell in vain attempts to counteract the results of a want of vigilance in the past. Help or hope there was none, and soldiers, women, children, Spaniards, friendly Indians, fell together in heaps of mangled bodies, the dying and the dead, scalped, mutilated, bloody, to be consumed ere long by fire, or to become food for hungry dogs and buzzards. In vain the young men, no longer dancing with the girls, and also the aged men and boys, fought the unrelenting savages with desperate fury. In vain did the brave Captain Bailey, left as the commanding officer, and who lived through all the carnage, animate the inmates to a resolute resist-ance. In vain did the women load the guns, bring water from the well, and do all that it was possible to do in sustaining the courage of the men."

To contend with foes within is not like contend-ing with foes without, whether in physical or in moral conflicts. The Spaniards referred to above

---

* Rev. J. G. Jones, of Hazelhurst, Mississippi, wrote, June 16, 1886, " I knew the brave and noble Captain Jack. He was quite a young man. He had just taken an additional course in our county school to complete his primary education when the news of the Creek uprising reached us."

were some deserters, so called, from Pensacola, who, while kneeling around the well and making the sign of the cross, fell beneath the Indian tomahawks.

The first destructive onset, resisted as bravely and as well as the dreadful circumstances permitted, lasted not more than two or three hours. Weatherford himself did not long remain, for in the middle of that afternoon, twelve miles from Fort Mims, he met his half brother, David Tate, told him of the massacre, and expressed his regret. On very good authority it is asserted that before he left the stockade he implored the savage warriors to spare the women and children, but those now infuriated Creeks refused to listen, and even threatened his own life if he tried to save any of the whites. That after the lull in the first storm of battle, when many inmates of the fort were living, there was a renewal of the work of destruction, is certain, but the authorities here are conflicting and how it was brought about is quite uncertain. Charles Weatherford explicitly denies that his grandfather, the Red Eagle, led the Indians to a second attack.*

Some assert that a new band of Indians arrived to complete the work of slaughter, and others that a reserve force of six hundred now came in from their concealment; but the probability is that after some slight rest, or respite for the doomed inmates of the fort, the thoroughly infuriated savages needed no leader to urge them to complete their bloody work. They succeeded by means of arrows in setting fire to the buildings within the inner enclosure. This is

*See the letter of Charles Weatherford, Junior, at the close of this chapter.

attributed by Woodward to the Shawnee Seekaboo, who was with them, and some of the McGillivray Negroes. Now, again, amid the fearful shrieks of women and children put to death in ways as horrible as Indian barbarity could invent, the work of death was resumed.

Those left alive now crowded into what they called the bastion. Says Pickett, " Soon it was full to overflowing. The weak, wounded, and feeble were pressed to death and trodden under foot. The spot presented the appearance of one immense mass of human beings, herded together too close to defend themselves, and, like beeves in the slaughter pen of the butcher, a prey to those who fired upon them. The large building had fallen, carrying with it the scorched bodies of the Baileys and others on the roof and the large number of women and children in the lower story."

Soon the flames swept over all, and while a few escaped, those, if there were any, not yet butchered by the Indians, perished in these flames.

As near as can be known the Indians retired from the burning mass of buildings and human bodies at about five o'clock, and that sad tragedy, known as the massacre at Fort Mims, was ended. The commanding officer had by his conduct invited it upon himself and upon the five hundred whose lives he was there to protect, and swiftly and terribly as a thunderbolt of war, the destruction at noon-day came upon them.

The bullets, the knives, the war clubs, the tomahawks, the flames, did their work, and more than half a thousand human beings in a few hours perished.

Although Pickett gives very definitely the number in the fort, and assigns to Weatherford one thousand warriors, yet in the nature of the case there must remain some uncertainty in regard to these numbers. Ramsay, the next best authority, gives six hundred as the number of the Indians, but he agrees very well with Pickett in regard to the number in the stockade. And from the territory represented by this fort, the Tensaw and Little River settlements, the number given cannot be too large.

Of the five hundred and fifty in the fort how many escaped is not quite certain; but at these and the authorities in regard to them we may now briefly look. Of the Mims family there escaped Mrs. Mims, and three sons, David Mims, Alexander Mims, and Joseph Mims.* There also escaped death by delivering themsevles up as prisoners, Mrs. Susan Hatterway, Elizabeth Randon a white child, and a colored girl named Lizzie.† Dr. Clanton of Leaf, Greene County, Mississippi, states that one of the inmates of Fort Mims, Samuel Smith, of mixed blood, informed him that fourteen at one time, near the close of the massacre, Smith, Steadham, Stubblefield, and eleven other men, having cut some of the pickets with an axe, broke through the enclosure and the Indians, reached the swamp, and escaped, Smith saving the life of Stubblefield in their flight

---

*See the letter of Mrs. Peebles who was Jane E. Mims.
†See Weatherford's Letter.

by shooting an Indian who was just in the act of striking Stubblefield to the earth.*

A colored woman, named Hester, manifested not a little resolution, for, although wounded, she made her way through the Indian warriors, reached a canoe in Lake Tensaw, paddled to Fort Stoddard that night, and gave to General Claiborne the first information concerning the massacre.

In the escape of Mrs. Vicey McGirth, a half Creek woman, wife of Zachariah McGirth, a gleam of human gratitude lights up the darkness of Indian barbarity. She was in Fort Mims with her eight children, while her husband happened to be on that day without.

The incident is so beautiful as a relief to the bloody deeds of that day that we may patiently listen to Pickett's full narrative: " Many years before the dreadful massacre at Fort Mims, a little, hungry Indian boy, named Sanota—an orphan, homeless and friendless—stopped at the house of

---

*Dr. A. B. Clanton gave in 1890 for publication in a Mississippi journal, recollections of what in boyhood he heard from the survivors of that massacre, especially naming as an informant Samuel Smith. He gives these, to use his own words, "as truthfully and graphically as my broken and somewhat confused recollection from so long a period will permit." He freely admits that much which he heard "has faded from his memory through the long lapse of time." Dr. Clanton relates on the authority of Smith, that "a large and powerful negro man" wielding an axe, "killed more Indians than any other man in the fort," but he fell at last, covered with wounds "from knife, and club, and tomahawk." Slave as he was, he fought bravely in behalf of the whites, and deserves to be remembered along with Captain Dixon Bailey and his brothers James and Daniel Bailey, and the other brave defenders of the women and children, although that bravery availed so little in saving life at the last.

Dr. Clanton gives not quite an hour as the length of the interval between the two attacks, and he says that during that time those in the fort drank too much whiskey. At this time it seems that some escaped who are not mentioned in Pickett's list.

Vicey McGirth. She fed and clothed him, and he grew to athletic manhood. He joined the war party, and formed one of the expedition against Fort Mims. Like the other warriors he was engaged in hewing and hacking the females to pieces, towards the close of the massacre, when he suddenly came upon Mrs. McGirth and his foster sisters. Pity and gratitude taking possession of his heart, he thrust them in a corner, and nobly made his broad savage breast a rampart for their protection. The next day he carried them off upon horses, toward the Coosa, under pretence that he had preserved them from death for his slaves. Arriving at his home, he sheltered them, hunted for them, and protected them from Indian brutality. One day he told his adopted mother that he was going to fight Jackson, at the Horse-Shoe, and that if he should be killed, she must endeavor to reach her friends below." He went and fought and fell, and she and her daughters did finally reach her husband at Mobile.

General Woodward and also Dr. Clanton attribute the protection of McGirth's family to the noted chief Jim Boy or High Head Jim, one of the leaders of the war party. That he was a friend to McGirth is evident from Woodward's statement that when the Indians were at Pensacola in the summer, and there met Zachariah McGirth, and some of the war party proposed to kill him, High Head Jim threatened with death any Indian who harmed McGirth.*

---

* How to reconcile these accounts I do not see unless the little Indian boy known as Sanota had become the chief Jim Boy, which does not seem to be possible. I accept Pickett's as the true account, because he received the facts from McGirth himself in 1834.—T. H. B.

General Woodward states that Jim Boy tried to save the lives of others at Fort Mims, and thus incurred the ill-will of the enraged warriors.

PICKETT'S LIST OF THOSE WHO ESCAPED FROM FORT MIMS.

Mrs. McGirth and her daughters, a friendly Indian named Socca, Hester, a negro woman, Samuel Smith of mixed blood, Lieutenant W. R. Chambliss, Dr. Thomas G. Holmes, Lieutenant Peter Randon, Sergeant Matthews, Josiah Fletcher, Martin Rigdon, Joseph Perry, Jesse Steadham, Edward Steadham, John Hoven,—— Jones, and —— Maurice. This last name can now be corrected from a newspaper record. A. J. Morris, died at Heflin, Alabama, April 5, 1891, nearly one hundred years of age. He is supposed to have been the last survivor of the inmates of Fort Mims. Five are mentioned in the "Birmingham Age Herald" by a special correspondent, L. E. M., as escaping through the pickets together. These were Martin Rigdon, Samuel Smith, Joseph Perry, Jesse Steadham, and A. J. Morris. And all these, it is said, went to Mount Vernon after several days' wandering. These names are all in Pickett's list. To these may be added, according to Dr. Clanton, Stubblefield, Cook, Montjoy, Aaron Bradley, and Elemuel Bradford. Dr. Clanton's authority was Samuel Smith. Pickett's informers were Dr. T. G. Holmes, Jesse Steadham, and Peter Randon. On the authority of Judge Meek may be added the name of James Bealle, and on the authority of the Rev. J. G. Jones of Hazelhurst, Mississippi, the name of private Daniels, of Jefferson county, Mississippi. There have already been given on good authority, the additional names of Mrs. Mims, David Mims, Alexander Mims, and Joseph Mims; also of Mrs. Susan Hatterway, Elizabeth Randon, and Lizzie, the colored girl. So that, in addition to the fifteen of Pickett, without counting the McGirth family of seven or eight, we have the names of fourteen others, making in all some thirty-six survivors out of five hundred and fifty-three. There were probably a few others whose names are yet unknown, and some of the hundred colored people were probably taken away by the Indians, of whom there would remain no trace.* About fifty seems to be a fair estimate of those who survived the horrors of that day and night.

The escape of Lieutenant Chambliss, as given by Pickett, was remarkable. After passing out from the stockade and the Indians around it, he at length took refuge in a log heap. To this in the night some Indians set fire, and when it seemed that he could no longer endure the smoke and the heat something called the Indians away and he escaped.

Captain Dixon Bailey, although severely wounded, left the fort with others, taking with him his little child, but he never reached a human habitation. Judge Meek states, that some time after, there was found in the swamp a gun having the name, Dixon Bailey, cut in the stock, and by it were the bones of a man and a child. Pickett states that a negro

---

* Jack Cato, a colored resident of Clarke county, in 1880, says he was a drummer in the war of 1812, was a drummer at New Orleans in 1815. He claims to have been at Fort Mims and gives a graphic account of scenes there. According to his statements he was in 1880 between eighty and ninety years of age. He was then living on a small farm and appeared to be a very old man.

carried a child of Dixon Bailey's in the effort to
escape, and that, becoming bewildered, in his excitement he ran back among the Indians, who immediately killed the trembling boy as he was calling on
his father to save his life.

We come now to the last scene connected with
this dreadful tragedy, THE BURIAL OF THE DEAD.

On the 9th of September, as has been incidentally
mentioned, a company of men under the command of
Major Kennedy, detailed for the purpose, reached the
place of the massacre to do what might be possible in
burying the dead. They found, as the result of Indian
barbarity, of the fire, of famishing dogs, of buzzards,
and of other wild animals, what had some ten days
before been human forms, in a condition too ho-
rible to be described with any minuteness. It will
certainly be the dictate of sympathy for the feelings
of the readers to spare them a review of the details
of what these men there found as showing the Indian
treatment of the women and children. Surely not
often, it is to be hoped never, not even in the Sepoy
rebellion in India, have human eyes looked upon a
more revolting spectacle. Some six or seven hundred human bodies—what there was left of them,
whites, Indians, "half-breeds," negroes, nearly all
in a condition that no friend could recognize or
identify, were on and around that once palisaded
acre. Trenches were dug, and so long as the men
could endure the horrible task, the mutilated,
charred, decomposing remains of human forms were
piled within the trenches and covered with earth.
No very thorough burial of all that had a few days
before been a part of living humanity could be com-

pleted, for the task was too much for human endurance, but doing the best they could, the company of resolute men left that dark and gloomy spot to be finally cleansed by the sunshine and the rain of heaven.

[28]

The Indians no doubt carried off the body of their noted chief Far Off Warrior, Hopiee Tustenuggee, who fell at Fort Mims, and also the bodies of their fallen prophets, probably of many others; but they left bodies enough there of their dead, grim warriors, to add no little to the task of the white men in committing to the earth the bodies of the slain.*

Among the five hundred dead of the inmates of that stockade, there were nearly every white woman, all but one of the hundred white children that were playing in the morning, and all those dancing girls.

The whites had good cause to remember the battle of Burnt Corn, while most of the Indian warriors lived not long to remember Fort Mims. Exterminating wars—perhaps sometimes needful—are ever to be dreaded; and surely no one can review this Creek War and not feel that the butchery of five hundred people, commencing at midday of

---

*One white man, Zachariah McGirth, had gone to Fort Mims on the night of August 30th. He searched there long, but of course in vain, among those mangled bodies in the smoking ruins of the fort, to find some remains of his wife and daughters. He gave them up as having been surely among the many, even then, unrecognizable dead; and when months afterwards, on the wharf at Mobile, where from their desolate home on the Alabama they had been conveyed by an American officer, they were finally presented to McGirth, as though they had returned to life from the dead, it is said that a "torrent of joy and profound astonishment overwhelmed him. He trembled like a leaf and was for some minutes speechless."—*Pickett.*

August 30, 1813, by infuriated savages, was perfectly
needless.   By needless, here, is meant that the com-
commanding officer could, and therefore should,
have prevented it.

Upon Fort Pierce, near by as it was, the Indians
made no attack, and the few inmates retired un-
harmed.   They reached the Alabama River, but
could not cross until Peggy Bailey, a sister of Captain Dixon Bailey, swam to the west side and procured a flat boat, on which they ferried themselves
over and safely reached the arsenal at Mount Vernon.   In acknowledgment of that daring act, swimming the Alabama in August, when alligators were
quite   abundant,   the   United States Government
bestowed a tract of land upon this heroine.*

NOTES.

1.   Captain Dixon Bailey was of mixed, or part
Indian blood.   He was a native of Auttose, and was
educated in Philadelphia.   His wife, say some, was
a white woman from South Carolina.†   He is represented as a man " of fine personal appearance,
unimpeachable integrity, and a strong mind.   His
courage and energy were not surpassed by those of

*Says Judge Anstill, of Mobile: " I have often heard my
father speak of ' Peggy Bailey' and her swimming the river. He
knew her well.   Her grant of land comprised what is now called
Choctaw Bluff on the Alabama River, opposite Carney's Bluff
on the 'Bigbee.   For a long time it was known as Peggy Bailey's
Bluff."—*Extract from a letter written March 5, 1894.*

†But other, and quite as reliable authority, gives as the wife
of Dixon Bailey a daughter of Mrs. Sophia Durant, thus making

any other man." It seems that he had at least two brothers, James and Daniel, and two sisters, Peggy and Polly. Peggy Bailey has been mentioned as aiding those who retreated from Fort Pierce. She is represented as having been a stout, heavy built woman, who could ride a horse and shoot equal to a man. Polly Bailey became the wife of Sizemore, who kept a ferry at what is now called Gainestown. She was an expert in swimming, and sometimes acted as ferryman. Sizemore lived on the west side of the Alabama and did not take refuge in Fort Mims. Peggy Bailey lived with her mother, an Indian woman, on the east side. Mrs. Sizemore lived to a great age in Baldwin county, and died in 1862. Her daughter, who became Mrs. Podgett, born on the Alabama River, was living in 1890, then one hundred years old.

2. It is difficult to reach certainty in regard to the various white men who married Indian women and became heads of families noted in the Creek history. It seems, that some time in the eighteenth century, Joseph Cornells, a white man, married an Indian woman, but her name has not been found. On the authority of Brewer, the Cornells family is placed among those claiming descent from the noted Sehoy. Three sons of this Joseph are named, George, Alexander, and James, the latter having been usually called Jim Cornells. And the name is often found written Curnells, as it was probably thus pronounced; but Colonel Hawkins and Charles Weatherford write Cornells. Besides these sons, Joseph Cornells had some daughters, one of them, named

a connection with the McGillivray family. These families seem all to be able to trace a line back, by various marriages, to the Princess Sehoy : McGillivray, Tate or Tait, Cornells, Bailey, Moniac or McNae, Weatherford, Durant, Tunstall, all wealthy and influential; in whose veins was variously mingled Indian, French, British, and American blood. Other families of mixed blood, those of Peter McQueen, of Smith, of the Fishers, and of McGirth, more or less noted all, do not seem to go back to the Princess Sehoy.

Anna, married a son of Big Warrior; one of them, Pickett says, was one of the wives of General Mc-Gillivray; and one of them was named Lucy. Alexander Cornells, the interpreter, is called by Brewer, Weatherford's brother-in-law.   He is recognized as an Indian chief as well as an interpreter, and his son, known by his Indian name of Opothele Yoholo, became "a distinguished chief," removed with his people to the Indian Territory, has always been a friend of the whites, and in the war of 1861 he declared himself on the side of the United States. James, known in this history as Jim Cornells, some years after the Creek war, died at the home of his sister, Mrs. Oliver, near the present town of Claiborne.

3. THE ESCAPE OF PAGE.

BY H. S. HALBERT.

Published in Alabama Historical Reporter, 1884.

Nehemiah Page was a hostler in the garrison at Fort Mims.   He was a somewhat dissipated young man, and the night before the attack on the fort was passed by him in a drunken frolic.   The next morning he went outside of the pickets into a stable, situated some eighty yards southeasterly of the eastern gate, and threw himself down on some fodder in the stable loft to sleep off the effects of his carousal. About midday he was awakened out of a deep sleep by the tramp of a body of men in rapid motion. Looking out through a crack, he saw the Indians in hundreds rushing past him towards the fort.   Page knew that the place was doomed.   For a few moments he was in mortal terror lest some of the Indians might enter the stable.   As soon as their backs were fairly turned upon him, he sprang out of the stable and fled for dear life southwesterly, towards the Alabama River. A little dog, which was following the Indians, saw the white man, and instantly leaving its red owners, ran after him. It seems that none of the Indians pursued Page, doubt-less thinking the fort before them a greater prize than a solitary fugitive. Still fear lent redoubled speed to Page's limbs, and he at last reached the river, with the dog close at his heels. He leaped into the river, and the little dog, whose actions were entirely friendly, plunged in after him. In swim-ming across the river, the dog, most of the time, kept close in his wake. But sometimes it would crawl upon his shoulders, and once or twice it even got upon his head. Page stated that several times it was with the greatest difficulty that he could keep himself from being drowned by the little animal's thus crawling upon him. During all this time he heard the terrible firing going on at the fort. At last, both the man and the dog reached the other shore, and for the first time Page felt safe. Fol-lowed by the dog, he then made his way to the white settlements. Page conceived a strong affection for the little Indian dog, which had so strangely fol-lowed him from Fort Mims. He would never part with it, but kept it as long as it lived.

Page was one of the first settlers of Neshoba County, Mississippi. About 1850 he emigrated to Texas, where he soon afterwards died. The above incident in his life was related to the writer by Mr. James W. Welch, of Neshoba County, who often heard it from Page's own lips. Page was considered a truthful man by all who knew him.

4. The last Sabbath at Fort Mims, from the ac-counts given by the survivors, must have been any-thing but a true Sabbath day for the crowded in-mates of that stockade. They were not of a class

accustomed to religious observances. In 1803
Lorenzo Dow had passed through there like a bright
meteor, and had preached at the Tensaw Boat Yards.
It is doubtful whether, in the ten years that followed,
any effort had been made to evangelize the Tensaw
people. They had in their stockade no camp-
meeting as did the inmates of Fort Easley. Pickett
puts it mildly when he says, abandoned to " fun and
frolic." Prayers in that stockade were very few.

5. One might almost suppose that J. F. H. Claiborne
thought that bravery, or what he chooses to call
bravery, would atone for all other neglects, for he
says, " Major Beasley, with the courage of despair,
ran to the outer gate to close it, and received half a
dozen bullets in his breast the moment he reached it."
Page 324. Again "Major Beasley was brave to desperation." 324. He speaks of him as " the brave
man who commanded there." Page 325. He says,
" Never did an officer more bravely seek to redeem
his fatal over confidence. He fell at the gate in the
blaze of a thousand rifles." 325. And as though
all this were not enough, he says once more, " The
courage of Major Beasley amounted to desperation.
Although often warned, he turned a deaf ear to all
idea of danger. At the onset of the enemy, in the
blaze of three hundred rifles, he rushed to close
the front gate * * * Here he fell." Page
336. (These extracts are from Claiborne's "Mississippi," a work to which I am indebted for some
valuable letters and official documents; a work which
contains very evidently some rhetorical embellish-
ments.)

We ought, sometimes, surely to call things by
their right names. If what all the accounts and reports show of the conduct of the commanding
officer at Fort Mims are the marks of a brave soldier,
rather would I have to help me defend a log hut
against Indians, a timid woman, for she would at
least shut the door and pull the latch string in.

I feel almost out of patience with Claiborne's persistency when I once more find him saying, pages 340 and 341: "The fall of Fort Mims, the butchery of so many women and children, and the defenseless condition of the settlements, aroused everywhere the sympathies and martial spirit of the people." This is well enough, but he goes on: "It was not the capture of Fort Mims—a strongly garrisoned post—well calculated to alarm the country, but the dreadful massacre of the captives that roused our people."

"Strongly garrisoned" truly! No doubt there were men there in sufficient number, and with arms and ammunition; but to call Fort Mims "strongly garrisoned" seems like a burlesque on words. How could the Indians have failed to take it? Weatherford had supposed it was garrisoned. He had heard that an officer was there with soldiers, and there is evidence that he did not expect to capture it until he saw its condition on that August morning.

Claiborne himself says, in another connection, when some of the facts he is almost obliged to tell, that Major Beasley "held the Indians in contempt, was angry at what he considered false alarms, and as a taunt and derision to the timid had the main gate thrown open." Page 324. And that main entrance was kept open. And yet Claiborne coolly tells us that the capture of this stockade, with the circumstances existing, which he well knew, was "well calculated to alarm the country." "Alarm" indeed! Had all the facts been known they would have aroused rather the indignation of the country.

This fearful massacre, one of the bloodiest in our land, has been placed as the beginning of the Creek War, and its responsibility laid almost entirely upon Weatherford, quite long enough. It is time that the real responsibility should be placed where it belongs. Had Captain Dixon Bailey, one of the true heroes at

Fort Mims, been in command of that stockade, there is no probability that it would have been captured. With a closed gateway, with the men at their posts, with sentinels on the watch, it would have been "strongly garrisoned." Had there been in the commanding officer true courage, had there been at Fort Mims no bravado and less whiskey, its capture and massacre would not have been a part of American history. And Claiborne virtually acknowledges all this, for he says: " Never men fought better; but such was the advantage given to the enemy, by neglecting the most obvious precautions, all their bravery was thrown away." And who gave them that advantage? Who " had the main gate thrown open "? Claiborne himself gives testimony. He says once more. "Had the gates been kept closed, and the men properly posted   *   *   * all experience shows that such a force might have kept at bay a thousand Indians."

Let us deal fairly with the well attested facts, and not lay all the blame upon Weatherford and the Creeks.

LETTER OF MRS. PEEBLES.

" LOWER PEACH TREE.
[Wilcox Co., Alabama, June 13, 1890.]
" Having received your letter and reading its contents I will give you all the information I can. I was the granddaughter of Samuel Mims that was killed at Fort Mims, and my father was Joseph Mims, his son. My mother's name was Jane Oniel. My age is seventy-one. I had two uncles, David and Alexander Mims, that escaped, and Grandma Mims, and also my father, Joseph Mims, but they are all dead, and I am the only heir in Alabama.

*   *   *   *   *   *   *

" I have a half-brother, Leonard Mims, in Texas.
I have some nephews and nieces in Texas, but I
can't tell anything about them.   *   *   *
" Mrs. Jane E. Peebles."

SECOND LETTER FROM MRS. PEEBLES.

" Lower Peach Tree, July 22, 1894.

" Mr. T. H. Ball—*Dear Sir :* I received your
letter several weeks ago, and would have written
before now, but I have been thinking over Fort
Mims and the massacre, and as I am old and forgetful, I will try and do the best I can for your history.
Grandma Mims was a white woman without any
Indian blood. She was not in the fort at the time
of the massacre. They all escaped together after
the battle, and went to Mobile in a flat boat.

" My grandfather, Samuel Mims, was married
when he settled Lake Tensaw, 1797. When the
battle was fought my grandma could hear the
Indians yell. I am so forgetful, I can't remember,
as I have been told by my father all about it. Be
sure to send me a book when it is complete. My
health is not very good, and has not been for a long
time.   " Your friend,
" Jane E. Peebles.

" P. S.—Peggy Bailey escaped from Fort Mims,
and swam the Alabama River."

Besides writing to Mrs. Peebles, I sent the following letter to Mount Pleasant, Alabama :

" Crown Point, Indiana, October 2, 1890.

" Mr. Charles Weatherford, Jr.—Dear Sir: I
am gathering material for an account of the massacre at Fort Mims in 1813. I wish to do no injustice
to the memory of that Weatherford, your grand
father I suppose, who is said to have led the Indians
to Fort Mims. I have Pickett's account of the
attack, and also the writings of others.

"Will you have the kindness to give me what you may have learned in regard to some particulars.

"1. Did Weatherford, along in the middle of that fatal afternoon, encourage the Indians to a renewed assault ? 2. Was he 'mounted upon a splendid black charger'?

3. "Did he take away from the fort, as has been said by some, 'an extremely beautiful' and spirited maiden of about seventeen or eighteen summers, named Lucy, daughter of Joseph Cornells ? Or is this story a fiction ?

4. "Should that name be written Cornells or Curnells ?

"How many times was Weatherford married ? Who were his wives ? And when did they die ?

"I have noticed that Claiborne, Meek, and Pickett do not agree exactly in their estimate of William Weatherford, the Red Eagle. I have no prejudice ; no partiality. If any facts are in your possession that would enable you to answer any of these question you would do me a favor to write on the back of these slips.

"As what I expect to prepare on Fort Mims is designed for publication, I should like to make it as accurate and reliable as possible. You can probably help me to do this.

"Your friend,
"T. H. BALL."

According to my request the following answers were returned. The numbers correspond to the numbers of the questions :

1. "No ! About the middle of the afternoon of that memorable day David Tate, Weatherford's half brother, met Weatherford twelve miles above Fort Mims. Weatherford told him of the massacre and expressed great regret. * * *

2. "No ! At the time of the engagement he was on foot. * * *

3. "No! I presume that is the embellishment of the story. * * *

4. "Cornells I believe is correct."

In addition to these answers written on the slips and returned to me as requested, the following letter was also sent, a letter which I consider of so much interest that I give it entire. I have omitted parts of the answers given above because they are given so fully in the letter :

CHARLES WEATHERFORD'S LETTER.

"Mt. Pleasant, Ala.,
"Oct. 17th 1890.

"Mr. T. H. Ball,—*Sir:* Your letter of the 2d inst. came to hand yesterday. Sir, your subject has become stale. The name of Billy Weatherford is almost forgotten, superseded by the names of such men as Lee, Jackson, and Grant. With the death of my father, Charles Weatherford, Sr., who is about ninety-five years old, the name of Weatherford will become commonplace. My father is the oldest and only living child of the notorious, and so called bloody handed, Billy Weatherford. And I, sir, am the only living child of Charles Weatherford, Sr. Now, sir, you know who and what I am.

"My grandfather, Billy Weatherford, died in 1826.

"I was born in 1834, therefore what I have to say will only be hearsay and from many lips, some prejudiced and some partial.

"According to the most authentic information Weatherford did not desire the massacre at Fort Mims. About the middle of the afternoon of that sadly memorable day Weatherford met his half brother, David Tate, about twelve miles above Fort Mims, and told him of the massacre and spoke of it with much regret. He told Tate that he tried to prevent it ; but under the excitement his warriors threatened his life if he interfered. **Tate** did not belong to the hostile party.

"Now as to Weatherford's being mounted at the time the engagement began, circumstances prove that he was not. I had an aunt who was a refugee in Fort Mims. I have often heard her say that she saw Billy Weatherford as he came in the gate at full run, at the head of his warriors, jump a pile of logs almost as high as his head. (Weatherford stood six feet two inches). She said, as he sprang over the logs he saw Captain Dixon Bailey who was a bitter enemy, to whom he shouted, ' Dixon Bailey, to-day one or both of us must die.'* So I judge by this that he was not mounted at the time of the engagement. But in the evening [afternoon] of that day, when he met Tate, Weatherford was mounted on the veritable black horse. I believe it is a recognized fact that all warriors of note ride either a milk-white or raven black steed. Now, sir, I being a man of peace, and altogether unlike my grand sire, ride an old sorrel mare.†

"The aunt of whom I have spoken as being a refugee in Fort Mims at the time of the massacre was Mrs. Susan Hatterway (nee Stiggins) who hated Billy Weatherford with a thorough hatred. My aunt's husband was killed early in the fight. She had no children. And when she saw that the fort would be reduced to ashes she took hold of a little white girl, Elizabeth Randon, with one hand, and a negro girl named Lizzie, with the other, and said to them, 'Let us go out and be killed together.' But to her surprise she saw one of the busy and bloody warriors beckon her to him. On approaching she recognized him. It was Iffa Tustunnaga, meaning

---

"*One of us two, Herminius, shall never more go home;
I will lay on for Tusculum and lay thou on for Rome."
                              "Lays of Ancient Rome."

†Those, at least, who have lived in the South can appreciate this touch of humor, as in imagination they see this old mare jogging along.

Dog Warrior. He took her prisoner with the two children. He took them to Pensacola, and gave them over to some of their friends, where they remained until the war closed, when they returned to their homes in Alabama. Soon after the close of the war my aunt married Absalom Sizemore. She died near Mount Pleasant in 1865.

"When Elizabeth Randon grew to womanhood she married Algier Newman, and lived many years on the Alabama river just below Fort Claiborne in Monroe county. Excuse me for the digression.

"I will get back to my subject by saying the Lucy Cornell's story must have been merely to embellish the story. But it would not have surprised me if he had done so. All great warriors do such things.

"I believe the name has always been spelled Cornells.

" Billy Weatherford was married three times, twice under the Indian law. His first wife, my grandmother, was Mary Moniac, originally spelled McNac. She died in 1804 at Point Thloly, which is in Lowndes county. His second wife was Sapoth Thlanie. I never heard where or when she died. His third and last wife was Mary Stiggins. They were married under the white law in 1817. She died near Mount Pleasant, Monroe county, 1832.

" I had an anecdote told me once by the mother of the late Colonel William Boyles, of Mobile, which is the only one that I have never seen in print. Mrs. Boyles was a widow and lived near Billy Weatherford in Monroe County. She kept what was called at that time a wayside tavern. Weatherford, in going to and from his plantation, passed right by her door. They were warm friends, and she frequently invited him to eat a meal with her. On this particular day she invited him to eat dinner. Just before the meal was ready four strangers rode up and asked for dinner. All were soon seated at table, and discussion commenced, in the course of which the strangers wanted to know where that bloody-handed savage, Billy Weatherford, lived. Mrs. Boyles said Weatherford's eyes sparkled. She shook her head at him to say nothing. The talk went on. Three of the strangers expressed a wish to meet Weatherford, assuring Mrs. Boyles they would kill the red-skinned, bloody-handed savage on sight. (Weatherford was fair, with light brown hair and mild black eyes.) Dinner being over, the gentlemen walked out on the gallery. To the surprise of the strangers, the man with whom they had sat at dinner stepped into the midst of the crowd and said : 'Some of you gentlemen expressed a wish while at dinner to meet Billy Weatherford. Gentlemen, I am Billy Weatherford, at your service!' But, Mrs. Boyles said, she never saw men more frightened than were the three belligerently disposed gentlemen. Not one of the trio was entitled to a raven black or milk white steed. They quailed under the glance of the Red Eagle's eye. The fourth gentleman, who had said but little, stepped forward and shook hands with Weatherford, and introduced himself as Colonel David Panthon.

" Exit.

" CHARLES WEATHERFORD."

CHAPTER X.

THE KIMBELL–JAMES MASSACRE.

RANSOM KIMBELL with his family came from South Carolina to the Tombigbee River, settling near McGrew's Reserve about 1807, but in 1812 the family removed into the Bassett's Creek Valley, near to the home of a settler whose name was Sinquefield. When the stockade was built bearing this pioneer's name, as a protection from the dreaded Muscogee incursions, the Kimbell family with the others in that neighborhood left their plantation home for a residence in the stockade. After a time, no Indians appearing east of the Alabama, and the small stockade being crowded, the Kimbell family and the family of Abner James retired to the cooler and more roomy plantation cabin. They were spending there the days of that last week in August, 1813, knowing indeed that there was danger, but not thinking how unexpectedly Indians from the eastward might come upon them.

On Tuesday evening, August 31st, quite late in fact into the night, as young Isham Kimbell and a daughter of Abner James were sitting up with a sick member of the household, "the dogs ran out furiously and barked violently, while the sounds of running human feet were so distinctly and alarmingly heard, that Miss James, with admirable presence of mind, blew out the candle."* Yet when the morning came the families neglected to return to the stockade. It was their last opportunity. It seems to be deeply imbedded in human nature not to heed warnings. On Wednesday, September 1, 1813, at about three o'clock in the afternoon, suddenly from the Creek bottom, Francis, called the prophet, and his warriors appeared. Ransom Kimbell was away from home. Abner James and a visitor named Walker were in sight within the house, upon whom the Indians fired; but neither man was wounded, and without stopping to make any defense for the helpless women and children, which in the circumstances was no doubt hopeless, taking along his son Thomas, fourteen years of age, and his daughter, Mary, Abner James with Walker started with all possible speed for Fort Sinquefield. These four reached the stockade in safety. Isham Kimbell, a youth of sixteen, with a little brother was at the blacksmith shop, distant from the house one hundred and fifty yards. Hearing guns and immediately after seeing the Indians in his father's dooryard killing the inmates of his home he also started at once with his brother for the stockade. The distance was a little more than a mile. The brothers avoided the roadway. The Indians saw them and fired a gun, the shot cutting the chincapin bushes near them but harming neither. Crossing a little stream that flows between the two localities, the elder brother fell. Regaining his feet and looking round, to his surprise his little brother

*Isaac Grant, Editor at Grove Hill, Alabama; for thirty-eight years a valued friend; a careful student of local history and a first-class authority.   T. H. B.

was not in sight. He was with him when the gun was fired, and was not hurt, and that seems to be the last certainly known of this child. Of his death or of his captivity among the Indians nothing was ever heard. Like the disappearance of Ginevra of Modena, all that was ever known was the brief record that he was not. On the first day of September, 1813, that young Kimbell boy passed strangely out from the knowledge of all the white dwellers in Clarke.

The young Isham Kimbell, finding himself alone, hurried on towards the stockade. Uncertain in regard to its direction, he walked up the inclined body of a prostrate pine to get a better view around him, but hearing Indian voices on the roadway, he hastened down from his exposed position. He was soon met, almost exhausted as he now was, by Thomas Matlock and John O'Gwynn, who had heard the guns and left the stockade to reconnoitre; and they returned with him to the fort.

Of the onslaught at the Kimbell home, in the door yard, quick, savage, and merciless as it must have been, there were no witnesses, except the helpless victims and the Muscogees. There was not much scattering of the families after the two men and the four children made their hasty retreat. The savage blows from clubs and tomahaws fell thick and fast. Scalps were removed, the domestic animals were killed, the house was pillaged, and in a short time the Muscogees were out of sight in the densely wooded region that bordered on the creek, leaving, of women and children, all supposed to be dead, fourteen bodies in the house and door yard. It is

said above, in a short time, and short it must have
been, perhaps not more than twenty minutes, for
Ransom Kimbell, away on horseback, hearing the
guns, started for his home.   He reached it in time
only to find the work of death completed, and the
Indians, like a destroying cyclone, gone, he knew
not where.   Seeing the fearful desolation at his
lately peaceful home, sick at heart we may well know,
he, too, retired to the stockade.   We might suppose
that on his arrival there with his grief-laden report, a
force would have immediately proceeded to the home
spot to care for the dead.   But the men were mostly
absent at their plantations, and when they came
in at night-fall, not knowing the number of the
Indian band, nor how soon their stockade would be
attacked, they were busy posting pickets and preparing for defense.   So the dead were left in the care of
God.   Night and darkness came, and then a gentle
rain.   One of the scalped women, Mrs. Sarah Mer-
rill, a daughter of Abner James, although struck
senseless by a war club, was not dead.   In the night,
perhaps with the cool rain drops falling on her, she
revived.   Her thoughts were soon for her little
child.   There were two children in the house, of the
same size and age, and how, in the darkness, among
the bloody, dead bodies, could she recognize her
own ?   The dress of one fortunately was fastened
with buttons, the dress of the other only with
strings.*   This the mother well knew.   She found
her little one, a boy one year of age, and its body was

---

*Authority : Mrs. Mary Bettis, sister of Major W. J.
Hearin, in 1882 a commission merchant in Mobile.   Mrs. Bettis
was born in 1804, and was a woman of a remarkable memory.

yet warm. She nursed it for a few moments and it revived. Its short hair had saved it from being scalped, and, with her living child in her arms standing with difficulty upon her feet, she, too, left that fearful spot, where there seemed to be no more life, and started slowly for the fort. At length, almost exhausted, she placed her child in a hollow log, and dragged herself along. In the early morning the inmates of the fort were startled by the slow approach of a feeble, scalped woman. Soon they recognized her, some went immediately for the child, and both mother and child lived.

The remaining bodies of the dead were brought up the next day and buried near the stockade. Ransom Kimbell did not long survive. He died at Fort Madison. [29]

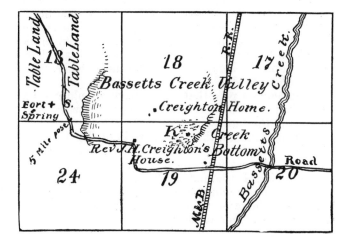

NOTE.

The preceding diagram shows the locality of Fort Sinquefield and of the massacre. The letter K. is used to indicate the latter as Fort S. designates the former. The squares, as marked out, are sections or square miles. The curved shading east of the fort indicates where the slope for the valley begins.

The table land here is about one hundred feet above the creek bottom, and gives to one standing there a fine view eastward to the Alabama.

In 1877, I made a special examination of the massacre locality, and wrote the following as the memorandum.

" Everything now on and around the scene of this tragic event is in keeping with what a poet or historian would like to find. Sixty-four years have passed away. The one survivor is an aged man. A growth of young pines, covering several acres, extends over and around the place of the massacre, extending westward about twenty rods. The shade is dark and deep in this pine grove. An old china tree, and the roots and decaying body of another, and a younger looking cedar, are near where the house once stood."

"It seems a pity that this solitude should ever be disturbed. It certainly ought to be left for the sunshine and the birds."

Isham Kimbell, the one survivor of the Kimbell family, became an influential citizen in Clarke county. He was for many years clerk of the Circuit court, and held other public offices. He started with nothing and accumulated by diligent effort property amounting in value to forty thousand dollars. He has many descendants now living.

ISHAM KIMBELL.

CHAPTER XI.

ATTACK ON FORT SINQUEFIELD.

TO the writer of this chapter it seems that full credence can well be given to a statement coming down from James Cornells in regard to a great council held by the hostile Creeks on the Alabama River (perhaps at the Holy Ground), some two weeks prior to the attack on Fort Mims. In this council it was resolved to divide the Creek army into two divisions, and make a simultaneous attack on two forts. Fort Mims was unanimously selected in the very beginning of the council as one of the forts, since a large number of its inmates were the antagonists of the Creeks at Burnt Corn,—mostly half-breeds, against whom the Red Stick party seemed to entertain a special animosity. A discussion lasting two days then ensued, in which it was debated whether the second fort should be Fort Madison or Fort Sinquefield. It was finally decided in favor of the latter, and a force of one hundred and twenty-five warriors was assigned to the Prophet Francis, with which to operate against that stockade. At what time or place Francis and his warriors separated from the main Creek army can not now be known.

We return to the Fork of the Tombigbee and the Alabama. It was near sunset on the last day of

August that the Tory Creek, Nah-hee, who had been out on an excursion, returned to Fort Madison and informed the garrison of the downfall of Fort Mims and of the presence of a large body of Creek warriors in the Fork, under the Prophet Francis. When this appalling news was heard, for a while the wildest panic prevailed. Some of the men grew deadly pale, women and children shrieked with terror, and many feared that Fort Madison would soon experience the same fate as Fort Mims. When the panic had spent its force, the garrison betook themselves zealously to their duties with the firm resolve to defend the post to the last. Nah-hee, who spent much of his time scouting, some days afterwards reported to Captain Dale that about the time of the massacre at Fort Mims, Francis and his warriors camped one night in the " Wolf's Den," a large deep ravine at the head of Cedar Creek, some three miles east of Fort Madison. Thence the Creek warriors moved northward, and on the middle of the afternoon of the first of September they committed the atrocious massacre on Bassett's Creek, of which a full and exhaustive account has been recorded in the preceding chapter.

When Colonel Carson, at Fort Madison, heard of this massacre, he sent early the next morning, the second of September, eleven mounted men, under Lieutenant James Bailey, armed with rifles, muskets, and holster pistols, up to Fort Sinquefield to assist in burying the dead and to learn the number of the Indians. John Woods, Isaac Hayden, and James Smith were of Bailey's party.

There were about fifteen arms-bearing men in
Fort Sinquefield. The inmates were mostly the families of the settlers on Bassett's Creek. Among these
was an aged man, named Charles Phillips, who had
a large family of children, several married, among
them Charles Phillips, Jr. In addition to the white
families there were also a few friendly Creeks, or, as
they were called in the language of the times, Tory
Creeks, who had taken refuge in the fort.

Upon the arrival of Lieutenant Bailey's party, as
has been stated, some of the garrison went with him
and his soldiers out to Ransom Kimbell's house, and
brought back in an ox cart the twelve bodies of the
slain. On the east side of the present Grove Hill
road, about seventy yards southeast of the fort, the
graves were dug for the dead.

It was now about eleven o'clock and a large
portion of the people were out at the graves attending the burial. About this time Mrs. Sarah Phillips,
wife of Charles Phillips, Jr., with two or three other
women, took a bucket apiece and went down to the
spring to bring some water. Several women were
already at the spring, busily engaged in washing.
A small guard had been detailed for the protection
of these women, but instead of accompanying the
women down to the spring, the guard only went
half way down the hill, there seated themselves on
a log and engaged in idle conversation.

The burial services were now drawing to a close.
At this time the elder Charles Phillips and Isham
Kimbell were sitting in front of the gateway, which
was on the west line of the picketing, near the southwest corner, and conversing about the massacre,

when Phillips happening to look towards the south, saw what he supposed to be a flock of wild turkeys coming towards the fort. Phillips called the attention of Kimbell to them remarking, " Look yonder, what a fine gang of turkeys." But the younger eyes of his companion saw at once that the supposed turkeys were a large band of Creek warriors advancing in a stooping position towards the fort. In an instant the shout of alarm was given and all were told to run into the fort. The party still lingering at the grave, rushed to the gate, the men seizing the smaller children and bearing them in their arms. The guard on the log also rushed into the place of refuge. The women at the spring, who had just finished their washing, heard the warning shouts, and began to flee for dear life, up the hill to the fort. As soon as the alarm was given, the Indians straightened themselves up and began to run forward with lightning speed so as to cut off the entrance of the burial party into the fort. They were about a hundred in number, armed with guns, tomahawks, and war clubs, and were commanded by the Prophet Francis. They were dressed in the usual Indian garb, their faces painted, their heads encircled with crowns or chaplets of upright turkey feathers, and many of them had a cow's tail tied on each arm from the shoulder to the wrist, the long hairs of the tail depending from the wrist. The Indians had run but a short distance, when seeing that they could not cut off the burial party, they saw then, for the first time, the women just beginning their flight from the spring. With appalling yells **and** waving of cow tails, they instantly whirled to

the left and rushed down a hill to cut off the escape
of the helpless females. To all human appearance,
the escape of the women was hopeless and an awful
death stared them in the face as they strained every
nerve in upward flight towards the gate. Closer
and closer did the swift-footed Muscogees press upon them and nearer and nearer did the savage war
whoop sound upon their ears.

At this juncture of terror and confusion everywhere, Isaac Hayden suddenly conceived a bold and
unique plan for the rescue of the women. Instantly
leaping upon a horse, to the saddle of which was
attached a pair of holster pistols, he cheered all the
dogs in the fort, about sixty in number, and galloped down the hill with the fierce yelling pack
upon the Indians. The Creek warriors, appalled
by the onset ôf these new and savage foes, were
compelled to halt and defend themselves for some
moments against their savage fury. It was a
singular encounter,—the fierce brutes, some baying
and others leaping on and throttling the red warriors.
In the struggle, some of the dogs were killed and
some wounded. In the meantime, the daring Hayden was not inactive. Seeing one of the women hard
pressed by an Indian, he galloped to her rescue with
pistol in hand and shot down the warrior dead in
his tracks, just as he had his tomahawk poised to
strike the fatal blow. Hayden's "dogs of war"
had by this time done their duty well and had so
checked the charge of the Indians, that all the
women, save one, safely escaped into the fort. A
negro woman, who was of the party, with wash-pot
on her head, was the first to reach the gate. Almost

bereft of her senses, when she heard the terrible cry of "Indians" she did not think to throw her pot aside, but bore it, poised with one hand on her head, all the way from the spring to the gate.

It was, indeed a terrible race for the women up that steep hill. One young woman, Miss Winnie Odom, had nearly reached the gate when she sank to the earth in terror and exhaustion. A soldier rushed out, gun in hand, and seizing her by the hair, thus dragged her into the gate. Such was the exigency of the occasion.

Mrs. Sarah Phillips was the unfortunate woman who failed to make her escape. Being in a delicate condition, she could not run fast and so was soon left in the rear. Three Indians, one of them a prophet, frightfully painted, sprang forward to intercept her flight. The prophet gave vent to the most unearthly screeching and yelling, at the same time waving aloft a cow's tail fastened to the end of a staff. The poor woman ran with all her might. She had reached about half way to the fort when, weakened with terror, she fainted and fell. But for this it was supposed that she might have made her escape. In a moment one of the warriors reached the spot where she lay, sank his tomahawk into her head, tore off the reeking scalp, and otherwise mutilated her person. It seems that Mrs. Phillips was slain just before Hayden had shot down the warrior mentioned above.

The daring Hayden, in his generous rescue, had done all that man could do. His task now over, for a moment, as he afterwards confessed, he was greatly bewildered what to do next, whether to dash off into the woods, or rush back into the fort. All at once, yielding to some strange impulse, he put his horse to the top of his speed and galloped entirely around the fort back to the front, and then dashed through the gate. The good horse had just cleared the gateway and was safe in the fort, when he fell to the earth, creased through the neck by a Creek bullet. It was an hour before he recovered and rose to his feet. Hayden, the bold rider, had run a narrow risk. Many a rifle had been fired at him, and five bullet holes were counted in his clothes.

The gate was now closed. The Indians then surrounded the stockade on all sides, but the main body massed themselves on the south, and the siege began in earnest. On the outside were still the faithful dogs, to whose furious onslaught on the Creek warriors the women were indebted for their safety. They now became frightened at the uproar of battle, and all fled, panic-stricken, to the neighboring forest, and, with but few exceptions, were never afterwards recovered by their owners.

The furious fire which was opened by the Creek warriors upon the stockade was vigorously returned. The garrison, numbering, soldiers and citizens, all told, about thirty men, were resolved to defend the post to the last. That very morning they had heard of the terrible downfall of Fort Mims, and were resolved, if it could be averted by human bravery, that no such fate should befall Sinquefield. A little incident, occurring at the very outset, gave the Indians great hopes of winning an easy prize. James Short, one of the citizens, was among the first to fire upon the besiegers. His gun, it seems,

had been loaded a long time, and the powder was
probably in a damp condition. As he fired it off
the gun gave a long, sputtering fire. The Creeks
noticed this and shouted to each other in exulting
glee, "They are almost out of powder." This
exclamation, which was either in the Muscogee or
the Alibamo tongue, was interpreted by one of the
Tory Creeks to the garrison, some of whom shouted
back, defiantly, in reply, "Come on and we will
show you whether we are almost out of powder." A
well directed fire, accordingly, undeceived the
Indians, and checked their nearer approach. It
was, perhaps, at this time that one of the pursuers
of Mrs. Phillips, the prophet, was slain. He had
approached near the gate, and began to leap to and
fro near a tree, sometimes behind it, sometimes
beside it, in full view of the garrison, all the time
waving his cow tail and eucouraging his warriors,
when a bullet from the fort. ended his prophetic
career forever.

In the garrison, at the beginning of the fight,
there was great excitement among the women and
children, who screamed and shrieked in their terror.
Some of the men thereupon went among them and
soon succeeded in pacifying them, telling them not
to be frightened, that they would certainly drive off
the Indians. The women and children were then
placed in the lower story of the block house, where
some of the women busied themselves in moulding
bullets.

During all this time a continuous fire was kept
up by both parties. The men had taken positions
at the various port holes of the stockade and some

in the block house. The Indians took their positions
behind trees and stumps, and quite a number behind
Sinquefield's abandoned log cabin, which stood about
seventy-five yards to the south. Others were in
more exposed places. These latter would rise from
the earth, deliver their fire, then throwing themselves again on the ground, and while reloading
would roll to and fro, keeping their bodies in constant motion, so as to baffle the aim of the marksmen in the garrison. The Indians all fought with
great bravery. If one was killed or badly wounded
his companions dragged him off the field, back to
the rear, as it was a custom of the Creeks never to
permit an enemy to get possession of the bodies of
their slain warriors if it were possible to prevent it.
Those behind Sinquefield's house would come to the
corners of the house and there deliver their
fire. One warrior even ventured into the
house and was there slain by a bullet
that came through a crack; and for several
years after could be seen the stain of his blood upon
the puncheon floor. Another warrior had his arm
broken not far from Sinquefield's house, and after
making some vain efforts to reload his rifle with one
arm, he retreated behind the house. Word was accordingly passed among the garrison to watch for
him and for two or three to keep their fire in reserve
for him. As was expected, it was not long before
the crippled warrior attempted to retreat, when
the sure aim of these marksmen stretched him
lifeless upon the earth. But some of his companions succeeded in dragging his body off the
field.

The post assigned to James Smith, Stephen Lacey, and a few others, who were all fine marksmen, was in the upper story of the block house, whence they poured a destructive fire upon the Indians. Whilst these men were thus busily engaged, Mrs. Lacey and Mrs. Thomas Phillips, for some purpose, came up from below. The attention of Lacey at this time was directed to a large pine tree, about seventy-five yards to the south, behind which were posted several warriors. Lacey fired at this party several times. At last, he shot one down, and turning to his comrades, he exultingly exclaimed : " I have turned over one of the red skins." A few moments afterwards, whilst peering through the port hole preparatory to another fire, the brave man fell backward at the feet of his wife, who happened to be standing behind him. He had received his death wound, a rifle ball passing through his neck. The men present instantly realizing that any loud wailings of grief would give encouragement to the Creek warriors, if heard by them, cautioned Mrs. Lacey to control herself and give vent to no noisy exclamations. They wished to keep the Creeks ignorant of the fact that any of the garrison was slain. The poor woman, though suffering an agony of grief over her husband, heeded their admonition. As the dying man lay upon the floor, the blood gushed in torrents from the fatal wound, and through a crack poured down upon the floor of the story beneath, where were huddled together the women and children—an awful sight to eyes unused to the carnage of war. It seems that the party behind the tree had, at last, observed the particular port-hole, from which Lacey had sent so

many leaden messengers of death, and concentrating
their fire upon it, one fatal bullet did its sure work.
Lacey's comrades stated that the ball came from the
very tree, behind which this party of warriors was
concealed.   Lacey was the only man killed in the
fort.   He was a good, upright citizen and lived
about two miles north of Fort Sinquefield.

About the same time that Lacey was killed,
James Dubose, a boy about ten years of age, while
on the stairway leading from the lower to the upper
story of the block house, was slightly wounded in
the back by a ball.

In the meantime, in the excitement and confusion of the fight, Charles Phillips was, for some
time, ignorant of the death of his wife.   He did not
even know that she had gone out with the other
women to the spring.   When, at last, the terrible
news was communicated to him that his wife was
lying outside a mangled corpse, he became frantic
with grief.   In his wild frenzy, he was on the point
of rushing out alone upon the Indians, when some
of his comrades seized him and held him until the
end of the seige.

The fight at Fort Sinquefield began about midday and lasted two hours, John Woods firing
the last shot at the enemy.   At the very
close of the fight, he saw a warrior partially
concealed behind a stump.   Woods fired and broke
the Indian's right arm. After reloading his rifle, he
saw that the warrior, owing perhaps to the pain of his
wound, had uncounsciously exposed his left arm on
the other side of the stump.   Woods fired again, the
shot again took effect, and the Indian sprang to his

feet and fled, a broken arm dangling helplessly at each side. The Creeks now despaired of success, and desisting from the siege, they retreated, taking with them all the horses hitched near the fort. Some of these horses belonged to citizens in the fort, others to Lieutenant Bailey's troopers. It was upon one of the latter that Hayden made his desperate charge. It may here be stated that three of the horses captured at Fort Sinquefield were, several days afterward, recaptured by Lieutenant Bradberry's command from a party of Indians, to which they gave chase, but which they could not bring to action.

As soon as the Indians had retired from the fort, Phillips went out with some of his friends and brought in the body of his wife. Over the mangled corpse, Philips gave vent to an agony of grief. A profound sympathy pervaded the garrison for the bereaved man and the motherless children, and many mingled their tears with those shed by the husband and the kindred of the dead. It was a heart-rending scene. The settlers all present knew Mrs. Phillips well. She was a kind-hearted, religious woman, and universally beloved. She and Lacey were buried that evening, but there is some uncertainty as to the particular place on the fort grounds where their graves were made.

About an hour after the departure of the Indians, some of the people took the trail and followed it about two miles. Upon their return, they reported this, and the people, fearing a possible return of the Indians in greater numbers, resolved to abandon the fort as early as possible and retire to

Fort Madison. A small portion of the people left Fort Sinquefield for Fort Madison late that evening. They did not move off in a solid body, but in quite a disorderly manner, some arriving at Fort Madison about the usual bed time, others, late in the night. In fact there were continuous arrivals during the entire night. Some of the women were badly frightened on their retreat, their fears frequently converting an innocent black stump into a blood thirsty Creek warrior, whereat they would give vent to shrieks of terror.

Among the inmates of Fort Sinquefield, was a man, named George Bunch. When he heard that the people were determined to go to Fort Madison, he cowardly abandoned his wife and children, struck out alone and was the very first man to arrive at the place of refuge. His poor wife—the family had but little worldly substance—in preparing for her departure, empied a bed tick and filled it with all the family clothing and such other domestic articles as she prized. Throwing this heavy bundle on her shoulders, and encumbered besides with the care of two small children, she left the fort with the evening party. She was not able to travel as fast as the others, and consequently was soon left alone in the rear. All night, on her weary way, with the horror of the lurking savage harrowing her soul, and taking only occasional intervals of rest, the poor woman staggered along under her heavy burden. At sunrise she reached Fort Madison. She had just passed the guards, when, at last, relieved from all anxiety, she sank to the earth in a swooning fit. But kindly hearts and hands quickly and willingly administered to her comfort. Such were some of the trials of the women of the frontier. Mrs. Bunch was the last arrival of the evening party at Fort Madison as her coward husband was the first. The world has its cowards as well as its heroes. Hayden is a type of one class, Bunch of the other.

The day after the attack on the fort, the soldiers and the remaining families arrived at Fort Madison, where the inmates of Forts Glass and Lavier had also taken refuge. As a trophy of the Sinquefield fight, some of the party brought down with them the prophet's magical banner. It was a large cow's tail, dyed red, and the end of a red staff inserted and tightly fastened in the orifice, from which the bone had been taken, the staff, altogether, being about five feet long.

The loss of the Creeks at Fort Sinquefield was eleven killed on the field. Their wounded were, doubtless, much more numerous. With the exception of the prophet, killed near the gate, all the slain warriors were dragged, during the progress of the fight, down the hill, towards the spring. There they were slightly buried by being covered with leaves and brush, and for many years after their bones could be seen. After leaving Fort Sinquefield Francis and his warriors retreated across the Alabama River to Burnt Corn Spring. From information given by some of Mr. Kimbell's negroes, who were captured by the Indians and afterwards recovered, many of the severely wounded Creek warriors died after crossing the Alabama River. It is very probable that not all of Francis' warriors crossed the Alabama. From the fact, as has been

stated, that a few of the horses captured at Fort
Sinquefield were, several days afterwards, recaptured
by Lieutenant Bradberry's command, it may well be
supposed that some of Francis' warriors may have
remained in the Fork.

The attack of Francis and his warriors on Fort
Sinquefield was not characterized by that stratagem
and sound judgment displayed by the other Creek
war party, which enabled them to be so successful
in the capture of Fort Mims. If during some day.
or night, previous to the fight, Francis had led his
warriors forward and secreted them near Fort
Sinquefield, and there patiently watched his opportunity, then seizing the supreme moment had rushed
forward, he might, by dint of overwhelming numbers, have taken the place by assault, and ruthlessly
massacred every living being within its walls, and
the name of Fort Sinquefield would have stood next
to that of Fort Mims in the catalogue of Indian
horrors.   But by the unsearchable decree of the
Supreme Ruler of events, such a dark chapter was
never to be recorded on the pages of Alabama
[30]   history.

NOTES.

In collating and compiling the facts for the
chapter on Fort Sinquefield, free use has been
made of the histories of Pickett and Meek, of Rev.
T. H. Ball's History of Clarke County, of an account
of Fort Sinquefield by Mr. Isaac Grant, published
in the *Clarke County Democrat*, and of a letter of
General F. L. Claiborne, dated September 21, 1813,
published in an issue of the *American Weekly Messenger* of that year.

In addition to the above printed authorities, several facts were derived from the late Rev. Josiah Allen, of Jasper County, Mississippi. Mr. Allen was well acquainted with many of the participants in the fight at the fort, as Isaac Hayden, James Smith, John Woods, and Isham Kimbell, and often heard them relate incidents of the fight. For many years too, he was intimately associated with James Cornells, and often conversed with him in regard to the war. The opening paragraph of the chapter states a fact related by Cornells to Mr. Allen, Cornells receiving this information from the Creeks after the war.

In 1886, the aged Mr. Clement Phillips, of Newton County, Mississippi, a son of Mrs. Phillips killed at the fort, gave the writer all the circumstances connected with the death of his mother, and other incidents of the fight, that he had often heard related in his father's family. The incident of the supposed wild turkeys was related by Mr. Phillips in substantially the same manner as described by Mr. Ball and Mr. Grant.

The writer is also indebted to the late Mr. Presly Odom, also of Newton County, for some incidents. Mr. Odom was a brother of Miss Winnie Odom, mentioned in the narrative. All his father's family were in the fort at the time of the attack.

Two slight incidents were received from the Rev. John Brown, of Lauderdale County Mississippi, whose eldest sister was a member of the fort.

Other parties, who had good opportunities for obtaining information, likewise gave incidents, but we consider it unneccessary to give their names, as these incidents were precisely the same as those given by the above quoted parties. It is sufficient to say that after reviewing and comparing all the statements, we conscientiously believe that the chapter gives an authentic account of the attack on Fort Sinquefield by the Creek Indians, and the circumstances connected therewith.   H. S. H.

CHAPTER XII.

THE NIGHT COURIER.

THE inmates of Fort Sinquefield had retired to Fort Madison. Colonel Carson at Fort Glass, it may be again stated, was the military commander between the two rivers. More than a thousand persons were now at these two neighboring stockades, Glass and Madison.

It became desirable, as great anxiety was here prevailing, to send a special communication to General Claiborne at Mount Vernon. Whether the selection was made by choice or whether it was a voluntary offer of services is not now known, but certainly a good messenger was found in the person of Jeremiah Austill, nineteen years of age, son of Captain Evan Austill, and now commencing an active and dangerous career in the service of the white settlers. Mounted on a fleet cavalry horse he set out alone in the still hours of night. It was needful to proceed cautiously so as not to lose the way and in order to avoid any lurking Indians that might spring out from some night ambush. In a straight line the distance to Fort Carney was about thirteen miles. And from Fort Carney to Mount Vernon twenty-four miles. By the only route that a horse could travel the whole distance must have been more than

forty miles.* The solitary and wary horseman passed on, meeting with no adventure till he reached the river bottoms, and there found himself uncertain whether he was above or below Fort Carney. Riding as near as practicable to the river bank, he gave a good imitation of an Indian warwhoop. Soon there came to his ears in quick response, the loud defying bark of some fifty dogs. He thus learned the exact location of the fort and turned his horse in that direction. It was distant about half a mile. He soon reached the gateway, announced himself, and found a warm welcome from the startled men, women, and children, who were all glad to find that the warwhoop which roused their dogs had not proceeded from Muscogee lips. After partaking of a warm supper and allowing his horse some time for rest and food, both horse and rider were ferried over the Tombigbee, and again the courier was on his way. Passing west of the Sun Flower Bend, and then of McIntosh's Bluff, in the dawn of the morning he reached Mount Vernon. General Claiborne was astonished, after receiving the dispatches, to learn that the young courier had made that night trip alone, and was disposed to blame Colonel Carson for sending no escort. But the bold, young Austill replied, that his ears were quick to catch sounds and that his eyes were keen, as quick and keen as the ears and eyes of the native Red men, and that companions would only have increased the danger; and that his own recourses and the sagacity and speed of

---

* I passed over alone, on horseback, in the hours of a not very bright day, the first part of this same line as far as Salt Mountain, and found it to be, in the day time, a wild, long, lonesome road. T. H. B.

his horse were the hopeful things on which to rely if
attacked by the Indians.   He bore back to Colonel
Carson an order, designed, as it afterwards appeared,
to be discretionary, but interpreted then as per-
emptory, to abandon forts Glass and Madison and
retire west of the Tombigbee to St. Stephens.   At
this old French and Spanish station were embank-
ments and earthworks, and it was considered, so far
as the Creeks were concerned, impregnable.   There
was severe disappointment and there was even
dismay at Fort Madison, on the reception of this
order, for it seemed, to the thousand assembled
there, that Claiborne was abandoning the whole
[31]   body of settlers in Clarke county.   Their crops
needed to be gathered.   Their plantations were at
this time deserted, the Indians they knew were
committing depredations, burning houses, driving
off their cattle, turning the hogs into the corn fields
that they might be well fattened for the feasts which
the Indians were designing that fall to hold ; and
these white settlers saw before them a prospect of
suffering from the want of food.   A   consultation
was held. Some eighty citizens enrolling themselves
under the two captains, Evan Austill and Samuel
Dale, determined to remain   with their families at
Fort Madison and   protect themselves and their
homes.   It was a sad parting as some five hundred
or more set out with Colonel Carson and his troops
for St. Stephens.   Then those who remained at Fort
Madison took additional precautions.   They placed
slanting pickets around on the outside of their stock
ade.   They contrived to keep up a light, which was
forty feet high, and this light—not electric—made by

that fat, heavy lightwood of the long leaf pine, illumined a circle into which no Indian could step with safety.

The following is an extract from a letter written by Judge H. Austill of Mobile, son of Major J. Austill, dated Mobile, March 5, 1894. It was written in answer to some inquires which I made.

"I have often heard my father speak of the light at Fort Madison, and have no doubt you got the account from him as to the height. I remember the particulars as follows: When the garrison of soldiers and most of the people left Fort Madison those who determined to remain elected my grandfather captain. He had a tall pine pole erected in the middle of the fort, and built around it a scaffolding with a hole in the center so that it could be raised by pushing it up the pole. On this, earth was placed so that the burning pine would not ignite the boards. On this a light was kept burning at night, and you will remember that our fat pine throws a light a long way.*

This was resorted to, to prevent the necessity of putting out pickets at night and reducing the fighting men. All those pioneers were in the habit of shooting deer at night by shining their eyes,—fire hunting, as it was called—and their aim to the limits of that lighted circle would have been deadly."

These pioneer settlers, with no troops to help them, did not mean to repeat the Fort Mims experiment of trifling with the Indians. They knew the Indians too well to despise them. Captain Austill

*Yes, we have hunted together in that "Bigbee" region too many nights for me to forget that. T. H. B.

had been with his family for fourteen years at the
Cherokee agency in Georgia, civilizing and helping
the Cherokees. He knew the Indian character well.
The younger Austill had grown up among the Cherokees. Captain Dale had been for years familiar
with Cherokees and Creeks. He had great respect
for the Indian character. The Creeks called him
familiarly Big Sam. Judge Meek calls him the
Daniel Boone of Alabama. These were the right
kind of men to be here in command. Well has
Judge Meek said of these, now pioneer citizen
soldiers: "They were men well calculated, both by
nature and habits of life, to meet such an emergency.
With no dependence but the axe and the rifle, they
had brought their families through the wilderness,
and made them homes upon the table-plains and
rich alluvial bottoms of our two principal streams.
The character and habits of the Indians they understood well, their stratagems in warfare, their guile
and cunning. With a flexibility of nature that still
retained its superiority, they accommodated themselves to these, and were prepared, as far as their
limited numbers would go, for the necessities of
either peace or war. To a spectator, the strange
buckskin garb, the hunting shirt, leggings and moccasins, the long and heavy rifle, the large knife
swinging by the shot-bag, the proud, erect deport-
ment, but cautious tread, and the keen, far-seeing,
but apparently passive eye, of the settler in the fork
of the Alabama and Tombickbee, upon the Tensaw,
or about Fort St. Stephens, would have spoken much
of the moral energies and purposes of the man."

Of this class were the eighty men at Fort Madison, proposing to defend against Muscogee warriors their families and their homes.

Some two weeks after the departure of the troops, General Claiborne went up to St. Stephens, and seeing the situation of the settlers between the rivers, he sent Colonel Carson and his men back to Fort Madison.

Such was the lone night ride, in the early autumn, of the young Austill, and such its results; and although the message borne was not so momentous, the ride itself, not yet immortalized by any bard, was one of greater danger and over a much wilder region than was, in April of 1775, that " midnight ride of Paul Revere."

NOTE—Captain Evan Austill, who settled in that Fort Madison neighborhood in 1812, died in October, the 18th, 1818, forty-nine years of age, " from exposure in Florida in the Indian strife." A marble slab stands by the roadside, near the site of Fort Madison, and the plain inscription upon it tells the passing traveller the place of the repose of his dust. It was for him a fitting burial place. Long may those few acres of land remain undisturbed by axe or spade or plow.   T. H. B.

CHAPTER XIII.

INCIDENTS OF THE WAR IN THE FORK.

IT was not unusual for the inmates of the forts in the Fork to go out occasionally to visit their farms and bring back with them supplies for their immediate use. These visits were always attended with danger, for small Creek war parties were continually travelling over the country, committing all kinds of depredations. It was often noticed as a singular and unaccountable fact that when the farmers housed their corn in cribs in the fields it was almost invariably burned by these predatory parties; but when stored in the regular cribs near their residences it was never disturbed.

On the morning of the sixth of September, a man named Josiah Fisher, with his three sons, left Fort Madison and went out to his farm, situated on the Alabama River about a quarter of a mile above Sizemore's ferry. Fisher had married a Creek woman and had a half-breed family. About sunset, Ben, one of the sons, while shelling pease in the yard, was shot in the back. Instantly springing up, he made his escape to the woods. His father, then in the cane, came running out, in a stooping position, to learn the cause of the firing, when he also was shot, the ball entering his breast and coming out at the back. He likewise fled to the forest. As he started to run a warrior shouted to him in the Muscogee tongue, with which Fisher was familiar, "That is the way to do it." The other two Fishers being in different parts of the field, fled to the fort and reported the death of their father and brother. The next morning Ben came in, bleeding from his wounds, from which he happily recovered. It was now supposed that the elder Fisher was dead. But on the afternoon of the succeeding day some of the people who happened to be outside of the fort, saw a man afar off, in a stooping position, coming up the ridge road. As he came nearer they recognized him as Fisher and went forward to meet him. His wound was, indeed, a most desperate one. Drury Allen, one of the party, remarked to him : "Fisher, I do not wish to discourage you, but you will die of that wound." "No," was Fisher's reply, " if it was going to kill me I would have died before now." He then told them the cause of his long delay in reaching the fort ; that when he exerted himself too much in walking it caused a flow of blood which almost strangled him ; consequently, he was compelled to walk very slowly and cautiously and in a stooping position.

Fisher recovered from his wound, but it ultimately caused his death. Some two or three years after the war he had a corn-shucking at his house. Happening to engage in a friendly tussle with one of the corn-shuckers, he ruptured a blood vessel in the region of the old wound and died immediately from the hemorrhage.

Moses Savel was an inmate of Fort Madison and the owner of a mill on Savel's Branch, a small tribu-

tary of Bassett's Creek. About the last of
September a detail of twelve men was sent
from Fort Madison to this mill to get
some corn ground. Late in the afternoon, when the
work was finished, the party started out on their
return, leaving behind a negro, named Phil Creagh,
to close up the mill, but telling him to overtake
them as soon as he could. When the party arrived
at the fort, it was noticed that the negro was not
with them. Five days afterwards, he made his appearance with a tale of captivity and escape. He
stated that while he was adjusting the things in the
mill, a party of Indians entered and seized him.
They took their captive up the Alabama River to a
point several miles below Lower Peach Tree, where
they had a canoe concealed. Here they crossed over
to their camp, which was occupied by their families.
It may here be stated that the Creeks did not regard
captured negroes in the same light that they did
white prisoners. Instead of putting them to death,
[32]　their custom was to keep them as slaves. The frontier negroes were aware of this fact. Phil stayed
with the Indians four days, and was kindly treated
by them, being fed bountifully on venison and
honey. Of the latter, the Indians had a large supply, kept in deer skins. Phil manifested no apparent disposition to make his escape, but seemed con-
tent with his situation, thus completely lulling his
captors' suspicions. Every morning the men went
out hunting, leaving their captive in camp with
their families. Phil, meanwhile, was patiently bi-
ding his time. On the morning of the fifth day, he
saw his opportunity. When the hunters had been

gone about half an hour, he quietly slipped off to the river, took the canoe, and paddled across. Just as he reached the other shore, some of the women saw him and shouted the alarm. Phil heard it and knew that some of the hunters must have heard it too ; so he began his retreat as fast as his legs would carry him. He struck after a while the ridge path and hurried along in it until he was completely exhausted. He then went out to one side, about fifty yards from the path, and laid himself down behind a log to rest. In, perhaps, about an hour, he saw four Indians coming along the path in hot pursuit. They passed him without discovering that he had abandoned the path and continued their onward pursuit. Phil thought it best to still lie close. In about an hour, as it seemed to him, he saw the Indians returning, having evidently given up the pursuit. After they had completely disappeared from sight, he arose, resumed his flight, and about sunset, arrived safe and sound at Fort Madison. Phil was satisfied with his Indian experience.

One morning, not long after the above incident, an inmate of Fort Madison, named Miller, employed a boy about sixteen years of age, named Ben Arundel, a brother-in-law of James Smith, one of the heroes of the canoe fight, to go out to his farm, situated about a mile and a half above the present Suggsville, and dig some potatoes for him. Several persons, among these Ben's own father, endeavored to dissuade him from going, telling him he ran a great risk from parties of Indians that might be in the country. But Ben was obstinate, swearing that he was not born to be killed by an Indian. Miller mounted Ben on his mare, lent him his musket and bayonet, and Ben went out to Miller's farm, whence he never returned. During the day Ben's father became very uneasy, mounted his horse and went out to find him; but he returned about sunset without his son. He told his friends that he knew that Ben was killed; for while on the way to Miller's house, he came across the tracks of two or three Indians going in the same direction, and soon he heard the report of a gun. He now knew that his son was killed, and he thought it prudent to return to the fort. The next morning Miller's mare returned, doubtless having broke loose from the fence where she was tied when the gun was fired. Lieutenant Bradberry then went with his company out to the farm. They found Ben lying in the pototo patch dead and scalped and the bayonet of his musket thrust in his throat. The Indians had taken the musket and the amunition. The party buried Ben and then marched back to the fort.

NOTES.

The above incidents were related to the writer several years ago by the Rev. Josiah Allen and his brother Henry, both of whom were inmates of Fort Madison and knew well all the parties mentioned. The incident of the Fishers can also be seen in Pickett's history, but here given more in detail from the recollections of the Allens.　　　　H. S. H.

CHAPTER XIV.

CHOCTAWS AND CHICKASAWS JOIN THE AMERICAN ARMY.

IN 1813, the nation of the Choctaws occupied that portion of the present State of Mississippi extending from the old counties of Wayne and Hancock on the south to Line Creek and Tallahatchie River, on the north and from the Tombigbee River on the east to the Mississippi River and Bayou Pierre on the west. The traditional policy of this tribe, from time immemorial, had been that of steadfast friendship towards the whites. In the exciting crisis of 1813, tampered with by British and Spanish emissaries, some slight temporary dissaffection, may, possibly, have arisen among the more ignorant classes; but the bulk of the nation, influenced, as they were, by their great Mingoes, and by the noted Indian countrymen in their midst, Pitchlyn, Leflore, Juzan, and others, did not swerve from their fidelity to the whites, and remained firm in their adhesion to the Federal Government. It is true, that on one or two occasions, during the troubled times of the fall of 1813, many persons believed that the Choctaws would join the Creeks, and, in consequence, one or more great panics occurred; but subsequent events proved that these panics and apprehensions of the frontier people were altogether groundless and unnecessary.

The Choctaw people, at this time, as subsequently, were living in three districts or fires, (ulhti), each district governed by its own Mingo. The south-eastern district was governed by Pushmataha, the western by Puckshenubbee, and the northeastern by Moshulitubbee. These Mingoes were independent of each other and sovereign in their respective districts, and only acted in concert in national affairs, when the whole nation assembled in council to decide on questions of peace and war. In each district there were thirty subordinate Mingoes or captains, who managed and directed the local affairs of their respective towns or beats.

In the early part of August, with a view of ascertaining the precise attitude of the Choctaws with regard to the war, General Claiborne despatched Major Ballenger to the Choctaw nation. Ballenger had an interview with Pushmataha, on the fifteenth, at Pierre Juzan's either at Coosha or Chunky, but unfortunately died there three days afterwards. What effect or influence this visit had on the mind of the Choctaw Mingo, we have no information. But it is certain that Pushmataha, who was the most enlightened and influential of all the Choctaw Mingoes, was desirous that the Choctaw people should take an open and active stand on the side of the Federal Government. With this object in view, early in September, he rode to St. Stephens and proposed to Captain Ceorge S. Gaines to raise several companies of Choctaws for the American army. Gaines was greatly pleased with the proposition, and accompanied by the chief, he hastened to Mobile and laid the matter before General Flournoy;

but the General, from some cause, declined to receive the Choctaws as United States troops. Deeply mortified at the result, Gaines and Pushmataha returned to St. Stephens. Just as they arrived into the town, and were surrounded by the citizens, who were giving vent to their indignation against Flournoy for his folly, a courier was seen in the distance riding rapidly towards them. The rider bore a message from General Flournoy, who had reconsidered the matter, and now authorized Gaines to go into the nation and raise troops. The people forthwith shouted and rejoiced greatly. All apprehensions of Choctaw hostility were now removed, and it was believed that through the influence of Pushmataha, the Choctaws would actually assist the Americans in the war against the Creeks. [33]

Pickett writes: "In company with Colonel Flood Mrs. Grew and the Chief, Gaines departed immediately for the Choctaw country, with no other provisions than some jerked beef. Colonel John McKee, agent of the Chickasaws, met them at Pitchlyn's house, situated at the confluence of Oktibbeha and Tombigbee, where they held a consultation, while Pushmataha went home to assemble his people in council. Having transacted his business, Gaines left Pitchlyn's and in a few days reached the council ground, where over five thousand Choctaws were encamped. Pushmataha harangued them in a long speech, full of eloquence and ingenuity, in which, [as interpreted], he said among other things: ' You know Tecumseh. He is a bad man. He came through our nation, but he did not turn our heads. He went among the

Muscogees, and got many of them to join him. You
know the Tensaw people. They were our friends.
They played ball with us. They sheltered and fed us,
whenever we went to Pensacola. Where are they now?
Their bodies rot at Sam Mims' place. The people at St.
Stephens are also our friends. The Muscogees in-
tend to kill them too. They want soldiers to defend them. (He here drew out his sword and flour-
ishing it, added:) 'You can all do as you please. You
are all free men. I dictate to none of you. But I
shall join the St. Stephens people. If you have a
mind to follow me, I will lead you to glory and to
victory.' A warrior rose up, slapped his hand upon
his breast, and said: 'I am a man! I am a man! I
will follow you.' All of them now slapped their
breasts, a general shout went up, and Gaines was
filled with joy at the result."

We supplement the above narrative of Pickett's
with a few facts gleaned from Choctaw tradition.
The tradition of the old Choctaws is that this council
took place in Neshoba County, at Kooncheto village,
situated about a mile and a half west of Yazoo Old
Town. This place was selected as being the most
central point of rendezvous for the warriors of the
nation. Puckshenubbee and Pushmataha were present, but Moshulitubbee, from some cause, failed to
attend. Pushmataha, Puckshemebbee, and a sub-
chief, named Tapenahoma, all made speeches favor-
ing a military alliance with the Americans against
the Creeks. At the close of Pushmataha's speech, a
number of warriors arose, slapped their breasts, and
exclaimed: "Nakni sia hokat! Chi iakaiyat ia
lashke!" "I am a man! I will go and follow you!"

The troops raised by Pushmataha, who was commissioned as Lieutenant Colonel, consisted of four companies, the entire force, inclusive of the chief and the other commissioned officers, being one hundred and thirty-five men. The commissioned officers of the first company were Mingo Hopaii, (Prophet Chief), Captain, and Tapena ishtaya (Rod-carrier), First Lieutenant, with fifty-one non-commissioned officers and privates. The second company, commanded by Slim King, First Lieutenant, with Nukpallichabi (the one who entices and kills) as Second Lieutenant, had twenty-two non-commissioned officers and privates. The third company, Edmond Folsom, Captain, Red Fort, First Lieutenant, Chukkaba (House above), Second Lieutenant, Okchaya homma (Red Life), Third Lieutenant, had forty non-commissioned officers and privates. The fourth company, commanded by Captain Thluko, who bore the rank of First Lieutenant, was composed of twelve non-commissioned officers and privates.*

With this force, Pushmataha reported to General Claiborne, at St. Stephens, perhaps, early in October. He was treated with great distinction by the general and his officers, and soon became a favorite with all. During his entire connection with the army, a social grade corresponding to his rank was accorded to the Choctaw chief on all public, social, or official occasions. Whenever an officer gave a dining, Pushmataha was always an invited guest. The Mingo, on the other hand, was very careful not

---

* The Continental sound must be given to the vowels in the above Choctaw names, including that of Pushmataha, and the accent must be placed on the penult. H. S. H.

to compromise his dignity as a great man and a warrior. He would only associate with officers of
higher grade, from captain upward. If a private, a
non-commissioned officer, or even a commissioned
officer of lower grade should accost him and attempt
to enter into conversation with him, he would wave
him aside with great dignity, saying in his imperfect
English: "I no talk with little Mingo; I talk with
big Mingo."

A story is related that a short time after the fall
of Fort Mims—perhaps the time when he was tend-
ering the services of his warriors to General Flournoy—Pushmataha visited General Claiborne's camp.
When he approached the general's tent, he was received by the lieutenant on guard, who invited him
to drink with him. Pushmataha answered only
by a look of scorn. He recognized no officer with
one epaulette. When the general came in, the red
warrior shook him by the hand, and said, proudly,
as to an equal, "Chief, I will drink with you."

Some of the officers at St. Stephens were married men, and had their families with them. During
pleasant weather, these officers were in the habit of
taking an evening promenade with their wives.
Pushmataha noticed this custom of his brother white
officers, and not to be outdone he sent for his own
wife from the nation. Upon her arrival, every
evening when the officers and their wives engaged in
their usual walk, Pushmataha and his homely spouse
—she was not considered a handsome woman—
arm in arm, would imitate their example. This act
afforded much merriment to the officers, and especially to the ladies; but they were very careful to

suppress their mirth when within ear-shot of the chief.

Although these little incidents seemed amusing to General Claiborne's officers, they had, nevertheless, a high regard for Pushmataha, and considered his warriors good allies. The Choctaw Mingo was a rigid disciplinarian. He seemed to realize that to make his warriors efficient troops, they must, to a great extent, conform to the requirements of the military service of the white man, and the wild independence of the Indian warrior must be restrained. He accordingly exacted from his men implicit obedience to his orders [34]

The agent of the Chickasaws, Colonel John McKee, mentioned above, was in Nashville, when a messenger arrived from Captain Gaines bearing letters to Governor Blount and General Jackson, giving an account of the massacre of Fort Mims. This must have been about the twelfth of September. General Jackson at once directed Colonel McKee to return immediately to the Indian country and "get out" as many Choctaw and Chicasaw warriors as practicable, and then march against the Creek town, situated at the Falls of the Black Warrior, under the rule of the chieftain, Oseeochee Emathla. Colonel McKee reached Pitchlyn's the very same day that Gaines and his party arrived there. The Colonel had no difficulty with the aid of Major Pitchlyn, in raising as many warriors as he desired for the expedition, and began his march a few days after his arrival. When he reached the Falls he found that Oseeochee Emathla and his people had made their escape and there was nothing left for the Choctaw and Chickasaw warriors to do but to burn the deserted cabins and return home. According to Pickett, when the returning warriors reached Pitchlyn's, they separated, one party going to their homes and the other party going to St. Stephens to join Claiborne's army

The union of the Choctaws and the Chickasaws with the whites was now secured and thus was gained a great point for the protection of the Mississippi Territory. And to Captain Gaines and Colonel McKee must be accorded the chief honor of bringing the warriors of these tribes into the military service of the United States during the Creek War of 1813.

NOTES:

The materials for the above chapter are drawn from Pickett's History of Alabama, the Alabama Historical Reporter of May, 1884, Claiborne's life of Sam Dale, the records of the Department of the Interior, Choctaw traditions, and conversations, in 1877, with the venerable Captain S. P. Doss, of Pickensville, Alabama, who, in early life, was an intimate friend of Pushmataha.   H. S. H.

CHAPTER XV.

THE BASHI SKIRMISH.

"A steed comes at morning; no rider is there;
But its bridle is red with the sign of despair."
—*Lochiel's Warning.*

IT is not certain when the events bearing this name took place. An intelligent citizen of Clarke county says, before Fort Easeley was evacuated. Pickett says early in October. The inmates of Fort Easeley and of Turner's Fort came for greater security to Fort St. Stephens, probably early in September, and from this neighborhood Colonel William McGrew, with some twenty-five mounted men, had gone up the river, into the Wood's Bluff neighborhood, to look after the Indians who among the various tenantless and exposed plantations were committing depredations. Before this small band of horsemen had reached a little stream called Bashi, that flows into the Tombigbee a mile or two north of Wood's Bluff, they suddenly found themselves among concealed Creek warriors. They were ambushed. A turkey tail was raised above a log by one of the concealed Indians, and this was the signal for attack. The Indians who had guns instantly fired from their places of concealment and the white leader, who had taken part in the Burnt Corn engagement, fell from his horse. Edmund Miles was

also killed, and Jesse Griffin severely wounded.
Colonel McGrew's men returned the fire of the
Indians, but without much effect. The Indians
from their places of ambush had largely the advantage of the mounted men, and these found it needful
to make good their retreat. Besides the commanding
officer three of the men were missing, Edmund Miles,
Jesse Griffin, and David Griffin. These two Griffins
were twins. One of them on the morning of that
fatal day seemed to expect some calamity, and they
agreed to stand by each other, the one not to leave
the other in case of danger. They came into the world
together, and they proposed, if need should be, to stand
or fall side by side, and go out of the world together.
According to the best information Jesse Griffin
was shot through the thigh and, being unable to
retreat with the others, his brother David, according
to their agreement, staid by him while life remained.
It is one tradition that the two kept up a fire upon
the Indians, as fast as they could load their guns,
until seven of the Indians were killed; but, however
that may be, it is very sure that among the few
whites and the Indians slain the body of David
Griffin was not found. His son, William Griffin,
born at Wood's Bluff in 1812, and at this time with
his mother either in Fort Easeley or at St. Stephens,
a resident at Bashi in 1879, states, as the account
that was given to him, that the last sight which his
comrades had of his father, as the Indians were still
firing upon them in their retreat, showed him in the
act of loading his gun, himself then with a broken
limb, but resolute in appearance, as determined to
fight to the last moment of his life. William Griffin,

was informed by those who had a right to know that the body of his father was surely never found. All that was found as a trace of him on that skirmish field was the breech of his gun. The barrel was not there. His body, like the body or person of the young Kimbell boy, disappeared, how, none of his friends ever knew.

Colonel McGrew's horse, like the dark gray charger of Mamilius in Macaulay's Lays of Ancient Rome, started for his home.

Says Alexander Carleton, Esq., of Clarke county, " On the next morning after the battle, the Colonel's horse was at St. Stephens, thirty miles distant, with signs of blood on the saddle, and only one pistol in his holster."

Some days afterwards, General Claiborne crossed the river from St. Stephens, and advanced into this Wood's Bluff and Bashi region. The bodies of Colonel McGrew, of Edmund Miles, and of Jesse Griffin were found and were buried with military honors. These men fell "about five miles east of Wood's Bluff, near the present Linden and Coffeeville road, and about a half mile south-west of the Bashi bridge."*

General Claiborne spent a few days scouring this wild region. He found some Indians. Several of his men were wounded in the skirmish engagements. Among those severely wounded was Captain William Bradberry, another of those officers who had fought at Burnt Corn. Says Hon. E. S. Thornton of West

---

* One frosty morning I passed this spot alone on horseback and the road was lonely enough then for Indians to have easily ambushed a traveller. A "frail memorial" had been erected there, but it was decayed and no longer of use. T. H. B.

Bend, he was shot "about two miles above the Lewis Mitchell place, and five miles above West Bend, on the old Coffeeville and Wood's Bluff river road." His wound proved to be fatal.

Claiborne and his men returned to Jackson below St. Stephens, on the east side of the river, then commonly called Pine Level, and there for a time they camped, hoping to receive orders or permission from General Flournoy to cross the Alabama and proceed into the Creek country.

CHAPTER XVI.

BEARD AND TANDY WALKER.

During September and October, 1813, many depredations were committed by small parties of Indians in the Fork, and occasionally some of the settlers were killed. About the last of October, one of Carson's men, named Beard, was killed near Fort Madison. The circumstances of his death, as detailed to the writer several years ago by the Rev. Josiah Allen and his brother Henry, both of whom knew Beard well, were as follows: Early one morning, two wagons, one driven by Jim Dale, the other by Malachi Sharbrough, with a detail of soldiers, were sent a mile or so above Fort Madison to get a supply of corn for the garrison. Not long after their departure, Beard, who was on the sick list and temporarily boarding with the family of Micajah Benge, borrowed the latter's horse, and equipped with sabre and holster pistols, left the fort and started out to Benge's farm to get a supply of potatoes and collards. A short distance from the fort, he met one of the soldiers of the detail, who had received permission to return to get more cartridges, as he found out that he had only a few in his cartridge box. Benge's collard and potato patch, comprising about two acres, was situated on the ridge, about half a mile north of the fort. At the

southwest corner of the patch, there had stood three
large pines. As these trees shaded the patch too
much, Benge cut them down. They had fallen
down the western slope of the ridge, their trunks
lying parallel and their tops interlocking. The
road leading northward from the fort—the road
which the soldiers and the wagon had taken—
had once run along the western string of the fence,
but on account of the fallen trees at this point, it had
been turned somewhat to the left, passing along by
the tree tops and entering the original road near
the northwest corner of the patch. Five Creek
warriors, bent upon some hostile deed, had secreted
themselves in these tree tops. As the wagons came
along they saw that there were too many soldiers to
venture an attack, so they lay close. After awhile,
when the wagons had disappeared from sight, Beard
came up. He rode along by the pine stumps, in the
original road, between the Indians and the fence.
He dismounted near the northwest corner of the
patch, tied his horse by the reins to the fence, then
climbed over and began to cut some collards. He had retained his sword, but left his pistols in the holsters. Meanwhile, the soldier, whom
Beard had met, having replenished his cartridge-
box, was hastening back on the road to overtake
the wagons. The soldier had arrived within about
two hundred yards of the patch, when he saw two
Indians spring out of the tree tops, run and leap
over the fence, and with a loud war-whoop rush
towards Beard. Beard dropped his collards, and
ran to the eastern string of the fence, which he
crossed, with the warriors close at his heels. He

then ran along the string of the fence to the south-
east corner, and there took a hog trail which led out
into the main road near where the soldier stood, for
the latter had halted on seeing the Indians. The
soldier threw his musket to his shoulder, but feared
to fire lest he might kill Beard, who was just in front
of the Indians, and on a line with them. At last
Beard came to where the trail ran somewhat to the
right, in the midst of some postoak runners. Here
the Indians shot him down, crushed his skull with
lightwood knots, scalped him, took his sword and then
ran away at full speed towards the east. All this
occurred in the space of a few minutes, and within
two hundred yards of the soldier, who afterwards said
that the postoak runners were so thick at the spot
where Beard was killed that he could not see the Indians, and they were out of sight before he could get
a good aim at them. Just after Beard was killed
the soldier said that he saw the three other Indians
spring from their lair in the tree tops, and flee at
great speed across the potato patch in the same
direction taken by their comrades. Lieutenant
Bradberry's company had just left the fort for an
excursion when they heard the firing, and instantly
wheeling, they came to the place at full gallop,
David Glass being the first man to reach the spot
where Beard lay. Soon afterwards the wagons
with the detail, coming back at full speed, arrived
on the ground, for they too heard the firing. Bradberry's troopers, after hearing the statement of the
soldier, made an excursion eastward in search of
the Creek warriors, but failed to find them. Beard's
body was placed on one of the wagons, brought

back to the fort and there buried. His horse, frightened by the Indian war-whoop, had fortunately broken loose, and returned to the fort. Beard was about thirty-five years old, and was said to have come to the Mississippi Territory from Illinois or Missouri.

During the occupation of Fort Madison, many excursions were made by the citizens and soldiers, sometimes, perhaps, merely in quest of adventure, and sometimes to gain information in regard to the movements of the enemy. The most noted of these excursions was one made under the lead of Tandy Walker, once government blacksmith at St. Stephens, recorded, with some slight conflict of statement, in both the narratives of Pickett and Meek, but more in detail by the latter. This party, consisting of Tandy Walker, George Foster, an expert hunter and a bold quadroon mulatto named Evans, left Fort Madison, early in November, crossed the Alabama river, and advanced, says Pickett, to the battle ground of Burnt Corn, but Meek, whose statement we prefer, says they advanced to the destroyed residence of James Cornells, at Burnt Corn Spring. We quote Judge Meek's narrative: "When near the place, Evans dismounted, and, leaving his horse with his companions, stealthily approached to make observations. In a field, he saw an Indian, at a short distance, digging potatoes. He at once shot him, and, after some minutes, not seeing any other Indians, he entered the field and took the scalp of his victim. Returning to his companions, they examined the premises and found, on the opposite side of the field, the camp and baggage of a considerable party of Indians who had fled at the sound of Evans' gun. With this booty, the three adventurers now hastened towards the Alabama. At Sizemore's deserted old place, near the river, they found a field of corn, nearly ripe, with plenty of fine grass. Though they saw many mocassin tracks and other signs of Indians, they determined to stop here to feed their horses and to pass the night. They accordingly went a short distance into the field, and, as it was a cool November evening, kindled a small fire and lay down to sleep. In the night, Foster had a strange and alarming dream, or 'vision,' as he termed it, which awoke him and filled him with apprehension. Arousing his comrades and telling his dream, he urged them to leave the spot, as he felt they were in danger there from the Indians. They made light of his fears, and lapsed back into slumber. He, however, arose, and going still farther into the field, threw himself down in the high grass and went to sleep. At the dawn of the day he was aroused by a volley of guns fired upon his companions, and fled with all haste into a neighboring cane-brake. through which he made his way to the river, and, swimming it, he safely reached the fort.

After two days, Tandy Walker came in, severely wounded, his arm being broken by several balls, and his side badly bruised by a ball which struck a butcher knife in his belt. It appeared that the Indians had waited until the first faint light of day to make their attack. They then fired some five or six guns and rushed forward with their knives. Evans was killed; but Walker, though wounded, sprang from the ground and ran through the corn

and high grass. Being very swift of foot, he out-
stripped his pursuers and soon got into the cane-
brake, where he lay concealed till night, suffering
greatly from his wounds. Then he proceeded to
the river, and making a raft of canes, to which he
hung by his well arm, he swam across. He was so
feeble from the loss of blood and from pain, that it
took him all that night and the next day to reach
Fort Madison."

Pickett gives the 5th of November as the date
of this affair on the Alabama. As a slight supplement to the story, we will state on the authority of
one of Walker's old friends, that after he had taken
refuge in the cane-brake, the Creeks searched for
him a long time, several times they came very near
his hiding place ; but finally, to Walker's great
relief, a note or signal sounded on a powder charger
caused them to abandon the search.

CHAPTER XVII.

THE CANOE FIGHT.

THE North American Indian has, with good reason, when on what is called the war path, been dreaded by the white inhabitants of the frontiers; for he was cunning, quick, sagacious, often merciless. He knew how to come unexpectedly upon exposed households, to strike fierce and murderous blows, and to make good his retreat, taking with him scalps and even helpless women and children. But in the earliest settlement of the Atlantic coast it was proved that, with all his shrewdness, and powers of endurance, and forest bravery, he was not, after all, a match, even handed, for the cultivated white man. In more ways than one, even in meeting them on their own ground, those words were proved true, that "the anointed children of education have been too powerful for the tribes of the ignorant."

The most noted hand-to-hand conflict between white men and Indians, in New England history, is the encounter between Captain Miles Standish, with three of his Plymouth comrades, and Pecksnot, Wetawamat, and two other Indian chiefs, all heads of a conspiracy formed to exterminate Weston's colony and then massacre the Pilgrims. Standish had gone among the Indians and waited for his opportunity. It soon came. The four Indian conspirators were "all entrapped in one cabin." The door was secured. The four white men were also within, and as a witness the friendly Habbamak. "A terrific death-grapple at once ensued. There were no shrieks, no cries, no war-whoops. Nothing was heard save the fierce panting of the combatants and the dull thud of the blows given and returned. Habbamak stood quietly by and meddled not. Soon the Englishmen were successful; each slew his opponent," Standish himself killing Pecksnot, "an Indian of immense muscular size and strength," who had said not long before to the captain, "You are a great officer but a little man; * * I possess great strength and courage."* Here there were four against four, shut in by cabin walls.

The Alabama-River Canoe Fight was a conflict where the whites, apparently, had greatly the disadvantage. There were not four against four, nor yet, as in the old Latin story of the Horatii and Curiatii, three against three, but three against nine.

The well attested facts are these: (The month is November.) Small parties of the hostile Creeks were committing depredations among the Alabama-River settlements—they were wanting food, were foraging,—when Captain Dale obtained permission from Colonel Carson, commanding at Fort Madison, to drive the Indians at least to the east side of the river. He had a force of thirty Mississippi volunteers under Lieutenant Montgomery, and forty militia of Clarke county, under Lieutenant G. W. Creagh. With ten more men than, according to

---

* Martyn's "Pilgrim Fathers," page 188.

Mrs. Hemans, the Cid, the noted Campeador of
Spain had, when

> "For wild sierras and plains afar,
> He left the lands of his own bivar,"

Captain Dale and his two lieutenants left Fort Madison on an expedition which was to enroll at least
three of their names among our noted Indian fight-
ers. During the first day's march northward among
the unoccupied plantations they found no Indians.
The second day they went in a south-easterly direction to the river, crossed it by means of two canoes,
at French's landing, then called Brazier's, and
camped on the bank. The night was cool, the men
thinly clad. The next morning, when the warm sun
arose, they resumed their march, Jeremiah Austill,
our "Night Courier," son of Captain Evan Austill,
having charge of the two canoes, and with six men
to aid him, commenced to pass up the river abreast
of Dale and his company who were marching along
the eastern bank. Soon a canoe load of Indians
was seen descending the river, but these Indians
on being discovered paddled immediately back and
passed from sight in the dense cane at the mouth of
Randon's Creek. The men on the bank also met
with Indians who retreated when the guns of Dale's
men were fired upon them. One Indian was killed and
several were wounded. It was soon found difficult to
proceed further along the eastern bank and orders
were given to recross to the western side. When
all had crossed over but twelve men, among them
Dale, Smith, Austill, Creagh, Elliott, and Brady,
and while these were preparing a late breakfast and roasting sweet potatoes in a little field, an

alarm of " Indians!" came from the western bank.
Leaving their breakfast they siezed their guns and
reached the river bank. They soon saw descending
the river " a large canoe containing a chief and ten
painted warriors." The Indians back of them, on the
eastern side, who had occasioned the alarm, for some
reason made no attack on these twelve men, and
they gave their whole attention to the large approaching canoe. Soon two cautious warriors sprang out and
made for the shore.   One of them Smith shot.   The
other made good his retreat eastward.   The canoe
man-of-war with the nine warriors continued to descend the river, and as only one small canoe, with a
colored man named Cæsar in charge, was on the
eastern shore, Dale ordered the larger canoe to be
manned and brought over.   Eight men started out
to obey the order, but alarmed, as it appeared, by the
threatening attitude of the nine warriors in their
large canoe, these eight returned to the western
shore.   Captain Dale was vexed and proposed to
his men to attack that canoe load with their own
little dug-out. Besides Caesar, who paddled, it
would carry but three, and Dale stepped in followed
immediately by Smith and Austill, the latter taking
his position in the prow. Those who have ever attempted to stand up, or even to sit, in one of these
little river canoes can appreciate something of the
disadvantage, on the side of the whites, for three
men, in such a frail support, to undertake a life or
death grapple with nine stout Indian warriors in a
much more stable boat, a canoe, so called, that could
carry eleven or more men. The expectant Indians
awaited the attack as their boat floated on, and

Caesar, at Dale's command, with the vigorous strokes of his paddle, sent the small canoe directly towards the large one.

THE "CANOE FIGHT" ACTION OPENS.

The three Americans with their guns in their hands attempted first to pour in a broadside, but one gun only was discharged, and that with little effect, the priming having been dampened in the other two. Caesar was now ordered to pull up along side, and then the real conflict began. It was the twelfth day of November, a day to be remembered in Alabama Indian border strife, when on the beautiful Alabama in that noted river bend, with nine American spectators on one bank and sixty-one on the other, and how many concealed Indians in the dense canes none knew—Judge Meek says nearly three hundred— this conflict of three against nine was waged. Neither Americans nor Indians could help their fellows. They could only await the issue of this unequal encounter. It was a perilous moment as the little canoe closed upon the other, with Austill, a young man of nineteen in the prow, watching how or where the first blow might fall. He was not left in uncertainty long, for as the prow of the American canoe touched the other, and before he could strike a blow or grapple with a red warrior, the rifle of the chief who, when the canoes were about two feet apart, had exclaimed in English words, "Now for it, Big Sam," came like lightning heavily down upon his head. That the blow did not kill him is strange. Dale and Smith sprang instantly to his rescue, and with their heavy rifles and strong arms soon dispatched the

powerful chief. His words of challenge were his
last. Cæsar then brought the canoes side by side,
and so held them during the remainder of the sharp
but short fight. It was give blows and take in rapid
succession, Austill having immediately regained his
feet and his prowess, and doing his part in the fearful fray. In the thick of this fierce onset he was
again struck down, now by an Indian war-club, but
was rescued by Dale, and once more regaining his
feet he wrenched the war-club from the Indian warrior and with it dashed him into the river. Smith
performed his full part in the conflict, and soon
every Indian warrior was slain. Eight dead bodies
were cast into the flowing waters of the Alabama
when this "tiger strife was over," and Austill with
the war-club had already sent one warrior adrift
[35]   upon the river.

THE CANOE FIGHT WAS OVER.

It was difficult at the time, it is impossible and
needless now, to detail the part performed by each
of these three heroic men in that conflict. Like the
old "dauntless three," Horatius, Lartius, and Herminius, who kept the bridge so well in the days of
ancient Rome, these three "border men, true repre-
sentatives of one variety of American heroism, share
together the fame of their exploit, as that day they
stood together in their small boat in the confusion o
the desperate struggle." That they should all survive, and that nine brave Indian warriors, with the
apparent advantages all on their side, should perish,
shows again what was exemplified in the days of
Captain Miles Standish, that the American Indian,

dreaded though he well may be as a foe, is not a
match even handed for the bold and hardy pioneer
white man.

"Samuel Dale was at this time forty-one years
of age, was about six feet and two inches in height,
and weighed one hundred and ninety pounds. He
possessed a large, muscular frame, and had no super-
fluous flesh."

"James Smith was now twenty-five years of
age, five feet and eight inches in height, very stout
and finely proportioned, weighing one hundred and
sixty-five pounds.

"Jeremiah Austill was nineteen years of age, six
feet, two and one-fourth inches in height, very
sinewy, with no surplus flesh, and weighed one hundred and seventy-five pounds.

"Such, physically, were the men who proved their
superiority," when, to them, fighting seemed to be
a duty, "over red warriors of the brave Creek
nation, men who, in a hand-to-hand conflict, shared
the advantages which were needful for ancient
heroes and for knights in the Middle Ages, of well-
trained and hardy muscle."[*]

Two or three score of such men, springing as
"boarders" upon the deck of a British man-of-war,
with or without such a leader as John Paul Jones
or Commodore Perry, would soon have cleared the
deck and brought the colors down.

By means of the captured canoe the nine men
on the east side, now crossed the river. The men
all went as far up the river as Cornell's ferry, and
finding no more Indians, returned that night to

[*] "Clarke County," page 168.

Fort Madison. The canoe fight was ready to go into American history along with Perry's victory on Lake Champlain gained two months before.*

Of the three men engaged in this conflict, from whose hands one only, of the eleven at first seen in the canoe, escaped, some further notice may justly be given. Of James Smith but little seems to be known. He was born in Georgia, was a pioneer settler in the river region, is described as a very brave and daring man, and is credited with having "contributed very materially to the success of the canoe engagement." He removed to East Mississippi and there died.

Of Samuel Dale, known as Captain Dale and then General Dale, abundant material for a life record exists. He was evidently a remarkable man. A brief abstract of events in his life is all that can here be given. Claiborne, with some flowers of rhetoric, has written his life very fully. He was born in Virginia in 1772. In 1784 his father removed to Georgia and occupied a farm near the Creek Indians. In a few years his father and mother both died leaving to him the care of seven children younger than him-

---

*The nearest parallel to the Canoe Fight which I have found occurred near the opening of the "Pequod War." John Gallup was sailing on the Connecticut "in his little shallop of twenty tons," with one man and two boys, when he discovered John Oldham's pinnace off Block Island, which the Indians had lately captured, and fourteen of them were on the deck. Martyn says, "Pilgrim Fathers," "Then one of the most remarkable instances of gallantry recorded in the annals of border warfare occurred." Gallup steered directly for the pinnace, with a fresh wind, struck it "stem foremost, nearly upset it," and six frightened Indians "jumped overboard and were drowned." He did the same thing again, and four more jumped and sank. Four only remained. He drowned two of these and two finally escaped.

Whether the Connecticut River action or the Alabama River action displayed the more daring, the reader must judge.— T. H. B.

self. He became a trader among the Indians, then a
guide and mover of families to the river settlements.
Before the " Creek War " he himself removed to the
Alabama River region. After that war he held
office not a little. In 1816 he was a member of the
convention to divide the Territory. In 1817 he was
a member of the Alabama Territorial Assembly. He
represented Monroe county, which for some time
extended west of the Alabama to the water-shed, in
the years 1819, 1820, 1821 ; 1823, 1824; 1825, 1828,
1829. In 1824 he was a member of the committee
to escort Gen. La Fayette to Alabama's capital. The
Alabama Legislature conferred on him the rank of
brigadier general. In 1830 he was appointed by the
Secretary of War one of the commissioners to
remove the Choctaws. In 1831 he removed to Mississippi. In 1836 he represented Lauderdale county.
He died at Daleville, Mississippi, in May, 1841.
Such were some of the positions held by the man who
suggested and led the canoe fight. He is represented as having declared that in every hour of danger he was cheered by a firm trust in God.   [36]

   Jeremiah Austill, known as Major Austill in all
the later years of his life, was also a much more than
ordinary man. Born in South Carolina in 1794,
spending several years of his youth among the
Cherokees, when eighteen years of age he came
with his father's family into the Mississippi Territory. After the Creek war closed he became a clerk
at St. Stephens, in the store of his uncle, Colonel
David Files, then Quarter Master for the army.
After the death of his uncle, in 1820, he became
Deputy Marshal. He removed to Mobile and was

appointed Clerk of the Court of Mobile. He was also appointed city weigher. He represented Mobile in the state legislature. In 1824 he commenced business as commission merchant. In 1837, in that great financial crash, he closed, having then four hundred customers, and finding himself involved in a loss amounting to one hundred and seventy thousand dollars. He reasoned in regard to his customers from his knowledge of Indian character, but he found, to his loss, "that in similar circumstances the white man would not deal like an Indian." He admired the Indian business characterestics as he had learned them among the Cherokees. He bought in 1840 the Tombigbee River plantation on or near which was located Fort Carney. He made his home there, on the upland, among the pines, a mile or two from the river, in 1844.

His marriage was preceded by circumstances somewhat romantic. This quotation is from "Clarke and Its Surroundings," p. 464.

" When on that memorable night in 1813, as bearer of dispatches to General Claiborne, he entered Fort Carney, the gate was opened by John Eades, and a daughter of his, a young, dark-eyed maiden— she was then eight years of age—glanced at the tall youth who took his supper with them, and who was so boldly performing a perilous enterprise."—His keen eyes must have fallen, at least for a moment, upon her bright face—" This maiden afterwards attended the academy at St. Stephens, and there as a school girl she met the young clerk, who thought to himself that one day she would surely become his wife. But another maiden came in between them and

through a combination of circumstances to her young
Austill was married. Before many years had passed
she died and left no child to represent her. Again
the tall sharer of the honors of the canoe fight met
with her, whom he had seen in the fort and who as a
school girl had stolen his first affections, and before
long they were married. A long and happy, but
changeful life they have spent together. They
have had two sons and three daughters."

In receiving or forming mental impressions
Major Austill was peculiar. In 1818 he was in New
York city for his health, having recovered from an
attack of yellow fever in New Orleans which had
reduced his weight from one hundred and eighty
pounds to ninety-six. While in New York he had
a presentiment that his father was dead. He
hastened home, making the return trip in twenty-
three days, which was then considered a speedy
transit. He found that his father was really dead.
Again, in 1841, when residing in Cottage Hill, near
Mobile, at three o'clock in the morning a stranger
appeared to him in vision or dream saying " Dale is
dead. He died this morning at three o'clock."
Several days afterward he received a letter from a
stranger containing these words.*

After carrying on his plantation for many years
Major Austill died December 8, 1879, in the eighty-
sixth year of his age, " possessed of the respect and
confidence of all the people, and revered for the
long life of usefulness, honor, and patriotism he had
lived on the soil of Alabama."

---

* I am unable to account for these and similar impressions.
I was well acquainted with Major Austill. I am sure of his

trustworthiness, and I had this account from his own lips in 1877.   T. H. B.

As that young girl in Fort Carney in 1813 has had a special mention, of whose well ordered home in 1854 I was myself an inmate, it will surely not be unfitting to append here this note. The notice that follows was written by that editor friend, Isaac Grant, of Grove Hill, and published in his paper June 19. 1890.

"Mrs. Margaret E. Austill, late of Singleton, this county, died in Mobile last Saturday, the 14th., in the eighty-sixth year of her age.   She was the widow of the late Jerry Austill of this county , one of the heroes of the celebrated Canoe Fight on the Alabama River during the Creek Indian War.   She was the mother of Ex-Chancellor Austill of Mobile.   One by one the links connecting the present generation with that of our territory's early settlement are being broken.   Only a few of them remain."

MAJOR J. AUSTILL.

CHAPTER XVIII.

BATTLE OF THE HOLY GROUND.

ON the 10th of November, General Flournoy wrote to General Claiborne, ordering him to proceed to Weatherford's Bluff and there establish a depot of provisions for General Jackson, who had written that he was more in dread of famine than of Indians, and that without a supply he could not carry on the campaign. In accordance with this order, on the 13th General Claiborne broke up his camp at Pine Level and took up the line of march across Clarke County towards the Bluff. The troops manifested the greatest satisfaction on learning their objective point, and were greatly elated by the prospect, as they supposed, of an active campaign towards Pensacola. On the route, the Choctaw Battalion, under Pushmataha, camped for a day and night at Fort Madison, where twenty fine new rifles were distributed among them. On the 16th, the army arrived at the Alabama River, opposite Weatherford's Bluff, there camped for the night, and the next day, by means of rafts, the entire army was landed on the other shore. Here General Claiborne at once began the construction of "a strong stockade, two hundred feet square, defended by three block houses and a half-moon battery,

which commanded the river." In about ten days
these works were completed, and the place received
the name of Fort Claiborne in honor of the commander. The town, where the fort stood, still bears
his name.

We here quote from Claiborne's Mississippi a letter from General Claiborne to Governor Holmes,
dated the 21st of November, 1813, which gives a
brief account of the operations at Weatherford's
Bluff.

"I am now on the east bank of the Alabama,
thirty-five miles above Mims, and in the best part
of the enemy's country. From this position we cut
the savages off from the river, and from their
growing crops. We likewise render their communication with Pensacola more hazardous. Here will
be deposited for the use of General Jackson, a
supply of provisions, and I hope I shall be ordered
to co-operate with him. Colonel Russell of the Third
U. S. Infantry has been ordered to co-operate with
the Georgia troops, and is now on his march to this
place. We have by several excursions alarmed the
Indians, and the possession of this important position will induce them to retire. I have with me
Pushmataha, who, with fifty-one warriors, accompanied by Lieutenant Calahan of the volunteers,
will march this morning and take up a position to
intercept more effectually the communication of the
enemy with Pensacola."

A statement has been made to the writer by two
contemporaries of the Creek War, that while the
army was at Weatherford's Bluff, Pushmataha went
on an excursion with some of his warriors to Burnt

Corn Creek. There he discovered a Creek camp, upon which he made a night attack and killed several of the enemy, whose scalps his warriors bore in triumph back to Claiborne's camp. It is probable that this excursion may be the very one which General Claiborne, in the letter above speaks of Pushmataha's making with fifty-one warriors in the direction of Pensacola.

On the twenty-eighth Colonel Gilbert C. Russell, the commander at Mount Vernon, arrived at Fort Claiborne, with the Third Regiment of U. S. Infantry. Agreeably to General Claiborne's desire, Colonel Russell had, at last, been ordered to co-operate with him. Pickett tells us : " General Claiborne wrote [the fifth of December] to General Jackson, congratulating him upon his victories, giving him an account of the operations in the Southern Seat of War, and acquainting him with the fact that an abundance of corn and other provisions were to be obtained in the neighborhood of Fort Claiborne. He also wrote to Governor Blount, apprising him of the arrival of more English vessels in Pensacola, and added that he wished 'to God that he was authorized to take that sink of iniquity, the depot of Tories and instigators of disturbances on the Southern frontier.' He had, a few days before, dispatched Major Kennedy and others to Mobile, to learn from Colonel Bowyer the particulars of the arrival of the British at Pensacola. They reported, [37] giving satisfactory assurances that a large quantity of Indian supplies, and many soldiers, had arrived there; and in addition, that the Indians were committing depredations in Baldwin County, having recently burned down Kennedy's and Byrne's mills. Lieutenant Colonel George Henry Nixon had succeeded Russell in the command at Mount Vernon. At his request, Claiborne permitted him also to man Fort Pierce, in the neighborhood of the disturbances."

The year 1813 was now drawing to a close, and General Claiborne, at last, prevailed upon General Flournoy to authorize him to advance with his army into the Creek nation. He accordingly resolved upon an expedition to Ikana chaka, the Holy Ground, situated about one hundred and twenty miles above Fort Claiborne. Many of Claiborne's officers were opposed to this expedition into the heart of the Creek nation. A written memorial or remonstrance, signed by these officers, giving their objections against the expedition, was placed in General Claiborne's hands. We reproduce this memorial from Claiborne's Mississippi:

"The undersigned, volunteer officers, as republican soldiers devoted to their government, and warmly attached to yourself, and disclaiming any authority to remonstrate or complain, nevertheless, respectfully ask permission to lay their opinions before you in relation to the movement into the Creek Nation. Considering that winter and the wet season have set in; the untrodden wilderness to be traversed; the impossibility of transporting supplies for the want of roads; that most of our men are without winter clothing, shoes or blankets; that a large majority of those ordered to march will be entitled to their discharge before the expedition can be accomplished; for these and other considerations, we trust that the enterprise may be reconsidered and abandoned, declaring at the same time that be your decision what it may, we shall cheerfully obey your orders and carry out your plans." Louis Painboeuf, C. G. Johnson, C. V. Foelkil, Ben Dent, Philip A. Engle, R. Jones, A. Wells, James Foster, H. Morrison, Captains; Alexander Calvit, Lieutenant and Aid-de-Camp; Ben. F. Harper, Surgeon; John Allen, John Camp, Wm. Morgan, R. Bowman, R. C. Anderson, Layson J. Lockridge, Theron Kellog, A. L. Osborne, Lieutenants; George Dougharty, B. Blanton, M. Calliham, H. O. Davis, E. Burton, Stephen Mayers, James Luckett, Ensigns.

Notwithstanding the truly forcible objections to the expedition presented in this remonstrance, General Claiborne adhered to his resolve. From Claiborne's Mississippi, we quote the following extract from a dispatch of General Claiborne himself, published in the Mississippi *Republican*, relative to this memorial:

" Their objections were stated with the dignity, feeling, and respect which these officers had always manifested. But these abused, calumniated defenders of their country, in a situation to try the stoutest heart, rose superior to privation and suffering. As soon as the order to march was issued, each man repaired promptly to his post. Many, whose term of service had expired, and who had not received a dollar of their arrearages, volunteered for the expedition, and with cheerful alacrity moved to their stations in the line." This includes every officer who signed the address. "Yes," continues the General, " when they were exposed in these swamps and canebrakes to an inclement winter, without tents, warm clothing, shoes or food; when every countenance exhibited suffering; when they were nine days without meat and subsisted chiefly on parched corn, these brave men won an important battle, and endured without a murmur the exigencies of the service."

On the thirteenth of December, the army left Fort Claiborne and took up the line of march towards the noted Holy Ground of the Creek Nation. The force consisted of the Third Regiment of U. S. Infantry, commanded by Colonel Russell, Major Cassel's Battalion of Cavalry, Major Smoot's Battalion of Militia, of which Patrick May was adjutant, and Dale and Heard Captains, the Twelve Month Mississippi Territory Volunteers, under Colonel Carson, and Pushmataha's Choctaw Battalion, numbering, according to Pickett, one hundred and fifty warriors. The entire army amounted to near one thousand men.

After several days' march in a north-eastern direction, the army reached the high lands south of Double Swamp, in the present County of Butler. Here General Claiborne built a depot, called Fort Deposite, where he left his wagons, cannon, baggage, and the sick, with one hundred men as a guard. On the morning of the twenty-second, the troops again took up the line of march through the pathless forest, and late in the afternoon made their camp within ten miles of the Holy Ground.

A full description of the Holy Ground of the Creeks may, perhaps, be an acceptable digression to the reader of these pages. We quote from A. B. Meek: "The Holy Ground proper was situated along the south bank of the Alabama, between

Pintlala and Big Swamp Creeks, in the present County of Lowndes. It received its name from being the residence of the principal prophets of the nation, and having been by them consecrated from the intrusion of white men. Wizard circles were described around its borders, and the credulous inhabitants were assured that no enemy could tread upon its soil without being blasted. It was empathically [38] called the 'Grave of White Men.' A more fertile and beautiful tract of country, especially when clothed with the vegetation of spring-time, does not exist in our State; and it was thickly populated by the aborigines. Near the mouth of Pintlala, stood a village of eighty wigwams. The chief town, a few miles below, contained two hundred houses, and here the council house of the Alibamo tribe was situated." It is with this chief town, to which the name, Holy Ground, will be restricted, that the main interest of our narrative is concerned. At the outbreak of the war many of the Indians carried their families into this town. After the massacre of Fort Mims, it became the headquarters of Weatherford, Hossa Yohola, Josiah Francis, and other chiefs. The town was designed by these chiefs, not only as a place of refuge for their women and children, but as a depot for provisions and military supplies, and a point to which those discomfited in battle might retreat,—in short, the base of Creek military operations. The site of Holy Ground Town is about two miles north of the present town of White Hall. Holy Ground Creek rises near White Hall and flows northward to the Alabama River. On nearing the river, which here runs nearly west, the creek deflects

somewhat to the northeast before emptying into the
river.   Within this horse shoe or peninsula formed
by the creek and the river stood Holy Ground
Town.   About half a mile above the mouth of the
creek, and on its west side, is a small spring branch
emptying into the creek.   It is now locally known
as Sprott's Spring Branch.   About midway between this spring branch and the mouth of the
creek, also on its west side, is another spring.   This
latter spring doubtless furnished the main supply of
water to the people of the Holy Ground.   Between
the two springs is a low hollow emptying into the
creek, which may have been a small branch in
primitive days, but now shallow from the washings
of the cultivated soil.   On the western border of
the Holy Ground are two ravines, each about two
hundred yards long, and emptying into the Alabama
River.   The course of one ravine is to the north, the
other to the northwest, and their mouths unite on
the banks of the river.   Meek states that the Holy
Ground was enclosed with pickets.   If so, we conjecture that the pickets must have extended across
the neck of the land from the lower spring on Holy
Ground Creek to a point on the river just above the
two ravines.   The enclosed area would embrace
about fifty acres.   In addition to the pickets, a
long low pile of finely split lightwood was laid, on
the outside of the town, extending entirely across
the neck of land.   The prophets assured their credulous people, that should the white people ever come
and attempt to make an assault on their town, they
would fire this consecrated fuel, whereupon every
white man would at once fall lifeless to the earth.

Such was the Creek Holy Ground, and its ignorant and fanatical warriors no doubt deemed that its sacred precincts would be forever secure from the intruding footsteps of an invading foe.

Notwithstanding all their vaunted professions of belief in the impregnability of their town, the authorities of the Holy Ground, early on the morning of the twenty-third, when they became aware of the approach of Claiborne's army, had the good sense to take the precaution to convey their women and children across the river and lodge them securely in the thick forests of what is now known as the Dutch Bend of Autauga County. About eleven o'clock, the same morning, the army arrived within about two miles of the Holy Ground. Here General Claiborne ordered a short halt,—we conjecture a few hundred yards north or northwest of the present town of White Hall—and made his disposition for attack on the place. His plan was to surround the town in such a manner that the enemy could not escape. He divided his troops into three columns. The centre, commanded by Colonel Russell, at the head of which was Claiborne himself, consisted of the Third Regiment of U. S. Infantry, with Lester's Guards and Wells' Dragoons acting as a corps of reserve. The right column consisted of the Twelve Months Mississippi Territory Volunteers, commanded by Colonel Carson. The left was composed of Major Smoot's Battalion of Militia and Pushmataha's Battalion of Choctaw warriors, both under the command of Major Smoot. Colonel Carson was instructed to attack the Creeks upon the upper side of the town, while Major Cassel's mounted riflemen were ordered to take a position on the river bank, west of the town, to prevent their escape down the river. The plan of battle now arranged, the army was put in motion towards the town. The central column, after marching a short distance, halted for a while so as to give the right and left columns time to reach their respective places on the upper and lower sides of the town. We follow the fortunes of Carson's column. It was evidently General Claiborne's instruction or at least his desire, that Carson's column should cross Holy Ground Creek and march down along its right bank so as to strike the upper side of the town. But in consequence of an impassable reed-brake, this could not be done, and Carson was compelled to march down along the left bank. It was a very cold day, and for nearly a mile, Carson's men, with great difficulty, marched, or rather waded, over a level piney woods country, covered with water from six inches to two feet deep. Upon emerging from the chilly waters to firmer land, the troops heard, issuing from the Holy Ground, the loud shouts and yells of the Creek warriors and the roll of their war drums, showing that the Indians were advised of their approach. Carson's men were the first troops to strike the enemy. About mid-day they came within sight of the town. A short distance from the town, and athwart Carson's line of march, was a branch emptying into Holy Ground Creek. At this lapse of time, it is impossible to determine whether this branch was the Spott's Spring Branch, or the hollow beyond, both referred to above. Our opinion inclines to the latter. In this branch, and behind a large, long log lying parallel with it and on the side

towards Carson, was posted a large body of warriors. As Carson's men, now in line of battle, came
within gun shot, they were suddenly greeted with a
volley of rifle bullets from the Creek ambuscade and
the battle began. The soldiers returned the fire and
pressed steadily forward. Taking advantage of
every tree and stump, they moved nearer and nearer
the enemy, who under the lead of Weatherford,
stubbornly held their ground. On the west side of
the branch, immediately in the rear of the Creek
gun men, were many warriors equipped
with bows, who sent an incessant shower
of arrows towards the American line; but
the missiles, shot too high, fell mostly harmless in
Carson's rear. A prophet was seen in the midst of
the Creek bowmen, frantically rushing to and fro,
waving a red-dyed cow's tail in each hand and utter
ing most appalling yells. Sometimes he would rush
behind a cabin, that stood near by, and then would
return at full speed, with his never-ceasing wild and
frenzied gesticulations. Some of the soldiers finally
making an oblique movement passed around the log
and gave the Indians a severe enfilading fire, where-
by several were killed and wounded. At the same
time some of the whites were wounded. But this
fire caused the Creeks to retreat across the branch.
Still from other points, from behind trees, and among
the fallen timbers, they continued to resist their
enemies. The battle had now lasted about half an
hour, when the other troops began to make their
appearance upon the field. Major Cassels had found
it impossible to reach the position assigned him on
the western side of the town, on account of the

extensive marsh connecting with Big Swamp, which lay in front of his line of march. This unforeseen obstacle caused him to fall back on the head of Carson's regiment. The Third regiment, Major Smoot's battalion, and Pushmataha's warriors had now taken a position in front of the Holy G ound, and the enemy began to give way. About this time, a soldier of Carson's command, named Gatlin, resting his musket against a tree and taking deliberate aim, stretched the prophet lifeless upon the earth, the ball shattering his arm and piercing his breast. Colonel Carson who had up to this time endeavored to restrain the ardor of his men, wishing merely to keep the enemy engaged until the town could be completely invested from the creek to the river, now saw that this object could not be effected; so he shouted to his men, "Boys, you seem keen! go ahead and drive them!" The eager soldiers took their Colonel at his word and rapidly pressed the retreating foe back into the town. The Indians now fled in all directions, many casting away their arms. In accordance with the laudable custom peculiar to the Creeks, they bore off all the wounded warriors that were unable to make their escape. Carson's men pursued the Indians through the town to a bluff near the mouth of Holy Ground Creek. The fugitives here crossed, and some fled to the neighboring cane-brake, while others crossed the river, some in boats, others, by swimming. One of the last retreating warriors received a mortal wound and fell upon the very edge of the bluff. Here he tossed to and fro for a few moments in mortal agony and then rolled headlong down the slope. The mouth of Holy Ground Creek was not the only avenue of escape to the discomfited Creek warriors. According to Pickett, hundreds of them made their escape, along the Alabama River, by the western border of the town. These warriors evidently made their escape at this point before the close of the battle. [39]

Weatherford was the last man to retreat from the Holy Ground, the defence of which he had conducted with judgment and courage. We here introduce from Major J. D. Dreisback's sketch of the noted chieftain, the story of his escape and his wonderful leap as received by Major Dreisback from William Hollinger, a friend of Weatherford's, to whom it was related by Weatherford himself.

" When Weatherford found that most of his warriors had deserted him, he thought of his own safety. Finding himself hedged in above and below on the river, he determined to cross the Alabama River. He was mounted on a horse of almost matchless strength and fleetness; he turned down a long hollow that led to the bank of the river; on his arrival he found the bluff about twelve feet high; he took in at rapid glance the situation, and determined to make the leap; he rode back about thirty paces and turned his horse's head towards the bluff, and then, with touch of the spur and the sharp 'ho ya' of his voice, he put the noble animal to the top of his speed and dashed over the bluff full twenty feet into the flashing waters below, which opened its bosom to receive the dauntless hero, who sought its sparkling waters as a barrier between him and the pursuing foe. He did not lose his seat; his horse and the lower part of his own

body went entirely under the water, he holding his
rifle high above his head.   The gallant horse struck
out for the opposite shore with his fearless rider
upon his back.   When he had advanced some thirty
yards from the shore, the balls from the guns of the
troopers who were above and below him began to
spatter around him like hail, but it appeared that
the 'Great Spirit' watched over him, for not a shot
struck either man or horse.   As soon as he reached
the further shore he dismounted and took off his
saddle, and examined his brave and noble horse to
see if he had been struck; one shot had cut off a
bunch, or lock of the horse's mane just in front of
the saddle.   Finding his noble 'Arrow' (the horse's
name) unhurt, he re-saddled him and mounted, and
sending back a note of defiance, rode off, to fight
again on other ensanguined fields."

A digression may here be permitted.   A Mr.
Sprott, a man of great intelligence, was the first
American settler on Holy Ground Creek.   According to a tradition coming down from him, and still
current with the people of the vicinity, the ravine
that runs northwest was the ravine down which
Weatherford rode when he made his wonderful
leap.   General Woodward, in his Reminiscences, has
attempted to cast discredit upon the reality of this
incident.   We quote his language: "Weatherford
was among the last to quit the place.   He made an
attempt to go down the river—that is, down the
bank of the river—but found that the soldiers would
intercept his passage, and he turned up [the stream]
keeping on the bluff near the river until he reached
the ravine or little branch that makes into the river

above where the town used to be.   There was a small
foot-path that crossed the ravine near the river; he
carried his horse down that path, and instead of going out of the ravine at the usual crossing, he kept
up it towards its head until he passed the line of the
whites.   So, now you have the bluff-jumping story."

General Woodward was evidently unfamiliar
with the topography of the Holy Ground.   There
are only two ravines at the Holy Ground—the two
already described—both of which are only two hundred yards long and quite shallow towards their
heads.   Weatherford could not have gone to the
rear of the American lines by riding up the bottom
of either of these ravines.   And as to "the ravine or
little branch that makes into the river above where
the town used to be,"—this was Holy Ground
Creek, which was certainly full of water on the day
of the battle, as it was a rainy season.   Weatherford could not have made his escape by riding or
leading his horse up the channel of this creek.   In
addition to this, Carson's men already had possession
of the mouth of Holy Ground Creek at the time
when Weatherford was making his escape.   These
facts should be sufficient to show the absurdity of
General Woodward's position.

As a rejoinder to General Woodward's unwar-
rantable skepticism and as evidence corroborating
Major Dreisback's narrative, we quote from the man-
uscript notes of the Rev. John Brown of Mississippi:
"In early life, I was well acquainted with James
Bankston, who was a member of Cassel's cavalry.
I have often heard Bankston say that he was of the
party that pursued Weatherford at the Holy

Ground, when he made his horseback leap into the Alabama River. And that when he was crossing the river, his pursuers fired their guns at him. On reaching the other shore, and thus being beyond the range of gunshot, Blankston said that Weatherford dismounted, unsaddled his horse, wrung the water out of his blanket and other articles, then again resaddling, he mounted and rode off. This was Bankston's statement of Weatherford's exploit, of which he was an eyewitness, and I believe that his statement is true in every particular."

The whole army was now in the Holy Ground, and the battle was over. It had been fought almost exclusively by Carson's men, the remaining troops only reaching the field of battle in time to participate in the closing scenes. If Major Cassels could have reached at the proper time, the place assigned him, on the lower side of the town, there is little doubt but large numbers of the Creek warriors would have been forced to surrender, or else as was the case at Tallasseehatchee, to accept the alternative of fighting until the last warrior was slain.

General Clairborne forbade his white soldier's pillaging the Holy Ground, but gave all the spoils of the place to Pushmataha's warriors. The Choctaws made a complete sack of the town, loading themselves with provisions, clothing, blankets, and many silver ornaments. Much of this booty—the clothing and blankets—is said once to have been the property of the illfated inmates of Fort Mims. From twelve to fifteen hundred bushels of corn were found, a sufficient part of which was appropriated for the use of the army, and the remainder destroyed. The most interesting trophy of the Holy Ground was a letter found in Weatherford's house, written by Governor Manique to the Creek chiefs, congratulating them on the victory of Fort Mims.

During the general search which engaged the attention of many of the soldiers, John Brown, one of Carson's men, entered a cabin, after it had been plundered, and a Creek woman, who had strangely escaped the notice of the Choctaw pillagers, came forth from her hiding place, and by signs, appealed to him for mercy and protection. The soldier conducted her to General Claiborne, who ordered that she should be well cared for, and that whenever practicable she should be restored to her friends.

In the middle of the Public Square of the Holy Ground, the soldiers took down a tall pine pole, standing at an angle of about sixty degrees, on which were huug three hundred scalps which the Creeks had taken at Fort Mims. They were of every description, from the infant to the gray head. This ghastly ' sight, as we may well imagine, filled the spectators with emotions of horror and revenge.

When the Choctaws had secured all their booty, Clairborne ordered the place to be burned. As a group of soldiers were standing idly gazing on the burning town, they saw a cabin door suddenly fly open, and a large mulatto negro bounded forth. He had scarcely cleared the threshold when a dozen rifles and muskets blazed forth and the negro fell dead. He was supposed to be a runaway slave, who had taken refuge among the Creeks, and wishing to avoid being captured, had secreted himself, as he supposed, safely in this cabin; but the fire drove him from his lair and he sprang forth only to meet the quick doom of death.

The American loss at the Holy Ground was one man killed, Ensign Luckett, and twenty wounded. This extremely slight loss, considering the bravery with which the enemy fought, must doubtless be ascribed to the scarcity of ammunition among the Creeks, which compelled many of them to have recourse to bows and arrows, the primitive weapons of their race. The Creeks had thirty-three killed, of whom twenty-one were Indians and twelve negroes, for on this occasion the Creeks forced their negro slaves to help bear the brunt of battle. The number of their wounded is not known, as they succeeded in bearing them all off the field. " Among the slain of the Indians," writes Dr. Neal Smith, " was found one of the Shawnee prophets, who was said to have first raised the disturbance with the whites, a singer in the Creek nation; and the leading prophet of the Creeks is said to have been mortally wounded and dropped a noted gun, which was well known." The Shawnee prophet was probably the man that was killed by Gatlin.

The Choctaws scalped all the Creek warriors slain at the Holy Ground. But with that contempt for the negro, which has always been a noted Choctaw characteristic, they scorned to appropriate the scalps of the dead negroes. They simply stripped off their wooly scalps and then instantly and disdainfully cast them aside, considering them trophies unfit for Indian warriors.

It may be well here to state that the Holy Ground was the only battle in the terrible Creek

war in which negroes bore arms in behalf of their
red owners. In all other engagements, Muscogee
valor alone sustained the tug of war. Kinnie Hadjo,
a Creek warrior at the Holy Ground, speaking of
this battle in after years, censured his countrymen
severely for making use of negroes in this engagement. He said that the proud and warlike Muscogees on this occasion had compromised the dignity
of their nation in stooping so low as to call to their
aid the services of such a servile and degraded race as
negroes to assist them in fighting the battles of their
country; that this act, too, was especially exasper-
ating to the whites and tended to increase the bitterness of their prejudices against the Creeks. [40]

The army camped, the night following the battle, near the ruins of the Holy Ground. The next
day was devoted to the destruction of the enemies'
towns, farms, and boats. General Woodward states
that after the massacre of Fort Mims, many of the
Creeks returned to a village, situated on a place
afterwards embraced in Townsend Robinson's plantation. This and every other settlement in the Holy
Ground territory was that day destroyed. A. B.
Meek relates an incident which must have been a
part of this day's work: In writing of Major Austill, he says that " he, in particular, distinguished
himself [at the Holy Ground] by crossing the river
in a canoe, with Pushmataha, the great Choctaw
chief and six warriors in front of the enemy's fire,
putting a large party to flight, and capturing a considerable quantity of baggage and provisions."

There is a tradition current among some of the
aged Choctaws of Mississippi, that the day after the

battle of the Holy Ground, in **some manner, a** Creek camp was discovered on the **west** side of the river. Pushmataha took some of his warriors in the afternoon, crossed over in a boat and approached this camp, without being seen. Pushmataha then gave the signal to his men by shouting, "Husa! husa! moma abi! moma abi!" "Shoot! shoot! kill all! kill all!"—whereupon his warriors opened fire and killed two or three of the enemy. The remainder fled. The Choctaws secured the booty of the camp and then returned across the river to the army. This tradition, no doubt, commemorates the same exploit recorded by Judge Meek, but perhaps embellished with some aboriginal exaggeration.

The same afternoon of this Choctaw exploit, while the cavalry were on their way up the river to destroy the town at the mouth of the Pintlala Creek, they encountered, not far from the town, three Shawnees, who retreated into a reed-brake. The troopers surrounded the brake, and, through an interpreter, called upon them to surrender, offering to spare their lives. But the Shawnees resolutely rejected every overture. Both sides then opened fire and a fight of two hours ensued. The Shawnees would load their guns, come to the edge of the brake, deliver their fire, then return to their covert, and there reloading, would again return to the post of danger. The soldiers at last prevailed, and the Shawnees were slain.

The firing of this slight engagement being heard in Claiborne's camp, he marched in that direction during the early part of the night and then camped on Weatherford's plantation, where the troops passed the remainder of the night, exposed to a cold drenching rain. A part of the next day, which was Christmas, was passed in still further laying waste the country, after which, there being nothing further to be done, the army marched back to Fort Deposite, and thence in three or four days to Fort Claiborne.

Tradition relates that while the army was on its return, the artillery men, on several occasions, fired off their cannon, supposing that this would strike terror into any revengeful party of Creeks, that might be dogging their march.

"On General Claiborne's arrival at Fort Claiborne," writes J. F. H. Claiborne, "Carson's Mississippi Volunteers and the calvary were mustered out of service, and there were only sixty men left, whose term would expire in a month. These troops, the General complains, had been permitted to serve without clothing or shoes, and had been disbanded with eight months' pay due them! What a commentary on the War Department of that day! What an illustration of the patience and patriotism of the volunteers of Mississippi!

The volunteers had served over and above their time; had remained from attachment to their General, and started on their weary journey for their distant homes on the Pearl, the Amite, and the Mississippi, without a cent of their pay. Their General soon followed, as poor as themselves, and, with a constitution broken by exposure, soon died."

In chronicling the disappearance of Claiborne's army from history, it may be but just to add that his red allies, under Pushmataha, were likewise mustered out of service at Fort Claiborne, and at once began their march to their homes beyond the Tombigbee. They bore upon their scalp poles the tokens of Muscogee defeat and disaster, and in every Choctaw village they entered they sang their savage war song and danced their exulting scalp-dance over the ghastly trophies of the Holy Ground.

The joy and enthusiasm with which the news of the defeat of the Creeks at the Holy Ground was received by the people of the Alabama frontier may be realized from the following extracts from a letter, dated December 31, 1813, written from St. Stephens by Thomas Vaughn and addressed to General Claiborne:

"Sir:—Ensign Burton arrived here last night about ten o'clock with the pleasing intelligence that you gained a complete victory at the Holy Ground. I made the communication to Captain Davis, and we had the fort illuminated, and gave you three cheers at the front gate, and the rear gate, and on grand parade, with appropriate music—an air named by Captain Davis, 'Claiborne's Victory.' The citizens by this time, had discovered the cause of our rejoicing, and illuminated generally. We then marched through the town with music, amid the joyful acclamations of the citizens. On every countenance the gleam of joy appeared to beam, and the name of Claiborne, his gallant officers and men, resounded from one end of the town to the other; and the night was passed with a general rejoicing, such as was never before experienced at St. Stephens."

The defeat of the Creeks at the Holy Ground practically closed their military career in South Alabama. Elsewhere, on other fields, against the armies of Floyd and Jackson, and in the Swamps of Florida, the struggle was still continued by this heroic race of red men with a courage, patience, and patriotism that have elicited the wonder and admiration of the historians of Mississippi and Alabama. "The achievements of the Creeks," writes Claiborne, "rival the prodigies of antiquity." Only a brief outline of the story of the remainder of this unparalleled struggle against the boundless military resources of the white man will be recorded in the subsequent pages. And now we flatter ourselves that we have fully redeemed our promise to our readers in giving them a full and exhaustive history of the Creek War in South Alabama.

NOTES.

The authorities used in writing the chapter on the Holy Ground campaign are the histories of Meek, Pickett, and Claiborne; a letter published in Alabama Historical Reporter, July, 1880, written January 8th, 1813, to Rev. James Smiley by Dr. Neal Smith, giving a short sketch of the battle; and manuscript notes on the Holy Ground by the Rev. John Brown, of Lauderdale County, Mississippi, giving facts derived from his father, who was a soldier in that battle. In addition to these sources of information must be mentioned some Choctaw traditions received from aged sons of two of Pushmataha's warriors.

In 1894 the writer visited the battle-field of the Holy Ground and thoroughly familiarized himself with its topography.

It may not be amiss in these notes to refer to a statement in Pickett's History of Alabama, that the

Creek prophets had caused many white persons and friendly Indians to be burned to death at the Holy Ground, and that when General Claiborne's army was "almost in sight of the town, Mrs. Sophia Durant and several other friendly half-breeds were mustered in the square and surrounded by lightwood fires designed to consume them." We have no desire to cast discredit upon this statement, yet it is singular that no contemporary records make mention of this matter. No reference is made to it in General Claiborne's official report of the battle of the Holy Ground, nor in N. H. Claiborne's Notes on the War in the South, published in 1819, nor in the letter referred to above, of Dr. Neal Smith, who was a participant in the battle. We will also add that no reference is made to it in the manuscript notes of the Rev. John Brown, which are, in reality, the recollections of another participant in the battle.

Some years ago this statement of Pickett's was brought to the notice of General Pleasant Porter, of the Creek nation, who is well informed on the ancient usages of his people. The General utterly disbelieved the statement. He said that he never heard a hint as to the Creeks' burning prisoners at the stake. He said that, on the contrary, such a practice would be a direct violation of their superstitious or religious beliefs; that dead bodies were shunned, as among the Jews, and that when a person was killed, there was a special detail of men to bury the corpse as soon as possible, as the spirits of the dead were regarded as disquieting or dangerous agents around them as long as their bodies remained unburied. And they would fear to torture the dying, lest their spirits should take revenge on them before their
[41]   bodies could be buried.   H. S. H.

The following letter was received from Mr. W. A. De Bardelaban after this chapter was completed. This letter shows how utterly untenable is General Woodward's statement in regard to Weatherford's escape at the Holy Ground.   H. S. H.

" White Hall, Jan. 24th, 1895.

"Mr. H. S. Halbert: *Dear Sir:*—Yours of 21st at hand. Will state in regard to the Holy Ground Creek, that it is now about twenty or thirty feet deep in water for at least half a mile up, taking in the crooks in the creek. In my best judgment it would have been utterly impossible for Weatherford to have made his escape that way, as the bluffs of the creek do not seem to be any deeper now than when I first knew the creek thirty years ago.   Yours very respectfully,

"W. A. De Bardelaban."

CHAPTER XIX.

The War in the Indian Country.

THE " Creek War," as waged by the whites
against the Indians, has been very fully
treated in those works that give an account of the
life of General Andrew Jackson.   Of these, twelve
or more are in the Chicago City Library, written by
Snelling, Eaton, Goodwin, Parton, Stoddard, Jenkins, Irelan, Waldo, Frost, and others, and some of
them are very reliable in regard to the battles in the
Indian country, now North and Central Alabama.

As on this part of the war such full accounts are
accessible to general readers, but little more than a
summary of the principal battles will here be given.

After the fall of Fort Mims, and that massacre
was not then regarded as a " philosophic historian,"
(quoting Gibbon), would regard it now—for the real
facts concerning it were not then made known—the
feeling among the whites was, Fort Mims must be
avenged.   The tidings went up into Tennessee and
Andrew Jackson, with Middle and West Tennessee
volunteers and militia, soon started for the Creek
country.   General Jackson is reported to have said
in regard to the Creek warriors, " Long shall they
remember Fort Mims in bitterness and in tears."

The following is the Creek War paragraph in
Venable's School History of the United States, one

of the best of the school histories which I have examined. T. H. B.   "In the year 1813, the South became the scene of Indian war. The Creeks of Alabama and Georgia had in August, attacked Fort Mims,situated on the left bank of the Alabama River, and massacred nearly four hundred persons of both sexes, who had flocked to that stockade for safety. The vengeance which followed was swift and bloody. General Andrew Jackson, the commander of the expedition against the Creeks, expressed himself as resolved to exterminate them. A large force of Southern militia, aided by Choctaw and Cherokee allies, carried havoc from village to village, and finally,having cooped up about one thousand of the Creeks at Horseshoe Bend, on the Tallapoosa River, charged upon them with such effect as to kill or drown six hundred and capture the rest.   Nothing was left for the remnant of the broken nation but to sue for peace."   Paragraph 189, page 153.

It was considered needful also by those in the Mississippi Territory and in Georgia that active measures should be taken against the Creeks for their own self-protection.

That the facts really warranted the action taken may be fairly questioned. It is to be feared that the American people, in their treatment of Indians, will have not a little for which to answer at the bar of the enlightened public sentiment of future generations.

It is a historian's duty to give facts and not to make pleas; but it may be added here that Colonel Hawkins, the Government Agent, residing among the Creeks, did not think it certain that the counsels of the war party would finally prevail. His views probably influenced General Flournoy, who, under date of August 10, 1813, wrote to General

Claiborne, "Your wish to penetrate into the Indian country, with a view of commencing the war, does not meet my approbation, and I again repeat, our operations must be confined to defensive measures." Had General Flournoy's policy been strictly carried out, had there been no Burnt Corn and a different officer at Fort Mims, the probability is great that there would have been very little Creek war. Pickett speaks of Colonel Hawkins as being "strangely benighted," but it is by no means certain that he was not correct in his forecast of events, for neither Colonel Hawkins nor the Indians could have anticipated the Burnt Corn engagement (which seems to have precipitated rather than checked the war upon the whites), nor the attack on Fort Mims terminating so unexpectedly as it did to both Indians and whites, which led to the destructive campaign now [42] before us. Brewer says, and his language seems to be that of a candid, truthful historian, "The savages highly incensed at the attack made on them at Burnt Corn, July 27, 1813, resolved to avenge themselves on the Tensaw and Tombigbee settlers." Thus he accounts for the attack on Fort Mims. And so it was one vengeance after another vengeance.

But whatever "might have been," the white settlers bordering on the Creek nation thought it was time to strike a heavy blow. They saw strong reasons for action. Three bodies of troops therefore, it may be said four, marched as speedily as possible in the circumstances, into the Creek country. One was from the river settlements, Mississippi volunteers; one from Georgia; and two from Tennessee. The Middle Tennessee troops met at their place of rendezvous October 4th, and on October 7th General Jackson joined them at Fayetteville.

Associated with Jackson was General Coffey, and leading the East Tennessee troops was General Cocke, and with him General White. General John [43] Floyd commanded the Georgians, and General Claiborne the Mississippians.

ENGAGEMENTS.

1. *Tallussahatchee or Talluschatchie town.*

This battle was fought November 3, 1813, General Coffee, with nine hundred Tennessee troops, conducting the attack. From General Jackson's official report. "November 4, 1813.—

"GOVERNOR BLOUNT.—*Sir:* We have retaliated for the destruction of Fort Mims." He reports "186 dead on the field," and about "80 prisoners," women and children. General Coffee says in his report made the same day, that "not one of the warriors escaped to carry the news, a circumstance unknown heretofore." [44]

2. *Battle of Talladega, Nov. 9, 1813.*

In this Indian town were friendly Indians beseiged by a force of hostile warriors, the strongest fact found to indicate any real war among the Creeks themselves. A noted chief had made his way out through the besiegers in the disguise of a hog skin and requested aid from the Tennessee troops. General Jackson was now at Ten Islands, on the Coosa, which was about thirteen miles above Tallussahatchee Creek. Talladega was about thirty miles below. At Ten Islands was built Fort Strother. Jackson himself, with some twelve hundred infantry and eight hundred cavalry, marched to the relief of the friendly Creeks. The siege was raised. Perhaps four hundred of the besiegers were slain.

Under date of December 18, 1813, at Ten Islands, General Jackson wrote to General Claiborne a long letter, given in full in Claiborne's "Mississippi," from which the following extracts are taken: "Before this reaches you, you will have heard of our battle at Talladega. It was fought on the 9th of November, and was indeed a severe blow to the enemy."

"It is impossible to tell, with any precision, the loss they sustained. We counted, however, two hundred and ninety-nine dead on the field; but this is known to fall considerably short of the number really killed. Could I have followed up that victory immediately, the Creek war, before this, had been terminated. But I was compelled by a double cause,—the want of supplies and the want of co-operation from the East Tennessee troops, to return to this place." Near the close of the letter is this suggestive statement: "It is not understood by the Government that this war is to be confined to mere temporary incursions into the enemy's country—such movements might distress them, but would produce none of those lasting and beneficial effects which are designed to be produced. Perhaps, too, there are ulterior objects, not yet avowed, which may be within the contemplation of Government."

Before leaving Talladega it may be stated that within were one hundred and fifty-four warriors with their families and a thousand hostile Creeks

without, around them. But it was no Fort Mims.
In all, it is said the Creeks had in the field, in the
war party, three thousand warriors; and in every
engagement they fought with what the narrators
call a "religious frenzy." Perhaps it might as
appropriately have been called "Spartan valor."
Weatherford had told the war chiefs, if we accept
General Woodward's statements, that going to war
with the whites would prove their ruin; the Cherokee interpretor had warned them that they would
lose their lands: and now, that the Americans were
actually at war with them, perhaps they felt that
the time had come for them to dare, to do, or to
die.*

3. *The Hillabee Massacre.*

This deplorable action took place Nov. 18, 1813.

A body of volunteers from East Tennessee had
marched to the seat of war under Major General
John Cocke. General White, with a thousand men of
General Cocke's division, marched to Turkey Town
and there reported to General Jackson that he
would receive his orders. General Jackson sent him

---

*Some of the remarks made by writers on Indian affairs seem
singular, as though Indians were not expected to share in ordinary human rights, as though they should tamely submit to whatever the white man exacted. The following is one of these
remarks. It is needless to name the writer. After saying that
some of the Creeks were friendly to the whites, he adds: "but
the main body of the nation fought as if their salvation depended
on defeating the Americans." One would hardly expect a man
to use the word salvation, here, in a religious sense, and if it
means their self-preservation, how else could they be expected
to fight? They did not wish, as a people, to be wiped off from
the earth because they were found to be in the way of the white
settlers, because the whites wanted their hunting grounds. With
what is called "religious frenzy," with determined resolution,
was the only way for them to fight.   T. H. B.

to Fort Strother at Ten Islands. The Hillabee Indians had opened negotiations with General Jackson for terms of peace, offering to surrender. While these negotiations were pending and the Indians were waiting for a favorable answer from Jackson, and General White was on his march to Fort Strother, he received orders from General Cocke, which orders he chose to obey, to attack these Hillabee towns. He fell upon and destroyed the very town that had already proposed to surrender to General Jackson, the inhabitants of which were waiting for the return of their messenger and had no thought that they would be attacked by Tennessee troops. It was a massacre and not a battle. "We lost not a drop of blood," General White reported to General Cocke, and Brewer adds "and Fort Mims was again avenged." It was a fearful mistake made by General Cocke or General White or by both—it is putting it too mildly to apply Tennyson's expression, "somebody blundered;" and it illustrates the danger of having in the same field two commanders, one not co-operating, as Jackson wrote, with the other. Pickett says that "Jackson was generally considered the commander-in-chief of all the troops from Tennessee," and the trusting Hillabees could look to no other. The surviving Hillabees could not learn that the attack was not made by his order; and, as one result, in the succeeding engagements, they fought with a vindictive fierceness. They considered that the attack made on their town, in the circumstances, was an outrage, and when they fought afterwards BLOOD WAS SHED.

4. *The Battle of Autossee, Nov.* 29, 1813.

Autosse was on the south bank of the Talla-poosa, near the mouth of the Calabee Creek, eighteen miles from the Hickory Ground, and twenty miles above the junction with the Coosa.

(The Hickory Ground, named above, was a large Indian town, one of the residence places of General McGillivray. The noted Tookabatchee was east from the Hickory Ground on the Tallapoosa.) General Floyd, with nine hundred and fifty Georgia militia, and four hundred friendly Indians, among them the chief Mad Dog, and the friendly Tooka-batchees, made the attack on Autossee. The Indians were driven out, about two hundred were killed, the town was set on fire, and some four hundred houses burned, some of them being fine speci-mens of Indian architecture.* At the same time, or about the same time, Tallassee was also destroyed. Little Tallassee, called the "Apple Grove," was on the east bank of the Coosa, five miles above the Hickory Ground. It was the birth place of McGilli-vray. After destroying these towns the Georgia troops returned to Fort Mitchell.   [45]

5. *Battle of the Holy Ground, Dec. 23, 1813.*

This action, as belonging especially to the Mississippi Territory conflicts, has already been fully described.

6.   January 22, 1814, about six in the morning, near Emuckfau Creek, General Jackson with nine

---

*McKenney and Hall, in their large work, call this also a massacre rather than a battle, for the Indians, they say, were "surprised in their lodges, and killed before they could rally in their defense."

hundred men and two hundred Cherokees and
Creeks, marching southward, was attacked by five
hundred Indians. "The fight lasted all day, both
sides suffering severely; but the assailants were
driven off." Jackson determined to return to Fort
Strother.

7. January 24, 1814, having reached a Hillabee
village, Enitachopco, "he was suddenly assailed with
great vigor by the pursuing red men. After an
obstinate combat they were repelled, though the
invading army was at one time in great peril."*
The Indians said, as their report of these engagements, "we whipped Captain Jackson and ran him
to the Coosa River." He certainly fell back; and the
Americans acknowledged that it was a severe engagement.

8. *The Calabee Valley Fight, Jan.* 27, 1814.

We return to the Georgia troops. Having his
force increased to about seventeen hundred men
and with his four hundred Indians, General Floyd
moved into the Calabee Valley and when about
seven miles from the present Tuskegee, "the savages
suddenly sprang from their lair in the undergrowth
of the creek and made a furious assault about day-
light." "A charge soon drove them into the recesses
of the swamp, with severe loss. But the cautious
Floyd was effectually checked, and his campaign
brought to a premature close." Says Brewer, from
whom these statements are taken, "The practical
results of the fight were wholly with the brave
[46]   natives."

*Brewer's "Alabama."

The
Jacksonian era

E 381 R 415

1989

9. *Tohopeka or the Battle of the Horse Shoe,*
March 27, 1814.

This was the great decisive battle.   The place
was a noted bend in the Tallapoosa River, which
from its shape took the name of Horse Shoe.   Here
a thousand warriors made their final stand.   It was
fortified in the Indian style.   If the breastworks
were taken it is supposed the warriors expected to
cross the river and escape.   When Jackson looked
upon this chosen spot with its Muscogee defences,
he is reported to have said, they have "penned themselves up for slaughter."   A flag of truce sent by
him was fired upon, whether through ignorance or
design is not known.   The Hillabee warriors might
have been expected to fire upon it.   The slaughter
here, when the action began, was fearful. Not many
of the thousand escaped.   This battle may well be
placed along side of that destruction that came
upon the Pequods in New England.   Of that,
Martyn says, "it was not a battle—it was a massacre."   The well informed reader will note more
than one point of similarity between the old Pequod
war and the Creek war.   Perhaps the one was as
needful as the other.   The one blotted out a small
tribe; the other subdued a great people.   And
Brewer says, "And the combined power of the
whites, the Cherokees, Chickasaws, and Choctaws,
assisted by a large portion of their own people, was
required to subjugate them; and only then when the
superior weapons of modern warfare had almost
annihilated the fighting population."

The following extracts from General Jackson's
report are dated March 28, 1814.

"Battle Ground, bend of Tallapoosa." Referring to the warriors, "Expecting our approach they had gathered in from Oakfuskie, Oakahoga, New Yorcau, Hillabees, The Fish Pond, and Eufaulu towns, to the number, it is said, of 1,000."

"Determining to exterminate them I detached General Coffee   *   *   *   to cross the river," which was to cut off retreat.

After describing the action and the little effect produced for some time upon the Indian defences, having determined at last to take the place "by storm," for which order the men were impatient, the report proceeds: "The history of warfare, I think, furnishes few instances of a more brilliant attack."

"The enemy were completely routed." "It is believed that not more than twenty have escaped."

Before leaving Tohopeka perhaps truth and justice require that another, a very unpleasant record should be made. It concerns the barbarity of some of Jackson's troops.

Jackson himself, although determining to exterminate the thousand warriors, made in this war, a good record for humanity in caring for the women and children and in saving the life of a motherless Indian infant, when even the Indian mothers would give it no nourishment; but the same cannot be said of all of his men.

Mr. Warren Wilbanks of Noxubee county, Mississippi, who died in 1882, ninety years of age, is authority for the statement that many of the Tennessee soldiers cut long strips of skin from the bodies of the dead Indians and with these made bridle reins. Also that when the Horse Shoe village was set on fire some of the soldiers noticed a very old Indian, a non-combatant, sitting on the ground, pounding corn in a mortar, as though unaware of the tumult and danger around him, and that a Tennessee barbarian, though called a soldier, deliberately shot him dead, assigning as his reason for so doing that he might be able to report when he went home that he had killed an Indian.

Mr. Archibald McArthur, an aged man of Winston county, Mississippi, is authority for this statement, that in the heat of the fight a lost, bewildered, little Indian boy, five or six years of age, came among the soldiers, when one of them struck him on the head and killed him with the butt of his musket. When reproached by an officer for barbarity in killing so young a child, he replied, that the boy would have become an Indian some day. An aged man, Mr. Evans, of Neshoba county, Mississippi, is authority for the statement that the party detailed to count the dead warriors found on the battle field of Tohopeka, so as to make no mistake in the count, cut off the tip of each dead Indian's nose so soon as the count was made. They counted up, says Pickett, five hundred and fifty-seven warrior bodies found on the field. The Indians take off the scalps. These soldiers took off the nose. [47]

Surely it was not needful, in avenging Fort Mims, as it was called, that the whites should imitate the barbarity of the Creeks.

It is claimed that the truly brave are nearly always humane, but many a sacked city and many a war-ravaged region can show that white soldiers may equal in atrocity and barbarity and far exceed in licentiousness the North American Indians.

War at the best is ever terrible, and too many whites despise more or less what they call the inferior races of mankind. "Only an Indian" is a poor excuse for justifying a barbarity.

CHAPTER XX.

CLOSING EVENTS. 1814.

A T Fort Jackson, the old Toulouse, the treaty of peace, by some called "Treaty of Conquest," was concluded August 9, 1814. By this treaty there was ceded to the United States Government, to defray the expenses of the war,—which, of course, the vanquished must pay—a large domain west of the Coosa; which was, says Brewer, " a very import. ant event in the annals of Alabama, for it threw open to the whites half the present area of the State." But although the treaty was signed "by the leading chiefs and warriors," and thus it terminated formally the war on the Tallapoosa, which had been virtually terminated, March 27th, by that bloody battle on the Horse Shoe Bend; many of the Indians fled to Pensacola. The British were permitted by the Spanish authorities to land some three hundred men here August 25, 1814, and the British officers were permitted by these same authorities to equip and discipline these fugitive Creek warriors that they might aid the British in an aggressive movement which they planned against Mobile and New Orleans. [48] General Jackson went down the Alabama to Mobile, reconstructed Fort Bowyer, which was attacked September 15th by a sea and land force from Pensa-

cola, the land force mainly Indians, the sea force
the British; but the fort was successfully defended.
Then General Jackson, with about four thousand
men, marched across the strip of country lying
between the Cut Off of the Alabama and Pensacola
and captured Pensacola, the 7th of November. Leaving Major Blue to scour the coast and drive out the
Indians from the swamps of the Escambia and the
Choctahatibee, he started back on the 9th of November for Fort Montgomery—a new fort a mile or two
north of the destroyed Fort Mims, erected by Colonel
Thomas H. Benton, who had command there in the
fall of 1814—and went down the river to Mobile,
and on the 21st he left Mobile for New Orleans.
Major Blue, with a force of one thousand men, suc-
[49]   cessfully accomplished his dangerous work. So that,
as the year 1815 opened, a year that was to cover
Jackson with glory at New Orleans, the last fighting, for that time, with these fierce Creek warriors
was over. As Brewer, Alabama's later historian,
says :

"Thus was ended a war so glorious to the brave
Musgogees, and yet so fatal! Their formidable
strength was shorn forever."

That neither Tohopeka nor the treaty at Toulouse actually ended the Creek War is quite certain.
Latour says, that the Creek Indians had been defeated and a treaty made, and he gives as its date
August 10th. But he adds, that a part of the Creeks
refused to join in it and remained still at war, committing depredations on the Alabama, Tombigbee,

and Mobile Bay, aided and abetted by the Spaniards who supplied them with arms and ammunition.

He says, that General Jackson demanded satisfaction from the Spanish, and as this was not furnished, Jackson took Pensacola. When this was done, the war was soon closed. See Latour's "Memoirs of the War in West Florida and Louisiana, 1816."

Before the treaty of Fort Jackson was signed, Big Warrior, in the name of the friendly chiefs, tendered to General Jackson and Colonel Hawkins a reservation of land, three miles square for each, to be chosen by themselves; and to the two interpreters, George Mayfield and Alexander Cornells, one square mile each. Colonel Hawkins, in a nominal acceptance of this gift, spoke of it as not originating in any intimation from themselves, but as the spontaneous act of the chiefs, as an expression of their respect for Jackson and himself. It is needless to say that by this kindly offer General Jackson was not enriched.

Surely some readers would like to see the text of the treaty made with these vanquished Muscogee warriors, a treaty to the terms of which they could scarcely refuse to agree, yet which they very reluctantly signed.

A generous, powerful, civilized government should not force a treaty that is unjust upon the helpless and unresisting. It may be questioned whether our Government has been accustomed to deal as did William Penn and Roger Williams and the Pilgrim Fathers, with the American Indians.*

"TREATY OF FORT JACKSON.

"Articles of agreement and capitulation made August 9, 1814, between Major General Andrew Jackson on behalf of the President of the United States and the Chiefs of the Creek Nation.

"Whereas, An unprovoked, inhuman, and sanguinary war, waged by the hostile Creeks against the United States, hath been repelled * * * in conformity with principles of national justice, * * * be it remembered that prior to the conquest of that part of the Creek nation hostile to the United States, num erless aggressions have been committed against the peace, the property, and lives of citizens of the United States and those of the Creek nation in amity with her, at the mouth of Duck River, Fort Mims, and elsewhere, etc., etc., wherefore:

Article 1. The United States demand an equivalent for all expenses incurred in prosecuting the war to its termination by the cession of all the territory belonging to the Creek nation within the territory of the United States lying west, south, and south-

---

*Of the Pilgrim Fathers it has been well said, "They were uniformly gentle and obliging to the savage tribes, and they were invariably and inflexibly just in treatment and in requisition."

In 1636 a lone Indian trader was murdered and his goods taken by some white men. Three of the murderers were caught, tried at Plymouth, found guilty, and hung."

"It was as certain death to kill an Indian in the forests of America, as to slay a noble in the crowded streets of London." "Pilgrim Fathers," pages 371, 372.

Such justice pleased the Indians well. They respected and trusted the Pilgrims. It would not be safe to say that the Puritans kept up the kind and just treatment commenced by the Pilgrim Fathers.

eastwardly of a line to be run and described by persons duly authorized, etc., * * * beginning at a point on the easterly bank of the Coosa River where the south boundary line of the Cherokee nation crosses the same, etc., etc.

Provided friendly chiefs are entitled to their improvements, land, etc.

ARTICLE 2. The United States guarantee the Creek nation all their territory east and north of said lines.

ARTICLE 3. The United States demand the Creeks to abandon all communication with British or Spanish posts, etc.

ARTICLE 4. The United States demand right to establish military posts, roads, and free navigation of waters in territory guaranteed the Creeks.

ARTICLE 5. The United States demand a surrender of all persons, property, friendly Creeks, and other Indians, etc., taken.

ARTICLE 6. The United States demand the capture and surrender of all the prophets and instigators of the war, whether foreign or native, who have not submitted to the United States, if any shall be found in territory guaranteed to the Creeks.

ARTICLE 7. The Creeks being reduced to extreme want, etc., the United States, from motives of humanity, will continue to furnish the necessaries of life until crops of corn can yield the nation a supply, and will establish trading posts.

ARTICLE 8. A permanent peace shall ensue from the date of these presents forever between the Creeks and the United States, and between the Creeks and the Cherokee, Chickasaw, and Choctaw nations.

ARTICLE 9. If in running the lines east, the settlement of the Kinnards falls within the boundaries of the ceded territory the line shall be run so as to leave it out, etc.

The parties to these presents agree to ratify and confirm the preceding articles, and do hereby sol-

emnly bind themselves to a faithful performance,
etc., etc.*

The surrender of Weatherford to General Jackson
has been described very fully by some of the writers
who have been considered well informed.　But from
what source did they derive their information?　The
sifting process which has been found needful in all
these Creek war researches leaves here a few quite
well attested facts.

　Eggleston, who wrote an interesting work called
The Red Eagle, a name applied to Weatherford,
whose Indian name was Hoponika Futsahia, in English, according to Woodward, Truth Maker, repre-
sents Weatherford as having been the great leader
in the whole Creek war, a kind of general or commander-in-chief of all the Indian forces.　But no
evidence for anything of this kind has been found.
There is no evidence of his presence in any conflict,
only for a short time at Fort Mims and in defending
the Holy Ground.‡

　It is sure that Weatherford made a voluntary
surrender of himself to General Jackson; not as
Waldo says, after exhausting his vocabulary in describing his terrible ferocity, then at last "flung himself into the hands of General Jackson and demanded

---

* The treaty of Ghent, which declared peace between Great
Britain and the United States, was signed December 24, 1814; but
as the treaty of Fort Jackson did not actually terminate the war
with the Creeks, so neither did this European treaty actually terminate the "War of 1812," of which the Creek War became a
part.　Pensacola had first to be captured and New Orleans to be
defended.

‡ See Woodward's Reminiscences.

his protection:" but coming with no demands, he
placed his life at the disposal of the conquering general.   He requested relief for starving women and
children and for the deluded Indians who had followed their chiefs and their prophets.   In reply to
the   charges of General Jackson, Weatherford
claimed to be innocent of much that had been
charged to him; "that he regretted the unfortunate
destruction of Fort Mims as much" as did Jackson
himself.   "He said it was true he was at Fort Mims
when the attack was made, and it was but a little
while after the attack was made before the hostile
Indians seemed inclined to abandon the undertaking;
that those in the fort, and particularly the half-breeds
under Dixon Bailey, poured such a destructive fire
into their ranks as caused them to back out for a
short time.   At this stage of the fight he advised
them to draw off entirely.   He then left to go some
miles" away, to look after the negroes of his half
brother, David Tate.   He also said to General Jackson that he joined the war party, for one thing, to
save bloodshed, and that "but for the mismanage-
ment of those that had charge of the fort he would
have succeeded" there.   These statements Woodward says were given to him by General Jackson
himself.   The speech attributed to Weatherford
lacks sufficient evidence of genuineness to insure its
credibility.   It is out of harmony with the well attested facts of his actual part in the war.   It seems
evident, and such is Woodward's statement, that
Jackson formed the opinion that he was a brave,
fair-minded, truthful man, whom circumstances had
forced into the war party.   Jackson spared his life,

gave him such protection as was needful, and his plantation life afterward on Little River as a good citizen is abundantly attested.

We learn from the records of the Department of the Interior that in February, 1814, a Choctaw force of seventy-five warriors, under the command of Pushmataha, made an expedition across the Tombigbee, just below the mouth of the Black Warrior. Neither history nor tradition has preserved any details of this expedition, the bare fact alone being revealed by the records of the Government.

We here copy the roll of the field and staff of a detachment of Choctaw warriors in the service of the United States from March the 1st to May the 29th, 1814: Pushmataha, Lieutenant-Colonel; Humming Bird, Lieutenant-Colonel; Louis Leflore, Major; John Pitchlyn, jr., First Lieutenant and Quartermaster; Samuel Long, Quartermaster-Sergeant; Middleton Mackey, Extra Interpreter.

On the 17th of August, 1814, a Choctaw company of fifty-three warriors, commanded by Pushmataha, with Moshulitubbee as second in command, was mustered into the service of the United States. This company of Indian warriors formed part of the detachment under the command of Major Uriah Blue, and assisted in bringing the Creek War to a close. They were mustered out of service at Fort Stoddart January 27, 1815.

The record of the Choctaw warriors during the Creek War was, in a high degree, honorable. Their nation proved itself a true friend of the American Government. Let us hope that posterity will never permit the name of their great and patriotic chieftain to pass into oblivion.

CONCLUSION.

"A historian dare not have a prejudice, but he cannot escape
a purpose—the purpose, conscious or unconscious, of unfolding
the purpose which lies behind the facts which he narrates."

IT was stated in the "Introduction" that the
authors of this work proposed to do justice to
the Indians and justice to the whites; which meant
that they proposed and expected to state the facts,
if they could reach them, concerning both the
Indians and the whites, fairly, truly; without coloring; without unduly extenuating the blunders or the
wrongs committed on either side; allowing only the
ordinary and just feelings of a true humanity to
influence them in any sympathy or feeling for the
Indians, in any sympathy or feeling for the white
settlers; holding themselves as impartial and friends
to all, while following the white thread of truth,
whether it should lead into the crowded stockade,
or was found at the red man's camp fire. All this,
and it is much, they hope the readers will feel that
they have accomplished with fair success. There is
another line, another thread, the golden thread of an
even-handed justice, which they would like to trace
by giving a brief summing up or review of this
border war. Of course every reader of mature
judgment will do this for himself, but as we both
have had many years of experience in life and are

no longer young, perhaps even such a reader would not object to take a look for a moment through our eyes.

There are 'certainly some well established facts.

There had been some aggressions committed by the Creek Indians. The treaty preamble calls them "numberless." A figure of speech, of course.

A part of the Creek confederacy proposed to make war upon the white settlers, perhaps hoping even to exterminate them.

Some of the war party went to Pensacola to obtain war supplies. They were quietly returning. And here comes in the first real action of the war, the Burnt Corn attack. Woodward declares that the Indian leader, "Jim Boy, said that the war had not fairly broke out, and that they never thought of being attacked." It was like saying, if they had been civilized: True, we were getting ready for war, but no declaration of war had been yet made on either side. As they were not civilized, and as the white settlers, not the United States authorities, considered it best to get the start of the Indians, they marched across their frontier line and issued their declaration of war in the first discharge of their muskets and rifles at Burnt Corn. The whites commenced the actual, the open war.

The next action, the first on the part of the Indians, but not the first of the war, was at Fort Mims. Brewer has surely stated the case fairly, when he says, (see Brewer's Alabama, p. 194), "A skirmish on Burnt Corn Creek, eight miles below Belleville, in this county, between the whites and Muscogees, July 27, 1813, was the commencement of the great Indian war." After briefly detailing the action, he says that the Indians were greatly elated by their success"; but he adds: "Inspired by revenge, a month later they fell upon Fort Mims."

And if the facts teach anything there they surely show that the Indians, as being Indians, could do nothing less than take the fort and butcher the inmates: nothing less, when the commanding officer, on Claiborne's own testimony, "held the Indians in contempt," "and as a taunt and derision to the timid," (those cautious backwoodsmen, probably, who warned him of danger, those truly brave Baileys and others who wanted to be prepared to protect human life), "had the main gate thrown open." The Indians could do nothing less, without ceasing to be Indians, than enter, kill, burn, and destroy.

Now two questions arise here, in this review, as we seek for the golden thread of justice. The first is, passing over what bloodshed there was in Clarke county, why did not Weatherford with his victorious thousand, if indeed they yet, as Pickett expressed it, "thirsted for American blood," pass over the Alabama and fall upon the stockades of the real, aggressive white settlers, who had put their cattle and put themselves on the Alibamo hunting grounds? Why? Perhaps there were prudential reasons. It was not so easy for the Indians to take food along for a campaign of many days. It was not so easy for a thousand men to cross the Alabama in a body, and then to re-cross it in haste if they should need to retreat. And there were soldiers at Mount Vernon whom they probably did

not care to meet.   But perhaps there were stronger
reasons.   They had learned something of the exact-
ion of justice by the whites in the Meredith and
Lott and Duck River tragedies; and now that they
had, beyond their own expectation, contrary to the
wish certainly of some of them, in one single day swept
off five hundred who could be classed, mostly, as
Americans,they were,perhaps,startled, as they looked
forward to the results.   As the chiefs, the leaders,
those who knew the Americans best, looked back
upon Fort Mims, it seems probable they did not
wish any further to incur the vengeance of the
whites, they scarcely wished themselves to engage
in such another butchery.

Reasons of some sort there must have been,
why Weatherford, if he was what the historians
claim him to have been, did not lead his warriors
across the Alabama.   Is it not more than possible
that Weatherford, who had joined the war party
reluctantly, and many others like him, were already
sick of the strife?

S. Putnam Waldo, in his memoirs of Andrew
Jackson, published in 1818, bears down very heavily
on Weatherford. He says that after the battle of the
Holy Ground, "Weatherford continued to fight
with the rage of a fanatic, the fury of a demon, and
the diabolical ferocity of a devil incarnate, until
saturated with the blood of Americans."   Such was
not the Alabama Weatherford.   He was for a short
time at Fort Mims; he defended the Holy Ground
so long as he could; and where else did he fight?
Weatherford was not thirsting for American blood.
After August 30th he waited nearly four months, till

attacked in his place of fancied security December 23d, without striking a blow. The other question that comes up is this: September having passed and October having passed, and no great acts of hostility having been committed by the war party of the Creeks, was it really needful and was it fitting that such a destructive campaign, almost to the verge of extermination of the war party of the nation, should have been visited upon them in November and December and January and March? Did the Fort Mims tragedy, provoked surely by the Burnt Corn action, justify that fearful retribution? And if, when the circumstances are considered, Fort Mims hardly justified the shedding in return of so much Creek blood, was it justice to require such an amount of land from the Creeks to pay the expenses, as claimed, of that subjugating war? Alas! We do not find that golden thread of an even-handed justice. And what did Jackson mean in his letter to Claiborne by those "ulterior objects" which he thought might be "within the contemplation of Government?"

There were land claims, and conflicting claims there had been, in the Mississippi Territory. Georgia had claimed, as granted by Charles II, king of England, all the land between the Savannah and the Mississippi rivers and between latitude 31° and latitude 35°, and this, so far as Charles was concerned, without regard to Indian rights. Congress bought, at length, the claim of Georgia for one million and a quarter of dollars. Was the Government looking forward to securing a more full title to some of this land? Since the first settlements on the Atlantic coast it has been true that many of the whites have always wanted the Indian lands, their hunting grounds, even their burial places; they are wanting their very reservations now. Indian wars end in the extinction of Indian titles to land, and it may well be feared that this is an "ulterior" object underlying many of these wars.*

We reach now, in our review, having already implied it and looked at it, the fact of the war waged against the Creeks, in which the larger part of their three thousand hostile warriors seem to have perished. And the conclusion reached here is, that the "Creek War," as waged by the whites against the Creeks, was out of all fair proportion as compared with the "Creek War" as waged by the Creeks against the whites.

Burnt Corn, Tallussahatchee, Talladega, the Hillabee massacre, Autossee and Talassee, the Holy Ground, and Tohopeka, outweigh the few aggressive acts committed by the Creeks, before the war opened, the blood shed in Clarke, and Fort Mims.

It was surely not all justice that influenced the movements of the armies of Jackson and Claiborne and Floyd. Well does Venable call it "vengeance," and that "swift and bloody."

Well would it be if nations heeded more the meaning of the Bible statement: "Vengeance is mine; I will repay, saith the Lord."

---

*Furthermore, the United States, in 1802, had entered into a compact with the State of Georgia to extinguish the Indian title in the bounds of that state so soon as they reasonably could, and the Georgians were in a hurry for their share of the Creek lands. They, after 1814, so crowded the Government that a treaty was made, purchasing lands, which cost the life of Major William McIntosh, and which Congress was obliged to set aside.

The remnant of the War Party and the friendly Lower Creeks, after the treaty of 1814, still held lands which were desired by the states of Georgia and Alabama, and in 1832 was ratified the treaty of Cusseta, the first article of which states: "The Creek tribe of Indians cede to the United States all their land east of the Mississippi River." They were not obliged to remove by the terms of the treaty, but by the crowding in of the whites upon them, and in 1836 war actually commencing, they were constrained to remove to the west side of the Mississippi. Here, in a part of what is known as the Indian Territory, they have found an abiding place. As nearly all of those among the Alabama pioneers who had any part in the events of 1813 and 1814 have passed away, so have the Creek warriors who passed over the great Father of Waters passed now, all or nearly all, over the viewless river which is to the white man and the red man alike the end of strife and of earthly sorrow and earthly joy. The descendants of these Creek warriors have adopted largely the civilization and the religion of the American white race, and they now have farms and mills,and books and papers,and schools and churches. It is to be sincerely hoped that the American Government will at length deal with them on the true principles of Christian equity, suffering no greedy white man to despoil them of their land, and according to them at all times that protection to which they are so justly entitled, And those who dwell along the bright waters which once were held by the free and brave warriors of the great Creek nation, should remember that the children of the forest and the

wild had the first and best right to all those beautiful streams, that the white pioneers have nearly
always been aggressors upon Indian hunting
grounds and burial places, and that the least they
can do is, cherishing no animosity for provoked
massacres committed in the past, to imitate such
virtues as the Creek warriors did possess, and to do
their part as American citizens in having henceforth
just treatment accorded to all the remaining American Indians.

APPENDIX.

THE PANIC.

The various passions and propensities of human nature give rise to singular events, some of them grotesque, some of them grand, some of them disastrous. About 1716 a scheme of wild speculation was started in France, which became known as the "Mississippi Bubble," after it burst in ruin, deep and pitiless, to multitudes. In the fall of 1813 took place, in Mississippi itself, connected with this Indian Creek war, what is called

"THE GREAT MISSISSIPPI PANIC OF 1813."

It was not a financial panic, but a panic arising through fear of Indian atrocities. There lies before me now a manuscript copy, fourteen pages of foolscap, of a full account of this alarm, written by Colonel John A. Watkins, born in Jefferson county, Mississippi, dated, New Orleans, April 10, 1890. The style is so pleasing I should like to reproduce the account entire, but only some statements and a quotation or two can here be given. Alluding to the attack upon Fort Mims, of which he says, "as it was negligently protected, nearly all the inmates * * * were put to death,"—he knew too much, evidently to say "strongly garrisoned,"—he says: "The news of this massacre spread rapidly in Mississippi. * * * The danger was so threatening that Governor Holmes * * * called for volunteers to form a battallion of mounted men, to be composed of one company from each of the counties of Adams, Wilkinson, Amite, and Jefferson." These soon reported for duty "and at once hurried to the seat of war." He says: "This was the famous Jefferson Troop, designated at the War Department as Dragoons, commanded by Major Thomas Hinds, which subsequently became prominent

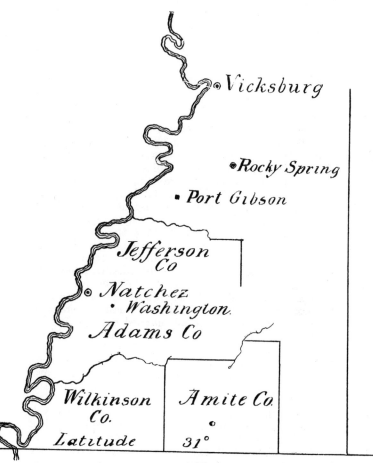

Natchez was the first capital of the Mississippi Territory. In 1801, the capital was removed to Washington, a village six miles from Natchez.

in the Indian war, and at the battle of New Orleans in
1815." And now Colonel Watkins comes to the panic.
" Rumors that an advance had been made by the Creeks,
and that in their progress they had been joined by the
Choctaws, began to be whispered around, at first so
vague that they could be traced to no reliable source, but
in a few days assuming a form, to which fear gave an
impulse, that resulted in a panic that I can only attempt
to describe from the recollections of more than seventy-
five years ago." He then mentions the preparations
made to send the women and children to the town of
Washington, (which the reader will find on this little
map of the southwestern corner of the Territory), and
adds: " By the time the non-combatants were ready to
move, the Indians were said to be at the
Rocky Springs, eighteen miles above Port Gibson, and the next breeze had wafted them
to the Grindstone Ford; some farsighted people could
even see the smoke of Colonel Burnett's house, a distance of seven miles. How these vague reports originated will never be known. Like the 'three black
crows,' they grew as they proceeded, until the alarm
became universal. * * * Runners were despatched
in every direction, warning the inhabitants, and direct-
ing them to seek safety in flight." At the door of the
school house where as " a small boy" he then was, the
announcement was made that the Indians were upon
them, and, he says. "we all hurried home to find our
mothers in tears and tribulation." They were packing
up for a hasty flight. The families there, he says,
were rich in " pigs, poultry, and children," and into
the wagons baggage and children were tumbled "pro-
miscuously, and without any regard to the comfort of
the latter; horses received their cargo of live stock, two
or three being mounted on each ; and now the caval-
cade is under way—if I may use that term when applied
to oxen." These drew the wagons. "At the ' Raccoon
Box'"—a distance of two miles from his home where
two roads met—"our party was joined by twenty or
more families, all on their way to headquarters. Carts,
wagons, children, horses, and dogs, were so promis-
cuously thrown together that the elderly dames found

much difficulty in keeping together their numerous off-spring. After much confusion and any amount of loud talking, the caravan finally began to move." * * * "The scene was ludicrous beyond description. Here three white haired urchins were pelting an old plow-horse into a fast walk; while there, a young mother, similarly mounted, was carrying a child in her lap, while two others were holding on desperately to avoid a fearful tumble; while further on, a rickety old cart, drawn by two stalwart oxen, was loaded with beds, boxes and children, thrown together by chance,—the latter crying lustily to be released from their vile im-prisonment, while the rod was occasionally applied to keep them quiet. Being a good walker then, as in later years, I avoided the ills to which many of my own age fell heir." At length, as this "caravan" was moving on, a deputation was sent to Port Gibson to learn the facts about the Indians, if possible. This scouting party found that place "almost deserted," but one of the principal merchants was still there, Mr. B. Smith, who "did not believe that there was a shadow of truth in the report" about the Indians; and who invited them to help themselves to such as he had, "powder and lead" and "good old bourbon." I quote one more sentence and then must leave this account. "With their whisky and ammunition our party, fully satisfied that there were no hostile Indians on this side of the Alabama River, took leave of Mr. Smith and hurried to overtake their fami-lies, and just at sundown came up with them near Greenville." All of those from Colonel Watkins neigh-borhood turned back; but others continued on till they reached Washington, and thus ended with them a memorable day.

Claiborne in his "Mississippi" says that the Fort Mims tragedy "spread consternation through the Terri-tory," "that a coalition of the Creeks and Choctaws was generally apprehended," and that "the alarm penetrated to Baton Rouge, St. Francisville, Natchez, Port Gibson, Winchester, and Walnut Hills." He quotes from a public record the proceedings of a meeting held at Port Gibson, September 18, 1813, of which Colonel Daniel Burnett was chairman, at which a committee was appointed, on motion of H. Blennerhassett, to inquire into the foundation of the late alarm and to report means for defense. The committee reported the alarm to have been "groundless and unfounded," but they recommended the erection of three stockade forts and made other suggestions. Evidently the "Mississippi panic" was no trifling affair, although with the whole breadth of Mississippi and the friendly Choctaws between these settlers in Jefferson, Adams, Wilkinson, and Amite counties and the hostile Creeks, there was no cause for alarm. But panics are always unreasonable.

When obtaining material for the history of Clarke county, published in 1882, I had free access given me to the court records of Washington county, an early county in Mississippi Territory, which included what was afterwards Clarke; and among thirty-six names there found for jurors on the *venire facias*, "at a superior court held for the district of Washington at McIntosh Bluff on the fourth Monday in September," 1802, the following I give here as familiar names now, showing that they were citizens of the territory then: Tandy Walker, Nathan Blackwell, Moses Steadham, Joseph Stiggins, John McGrew, and Samuel Mims. On the first grand jury were Tandy Walker and Samuel Mims. The next term of this court was held in May, 1804, and additional names were Thomas Bassett, John F. McGrew, John Callier, and James Caller.   T. H. B.

HIGH-HEAD JIM OR JIM BOY.

In prosecuting their researches into the history of the Creek War of 1813, the writers of this work found some difficulty in determining whether the Jim Boy who commanded at the battle of Burnt Corn was the same man as the Jim Boy who figured in the Florida War of 1835. The inference could be drawn from the sketch of Jim Boy in McKenny and Hall's large work that they were two separate and distinct characters. But the authors of that work seem to be strangely benighted or bewildered as to the facts in the early life of Jim Boy. To determine the truth of this matter—the identity of the Jim Boy of Burnt Corn and the Jim Boy of the Florida war—a correspondence was opened with Mrs. A. E. W. Robertson, in the Creek nation. The matter was brought by her to the especial attention of ex-Governor Ward Coachman, Colonel William Robison, and Judge N. B. Moore. These highly intelligent Creeks, after consulting the oldest men among the Creeks, gave it as their deliberate verdict that the Jim Boy of Burnt Corn and the Jim Boy of the Florida War was one and the same man. That the oldest Creeks had never heard of but one Jim Boy. Jim Boy then must have been quite a young man in the war of 1813, as he was in active military life in 1835. He died near Wetumka, Creek nation, about 1851. The wife of Jim Boy, Ni-het-ho-ye, was the aunt of Colonel William Robison . Rev. William Jim Boy, a well known Methodist minister in the Creek nation, is a grandson.   H. S. H.

DEATH OF PUSHMATAHA.

As a matter of interest to our readers we publish a letter written from Washington by Captain David Folsom to Rev. Cyrus Byington, Mayhew, Choctaw Nation, which gives some particulars of the death of Pushmataha. The original letter is in the possession of Mrs. C. Robb, of the Choctaw Nation. Captain Folsom attended the delegation to Washington in the three-fold character of delegate, treasurer, and interpreter. Notwithstanding his imperfect education—he had attended school only six months in his life—Folsom became a great and influential man among his people. He was chief for many years, and was considered one of the first orators of his day. He died about 1847, and was buried at Doaksville, Indian Territory. His dwelling house in Mississippi is still standing, on the Robinson road, in Oktibbeha county. Mrs. Robb, mentioned above, Captain Folsom's neice, is a prominent Baptist in the Choctaw Nation, the author of a number of Choctaw hymns. She edited a Choctaw hymn book.

WASHINGTON, December 24th, 1824.

"DEAR FRIEND:—I take up my pen to you inform that Chief Pushmataha is no more. He died last night about 12 o'clock. He has complained almost ever since he has been here of a scabby spot in his throat. But when he did not drink much strong drink, he felt better. But his drink was great, and I noticed whenever he drank too much, he was worse. I finally concluded that he would never see home. Two nights before he died, he wheezed very much and struggled very much in his sleep. But notwithstanding all this, he would expose himself in every line of exposure, and finally on the 23d instant, about 9 o'clock A. M., he was attacked out on the street. He could hardly get his breath. Two doctors were immediately called, and efforts were made, but done no good. He died about 12 o'clock P. M. He had every attention and friendship shown him by the citizens of this place, besides strangers, who here came and visited us at this, our great trial moment. I was unable to do anything about his burial. However, it was conducted by others.

"December 25th.—I am much better to-day, and feel quite well. It was agreed that our chief should be buried with the honors of war, and several companies turned out, as well as the marine of the Navy Yard, and two bands of music, and with a great procession, we took the body of our departed friend, in presence of several thousand people. We marched in company of and in the way of these people to the burial ground. He was laid in the grave; he was covered with cold clay, and we left him in the midst of many hundred people.

"I assure you, my dear friend, I am thankful there was so much honor paid to our departed chief and towards us. Many of these Congressmen treated us as well as General Jackson. I can truly say, I have and we have received every mark of friendship and brotherly love towards us amongst the whites since we have been amongst them; more particularly since the death of the two chiefs.*

---

* In addition to Pushmataha, reference here is made to Puckshenubbee, who died on the way to Washington.

"I can truly say, as for myself, I feel my love towards the American people. Some say it was a croup or quinsy that killed Chief Pushmataha. But I am induced to believe he was completely burned out by hard drinking. I have noticed him particularly, and I am fully satisfied to say, it is strong drink has finally killed him. I must say, beware of the hard drinkers of the Choctaw people.   *   *   *

"We are still here doing nothing. That is all, have done nothing as yet. And I do not know when we will start for home. But I think our negotiation will come to a close soon. I am sorry to inform you that I cannot be useful to the delegation, because they will have their own way and will not have an ear for such a poor person as I am. But I set very independent before them, but kind and affectionate towards them. It will be a wonder to me if they all get home in safety. Pitchlyn, Moshulitubbee, McDonald, and McCurtain are all well, but the rest are not very well; but it is all on account of their wickedness. I must not write much more. God is not for us. But he is against us on account of our wickedness. God is just and right in taking those chiefs from among the people, so that there may be better men raised up in their places. We have been and have done all those things which would justify our Maker to cut us all off; and he would be right in saying to us wicked delegation of the Choctaw Nation—Why should they cumber the ground any longer? I am fearful that four of our number will never reach home. Don't read my letter to every one.

The 26th:—I am thankful to my Maker that I am as usual, and that my health is good. excepting a little deafness. I am so much confined and compelled to stay with the delegation that I have no chance to become acquainted with the great men of this city. The clergymen and some of the congressmen I should have been glad to become acquainted with them. I hope I have done a little good in the cause of schools and the Gospel in my Nation by coming here ; which is not convenient to mention here. My best respects to all my friends of the mission family. If my life is spared, I hope to see them some time in February.

"From your friend,   "DAVID FOLSOM."

After the death of Pushmataha, his nephew, Oklahoma, succeeded him in the chieftain's office.   But on account of his dissipated habits, Oklahoma was soon deposed, and another nephew, Nettacarchee, was elected Mingo in his stead.   Oklahoma died at Coosha, about 1845.

The statement in Claiborne's life of Sam Dale that Pushmataha was six feet two inches high, is an error into which, in some manner, Colonel Claiborne has drifted.   At intervals, in bygone years, in regard to this matter, I have interrogated a number of aged persons, both whites and Choctaws, who knew or had seen Pushmataha, and all concurred in stating that he was a man of middle stature, about five feet nine or ten inches high, and of portly build.   H. S. H.

A Christian civilization, especially the Christian part of it—civilization without the Bible does not amount to much—has made great changes with the descendants of those brave and fierce and wronged Muscogees with whom the whites in Alabama and Georgia came into conflict.   There is now before me a letterhead, the letter written in Indian Territory, December 24, 1894, which contains the words: "Wetumka National Labor School, Col. Wm. Robison, Supt.," and among the names of the faculty I find as matron, Miss Hannah Monahwee, who is a grand-daughter of that noted chief who commanded the Creek warriors at the great battle of Tohopeka.   His name written by some Menawa, by some Monahwee.   And a grandson of the noted High Head Jim, as mentioned elsewhere, is a highly respected Methodist minister in the Territory, the Rev. William Jimboy.   The introduction of Christianity into the Creek, or as the educated Indians now write, the Muskogee Nation, opens an interesting chapter in the progress of the Gospel.   No white missionaries first bore the Gospel to them, but "an old negro named Billy" taught it to a young Indian man in the Indian Territory, Joseph Islands, and they two commenced a work which, with the help of white missionaries, has been growing until now. See a little tract called "Joseph Islands, the Apostle of the Creek Indians," written by Dr. I. T. Tichenor, published at the Maryland Baptist Mission Rooms 10 E. Fayette street, Baltimore. Price, two cents. T. H. B.

As connected with the real interests which it is hoped this history may promote, some extracts from letters written by a Presbyterian missionary in the Indian Territory, Mrs. Robertson, will certainly be appropriate in this Appendix. Some facts in regard to her I give first; and for these I am indebted, in part, to an interesting article in the *Chaperone Magazine*, of St. Louis, August, 1894, and in part to a letter written by herself in February, 1895. Mrs. A. E. W. Robertson, Ph. D., was the daughter of a distinguished missionary among the Cherokee Indians, Rev. S. A. Worcester, D. D., and was born near that noted Chicamauga River in 1826. She was educated as became a minister and a missionary's daughter, spending her years from sixteen to twenty in an academy in Vermont, where she learned the Greek language, and at the age of twenty, in 1846, became teacher at Park Hill, Cherokee Nation, Indian Territory, and in 1850, April 16, she was married to Prof. W. S. Robertson, A. M., Principal of a then new "Manual Labor Boarding School," at Tallahassee, among the Muscogees or Creeks. Since 1850 she has devoted herself, besides caring for her husband and children, to the language and interests of the Creek Indians in Indian Territory, among whom she has resided, her home now being at Muscogee. Her talents, her opportunities, and her devotion to her work have placed her high among the "famous women" of the land. The article in the *August Chaperone* is headed "Famous Women." From that article I quote the following: "The subject of this sketch, Mrs. Ann Elisa Worcester Robertson, of Muscogee, Indian Territory, has had the very highest honor ever conferred upon woman, bestowed upon her by the Trustees of Wooster University, Ohio, namely, the title of Doctor of Philosophy, in recognition of her scholarly attainments especially in linguistic studies, she having just completed a translation of the New Testament from the original

Greek into the Creek language.   This work is the out-
come of twelve years' labor."   Much of her knowledge
and skill, in translating, she gained while aiding her
husband in his missionary work.   She is an authority
on the Creek language and is now translating the Old
Testament. Some of the words of such a talented, noble,
devoted, Christian woman, as written to her friend, H.
S. Halbert, I am glad to have the privilege here to repeat.   Under date of July 19, 1894, she says:

I am very glad you are giving *Christian* instruction
to the Mississippi Choctaws.   Nothing else will save
the Indians, or, indeed, any people. Our "Five Tribes"
here are in great trouble now on account of the per-
sistence of the Dawes Commission in trying to get them
to surrender their tribal rights in this Territory.   The
commission is giving special attention to the Choctaws,
in the hope that they can do more with them than with
the other tribes, but I think they make very little real
headway, if, indeed, they are not causing, if possible,
a stronger feeling against it than before.   They understand full well that the United States cannot take the
disposal of their lands into their hands (without their
consent) without actual robbery, and the survivors of
the emigration know by sad experience what it will be
to have the Territory thrown open.   I hope with all my
heart they will persist in their refusal to have a hand
in their own destruction, and leave the responsibility
with the United States Government, if the breaking up
must come.

"The poor Florida Seminoles are not faring so well
as your Choctaws, and I do feel for them.   I am glad
that Mississippi has room for the remaining Choctaws,
and seems likely to protect them until they may become
a truly Christian people.

"But what is to become of our own great country?
'The Lord reigneth' is the one comforting reply.
"Sincerely your friend,
"A. E. W. ROBERTSON."

Under date of December 26, 1894, she wrote: "I
suppose you see many of the exaggerated or false reports
about our territory, and know enough about the covet-
ousness of our people [the whites] in regard to these

Indian lands to understand that 'the wish is father to the thought.' They want our Government to have an excuse for robbing these tribes of their own territory. I hope you will join in the prayer that such a calamity may be averted."

As late as January 28, 1895, Mrs. Robertson writes, after expressing her hope that covetous white people would not crowd in upon the Choctaws now in Mississippi. "Even the few Seminoles remaining in Florida are now suffering from the greed of white people; and it begins to look as if these Five Tribes are to be robbed of their possessions in spite of their earnest protests."

The work of spoilation still goes on. It has gone on since the days of the Pequods and Narragansets. And ere long the prospect is—although the New York millionaires may fit up their great parks like the European noblemen—that in all the broad area of these United States there will not be left one hunting ground where the American Indians can shoot the deer or spear the mink. But if our words could reach the halls of Congress we would implore our statesmen there, if any with true hearts are left, to do justice, full and complete, to the descendants of the Southern Chickasaws and Choctaws, Cherokees and Creeks and Seminoles, and let not the greedy white man despoil them of their latest homes.

ALABAMA'S FIRST CAPITAL.

Old St. Stephens.

The State of Alabama, admitted into the Union in December of 1819, has had, with the present seat of government, four capitals, all situated on rivers. The first was St. Stephens on the Tombigbee. The second was Cahawba on the Alabama. The third was Tuscaloosa on the Black Warrior. The fourth is Montgomery on the Alabama.

Of the territorial and first State capital little is known by the youth of the present generation.

South Alabama, once included in West Florida and still earlier in Louisiana, was first crossed by a band of European adventurers, (the Spaniards under DeSoto,) in October of 1540. It was next seen and taken into nominal possession by French explorers and colonists in about the year 1700, the year in which was born at Coweta on the Chattahoochee, which is now in Alabama and was then in Louisiana, that Indian princess, Consaponaheeso, better known as Mary, who became the friend of Oglethorpe and the Pocahontas of the Georgia colony.

In 1763 South Alabama passed into the ownership of Spain and then immediately was transferred to Great Britain. It came back into the possession of Spain as late as 1780, and in 1799 became a part of the United States as far south as the line of latitude 31 degrees.

In the early part of the eighteenth century, about 1714, Fort St. Stephens was probably established by the French. It was held by the Spanish, who themselves built a fort, a church and a parsonage, from soon after 1780 till 1799.

In 1802 an American trading house was there established by our government for the Choctaw Indians, the Spanish block house being used for a store room and the parsonage of the Spanish church for storing the fur and the hides purchased from the Indians.

In December 1804, the place was visited by the gifted and eccentric Lorenzo Dow, then passing as a flying evangelist through the narrow American settlement, seventy miles in length, which then skirted the "Tombeckbee." Dow says that at St. Stephens there was but one family, "but it will be a place of fame in time."

In 1807 town lots were laid off with streets over one hundred feet in width, inhabitants came in, a village and then a real town was formed, and in 1817 it became the territorial and afterward the State capital of the young Alabama. In 1818 it was visited by refugees from France, noted generals "who had won laurels on the proudest fields of European valor," and ladies "who had figured in the voluptuous drawing rooms of

St. Cloud," then on their way to their own American settlement at Demopolis. These found St. Stephens "a place of some size, with refined and lively inhabitants." A number of the earlier most noted public men of Alabama, who became lawyers, judges, senators, congressmen, coming as young men from the older States, began here their prosperous public career. But in 1820 Cahawba on the Alabama became the new capital, and St. Stephens remained only as a county-seat, a place of trade and commerce, as being at the head of sloop navigation, and the seat of the United States land office. It is claimed that at this period it contained five thousand inhabitants. Others place the population at fifteen hundred. In 1821 decline began. The best buildings, built of brick, of stone, and of the characteristic fine white limestone of the region, were removed to Mobile. Another locality was selected even for the county seat, and about thirty years ago, as a dwelling place of the living, St. Stephens ceased to exist. As few state capitals in this broad land have become what this locality now is, let us look at this spot as it now appears.

In April of 1881, as a Southern tourist, it was my privilege to visit what is now called Old St. Stephens. The locality is on the west bank of the river, one hundred and twenty miles by water from Mobile, on the top of a large limestone bluff, one hundred or more feet in height, with walls of solid limestone down to the bed of the river. Honey bees for many years made their homes in the crevices of the rock, storing their honey out of the reach of man. Red cedar trees are abundant, skirting the edge of this rocky height, and back of these are pines and oaks, the locality of most of the old town being now well wooded. The following sentences are extracts from the journal record made in that solitude. April 12. "The flowers of spring are here, even the yellow blossoms of the sorrel; the birds are here; the pleasant breeze, the sunshine and the shadows, for the day is not cloudless, the ever-flowing river, these all are here, as they were in the almost forgotten years; as in the years when on this height, where now I am alone, the youth and maidens walked in the cool of

eventide; where but a little way from here were heard
the merry voices of childhood, as boys and girls were
playing in the now almost obliterated streets; where the
hum of business from thirty stores was heard at midday;
and where at nightfall mothers gathered their little ones
in, and heard their prayers, and laid them to rest on
their white couches, and night settled down over the
town and the stars above gave light. But now solitude,
grandeur, gloom, with the uncorrupted and undefiled
magnificence and beauty of nature reign here."

"A pathway leads across the site of the old town.
The long line of what was probably the principal street
is yet distinct. The rock foundations remain of many
buildings that were probably showy and imposing in
their day. Nearly every trace of any wood work has
disappeared."

Besides the yellow blossoms mentioned above I found
in some places the rich green sward of the former streets
and gardens and court-yards literally blue with some of
the spring flowers of the South, and the warm, bright
sunshine, then mantling everything with its own love-
liness, made the day in those lone woods delightful.
The old cemetery, where some distinguished and many
nameless dead are sleeping, I found to be a place for instructive meditation. It is on a high broad ridge, a
roomy spot, as was fitting for a city burial ground. Many
memorial stones are there.

Five or six building spots can still be identified.
These are the localities of the Spanish fort, of the American fort and trading house, of the Crawford family
mansion (the memorial monument standing near having
cost five thousand dollars), of the old brick bank, and
of the St. Stephens' Academy, the foundations of which
I discovered in a field on a hill-top, a breezy and pleasant spot for study for the light-hearted and beautiful
southern girls of seventy years ago.

This was the first chartered academy in what became
Alabama, having been chartered in 1811, the first American school in Alabama, so far as is known, having been
opened in this chain of river settlements in 1799.

An extract from the journal, April 13, says: "The
family homes and the business houses standing upon

the rock foundations which I observed yesterday, and upon the little earth hillocks, and along the lines of those dimly outlined streets among the pines and cedars and deciduous trees, cannot be specified by names. Little remains here of the works of man above the surface of the earth except the hard, dark-gray limestone rock, the brick work, and the memorial marble. French, Spanish, British, and American, and the long Indian times, have passed over this apparently sightly and attractive spot, but no human being dwells here now." As I was waiting that day for a steamboat at the landing below the bluff, some hunters brought in two wild turkeys which they had just shot on the grounds of the old capital.

Such is old St. Stephens now. Once containing, probably, a French, certainly a Spanish, and a noted American fort; a center of trade, when the nineteenth century was opening, for the brown Choctaws; a commercial town and cotton market for the early American settlers in South Alabama; for a time a gay capital, where the second newspaper of the present Alabama was started in 1814, the first steamboat company incorporated in 1818, where was a bank, and an academy, and busy life; and now surrendered back to nature to be re-clothed in all her new and fresh and ever beautiful forms.

Not soon shall I forget the physical and intellectual enjoyment of those two days in the cheerful solitudes of Old St. Stephens. T. H. B.

INDIAN NAMES.

I had proposed to give here the meaning of a number of Indian names to be found in this book; but learning from a correspondence with Mrs. Robertson of Indian Territory, that, while many names have meanings easily recognized, the meanings of others, if they have any, elude careful study; and learning from the writings of Mr. George Catlin, the great Indian painter, (who visited forty-eight tribes and secured about six hundred paintings,) that "a great proportion of Indian names admit of no translation," I abandoned the attempt.

Referring to a number of "proper names of tribes," Mrs. Robertson says that "the meaning is uncertain." And Mr. Catlin says that many names can no more be translated than can the English names of Jones, or Bailey, or Roberts, and other such names. He also says that interpreters often join to the names some qualifications for which the individuals are distinguished as Oondischta, the salmon-spearer, as we would designate in English, "Jones, the shoemaker, or Jones, the butcher," etc. But these designations are not the meanings of the Indian names, as we know they are not of the English. Mr. Catlin further says "that most Indians of celebrity have a dozen or more names, which they use according to caprice or circumstances." One statement may be of interest here in regard to general "Indian Nomenclature." Changes have been made in names of tribes since the published lists of names of 1822 and 1832, especially in the Office of Indian Affairs at Washington as names have been corrected and approved by Major J. W. Powell, chief of the Bureau of Ethnology. Major Powell says that a single name was often applied to different tribes, and he accounts for it, in part, from the fact that "the names for gentes, tribes, and comfederacies were confounded." See Smithonian Report for 1885.   T, H. B.

INDIAN BORDER WARS.

The list of Indian wars here given is not complete, but the principal ones are probably named. Those only are mentioned that were within the present United States. When the first settlements were made by the whites on the Atlantic coast, of course the " border " line was then there. As settlements have gone across to the Pacific, the line has been constantly changing.

1. The Virginian Indian War, commencing at noon, March 12, 1622, when three hundred and fifty

whites were massacred, and continuing till the Virginia Indians were exterminated.

2. The Pequod or Pequot War, 1637, ending in their extermination.

3. King Philip's War, 1675, lasting three years.

4. The Tuscarora War, 1712, in North Carolina, beginning, as did the war in Virginia, with a massacre of whites.

5. The French and Indian wars, or Indian wars, instigated by the French, from 1688 till the Revolution, particularly in New Hampshire, extending with some intervals of peace, through a period of eighty years. Says Ramsey: "The colony of New Hampshire was among the greatest sufferers from Indian wars."

6. The Maryland Indian War, commenced in 1642 and lasted for several years.

7. The Janodoa Indian War, also in Maryland, in 1662.

8. The Yamassees War in South Carolina from 1715 to 1718, commencing with a massacre.

9. Cherokee wars in South Carolina from 1755 to 1763. Also 1776.

10. The general French and Indian War, 1755. Says Ramsay: "These wars took place, more or less, along the whole western frontier of the colonies, from New Hampshire to Georgia, and from the year 1690 to the peace of Paris, 1763. Through that wide range, and for that long period of seventy-three years, with occasional intermissions, Indian hostilities, fomented by the French in the north and the Spaniards in the south, disturbed the peace and stinted the growth of the English colonies." And Venable says:

"In these early French and Indian wars 30,000 colonial soldiers perished, and $16,000,000 were expended."

11. Pontiac's War, 1763.

12. Expeditions in 1779 destroying the Onondago settlements in April; in August and September ravaging the Mohawk country—"the quantity of corn destroyed was immense," orchards were cut down, gardens laid waste;—and, also in August, an expedition from South Carolina against the Indians on their fron tier, destroying the corn of eight towns and driving

further back the Indians. Also, in August and September an expedition against the Mingo, Munsey, and Seneca Indians, destroying "five hundred acres of corn."

13.   Another Cherokee War, 1781; General Pickens leading three hundred and ninety-four horsemen burned thirteen towns and villages in fourteen days.

14.   Massacre of the Moravian towns by the whites, cruel and unprovoked, in 1782. Avenged in part by the Delawares, Wyandots, and other Indians, who met the whites on their way to destroy the Indian towns near Sandusky.

15.   Kentucky Indian War in the days of Daniel Boone, from 1769 to 1782.

16.   The Shawnee and Miami Indian War, General Harmar and General Arthur Saint Clair defeated, General Wayne victorious, 1790 to 1795.

In these various and constantly recurring wars there was much cruelty manifested on the part of Indians. And, says Ramsay, "On the other hand, there have been instances of justice, generosity, and tenderness, during these wars, which would have done honor to a civilized people." "They would sometimes carry children on their arms and shoulders; feed their prisoners with the best of their provisions; and pinch themselves rather than their captives should want food. When sick or wounded, they would afford them comfort and means for their recovery. But the most remarkably favorable circumstance in an Indian captivity was their decent behavior to women. There is no evidence that any woman who fell into their hands was ever treated with the least immodesty; but testimonies to the contrary are very frequent. Whatever may be the cause the fact is certain; and it was a most happy circumstance for female captives that, in the midst of all their distresses, they had no reason to fear from a savage foe the perpetration of a crime which has too frequently disgraced, not only the personal, but the national character of those who make large pretences to civilization and humanity."—Ramsay, Vol. I., page 289.

The same kind of testimony is given by Luzerne Ray in "Indian Miscellany," page 292. He says: "During the wars which he so frequently and fiercely waged against the whites, many of their wives and daughters were taken captive and carried into his own country. Although these prisoners were entirely at his disposal; although they were subject to insult and injury of every other kind; there is yet no instance recorded of the perpetration of that violence which female virtue reckons worse than death."

We now enter the nineteenth century.

17. Tecumseh's War, 1811.
18. The Creek War of 1813 and 1814.
19. The First Seminole War, 1817.
20. The Black Hawk War, 1832.
21. The Second Seminole War, from 1834 to 1842. In this war Osceola became noted.
22. The Creek War of 1836.
23. The Indian War or "Indian Trouble," in Oregon and Washington, 1855, 1856.
24. The Modoc War of 1872 and 1873.
25. The Sioux War of 1876.

The raid of the Cheyennes or Shiyans of 1878 in Kansas and Nebraska, and troubles with other Indians in these later years are not here enumerated.

Thus, for a hundred and fifty years of colonial times, and through a hundred years of national life, wars with the Indians have been carried on; and the end is not yet. The origin of the aborigines or Red Men of these United States, so different in some respects as they are from all the other great divisions of the human family, is yet unknown; but their extermination seems to be written all over the land in characters of blood. Nothing, apparently, can save the scanty remnants of the broken tribes that yet remain but the protection, the mercy, the grace of God. In a Christian civilization rests their only hope of avoiding a complete and utter extinction in the broad land of their forefathers.

T. H. B.

Population of the Five Indian Nations, furnished by Mrs. A. E. W. Robertson, of Muscogee, Indian Territory, February, 1895.

NAMES.	Indians.	Freedmen	Total.
Creek..........................	9 291	5,341	14,632
Choctaw	9,996	4,401	14,397
Chickasaw	3,464	3,718	7,182
Cherokee......................	25,357	4,242	29,599
Seminoles.....................	2,539	22	2,561
	50,647	17,724	68,371

CARD OF THANKS.

Having had the responsibility and also the mental pleasure of seeing this book " through the press," of aiding in the proof reading, and of seeing to the "make up," as well as bearing a part of the responsibility of authorship, I wish here to recognize some special obligations and to return some special thanks. First of all I may mention the great courtesy and kindness shown by the different ones connected with the large printing establishment of Messrs. Donohue & Henneberry, who are not only publishers, but who carry on one of the very largest printing and binding houses of the country and of the world. I return thanks to them. And I return special thanks to the astronomer of the Harvard College Observatory, to Mr. H. W. Beckwith, to Mrs. B. B. Cheshire, to General T. J. Morgan and his officials in the Indian Bureau, to Mr. Charles Weatherford, to Mrs. Peebles, to Mr. Barron of Montgomery, to Mrs. A. E. W. Robertson, to Judge H. Austill, to Mr. Isaac Grant, to Rev. J. H. Creighton, and to my nephew, young Jamie Chapman, of Jackson, Alabama, the last one named having procured for me the likeness of Mr.

Isham Kimbell. Also I return thanks to the post-master at Burnt Corn for the use of a history of Conecuh county and to Capt. P. D. Bowles of Evergreen. Also to Col. J. W. Portis of Suggsville. For special courtesies I return thanks to the Librarian of the State Library at Indianapolis, the Librarian of the Illinois Historical society, and to the lady in charge at the Newberry Library of Chicago. Some of these may possibly not be living when this book passes out from the hands of the binders, but so far as I know, at the date of this writing, they are all where words of recognition and of thanks can reach them.   T. H. BALL.

BOOK NOTICES.

ANNIE B., THE DYING GIRL. A small, handsomely bound book, of **48 pages**, on heavy white paper, edges all gilded. Price **by mail, 50 cents**. A beautiful gift book.

The following are some notices which have reached the author: 1. From the *Hammond Tribune*, "Book Notes. 'Annie B., the Dying Girl,' from the pen of Rev. T. H. Ball, of Crown Point, Indiana, is a dramatic poem with a purpose and an excellent purpose at that. As the title shows, it is a story told in verse, of a young girl whose young life is slowly ebbing away. In it four life-like characters figure: An old gray-haired family physician, the spiritual adviser, Annie B., and her faithful lover, Edward G."

"To tell the story which runs through the work one would have to quote the entire poem. Suffice it to say that it is seldom so much of poetic and dramatic interest centers on a young woman as in 'Annie B.' It is a tender, clean and interesting poem well told and worthy of reading. There is food for deeper thought in the story, and it will be found by serious readers to be the breath and finer spirit of a thoughtful man, and to carry with it a noble lesson of human sympathy and lofty ideals of mind and of duty "

2. From the President of Franklin College. "'Annie B.' came to hand yesterday, and I read it at a sitting. It is an excellent little poem."

3. From W. H. Levering, former President of Indiana S. S. Union. "The little volume, 'Annie B., the Dying Girl', came, and I have read it with pleasure and profit. It is a beautiful lesson, drawn from a beautiful life, beautifully told, and will be a beautiful legacy to youth when thou art called 'to mansions in the skies.' It is also a beautiful souvenir. * * * Mrs. Levering joins me in warm regard and best wishes. She has read 'Annie B.' and gives high commendation."

4. From Miss B. B., of Chicago. Referring to the book she writes: "I really think I received more good from it than any other book besides the Bible. I read it over and over, and thank you very much for sending it to me."

5. From Mrs. C. A.: "I read it all through soon after it was brought home. It is a lovely poem."

6. From Mrs. M. E. C., of Alabama: "It is surely a beautiful poem, so full and expressive. It is numbered with my treasures."

7. From Mrs. M. H. C., of Alabama: "The story and its teachings are beautiful—even the binding, the type, the finish is lovely. * * * We all have enjoyed reading it. Hope the author will live to write many such good thoughts."

8. From Miss L. W. "I am delighted with it, and think the book will do much good."

THE GUIDANCE OF THE HOLY SPIRIT IN INTERPRETING SCRIPTURE. By T. H. Ball. This is a pamphlet, pages 25, paper cover, price by mail 20 cents.

Says Rev. Dr. Hovey, President of Newton Theological Institution: "'This is an excellent discussion, full of 'sweetness and light.' I do not see how it could be improved in substance or form or temper. * * * The subject examined is one of peculiar interest at the present time, and the treatment of it is at once vigorous, direct, and solid."

THE LAKE OF THE RED CEDARS. By T. H. Ball.
Pages 357, 12mo. Price, by mail, 75 cents.

1. From the *Journal and Messenger :* " The glimpse
of the home at the lake is a charming one. The book
is written in a clear, straightforward style, by one evidently accustomed to the use of the pen."

2. From the *Sunday School Times :* " It gives much
interesting information, chiefly of a denominational and
local character."

NOTES ON LUKE'S GOSPEL. By T. H. Ball. Pages 120,
well bound, price 50 cents.

The press notices of this book are not now at hand.
It differs from all other commentaries in this, that it
makes a point in every chapter to discriminate between
general and limited or special teachings.

A GLANCE INTO THE GREAT SOUTHEAST, or Clarke
County, Alabama, and its Surroundings. From 1540
to 1877. Number of pages 782.

A few copies of this large work may yet be obtained
from Mrs. E. H. Woodard, Grove Hill, Alabama.
Price by mail $2.50.

Any of the other books can be obtained by sending to
T. H. Ball, Crown Point, Indiana.

THE CREEK WAR OF 1813 AND 1814.

In Alabama send orders to White, Woodruff & Fowler,
Montgomery.

Those elsewhere send to Donohue & Henneberry, but
address all orders or inquiries " Creek War," Box 79,
Crown Point, Indiana, and they will receive prompt
attention. Single copies sent by mail to any address on
receipt of $1.50. Address as above.

The Following ADDRESS or PAPER is placed here for Citizens of Alabama.

HISTORICAL PAPER.

PREPARED FOR THE ALABAMA HISTORICAL SOCIETY
JUNE, 1883.

I closed up my last work as a teacher in Clarke county, Alabama, in the summer of 1883. I was hoping to attend the annual meeting of the Historical Society at Tuscaloosa that summer, and so prepared a paper or an address which I expected to have the privilege of reading. I was disappointed in regard to attending that anniversary; so the address was laid away and ten years have passed along. I have not been able to revisit Alabama since, but having received many courtesies and kindnesses there, and feeling that I have much interest in common with the historical writers and literary men of Alabama, I take the liberty to place this historical paper here, as a prepared but unread address, hoping that it will prove an acceptable contribution to the interests which it was designed to promote.

T. H. B.

Crown Point, 1893.

NOTE.—I find on a final reading of electrotype proof the word Maubila printed Manbila. Please read all through this paper Maubila.

Not far from the center of the county of Clarke, in the State of Alabama, is a beautiful landscape.

Born as I was in the most fertile portion of the Connecticut River Valley, in the heart of New England, nine miles south of Mount Tom, amid the historic towns of North-Hampton and Springfield, Westfield and Chicopee, in what is now the Indian named town of Agawam, a descendant of Puritans and Huguenots, with ancestral homes going back to 1640,—it is quite possible that this landscape possesses more attractions for me because it includes what was the Bassett's Creek Valley home from 1835 to 1855, of an Alabama maiden, whose destiny thenceforward was to be linked in with mine for life, and, perhaps, in some sort, forever.

Nevertheless, that landscape view is beautiful, aside from all personal or all historical associations. And as I have stood on its western height, near the site of the old Fort Sinquefield, in spring time, in summer, and in autumn, and have looked eastward over the two slopes, and along the Bassett's Creek valley, looking upon the varied green hues of long-leaf pine and short-leaf pine, of the rich vegetable growth of the creek bottom, especially when an October sun was pouring its warmth and brightness down upon every growing and living thing, and upon the sand and gravel and clay beds and rock that characterize this region, mantling everything with the brightness and beauty of sunlight,—I have thought of the historic interest connected with this then bright landscape; a landscape amid the scenes of which there dwelt three hundred and fifty years ago the sisters of the beautiful dancing girls who fought and fell at old Manbila; within sight of the eastern crest of which passed in 1540 Spanish invaders; where afterwards came French traders; then Creek and Choctaw Indian strife reddened the hillsides; and at length came children of American pioneers, whose young hearts were upwards drawn " by influence sweet," and who learned to send their fervent prayers upward to the eternal throne: but where, especially in September of 1813, soon after the horrible massacre at Fort Mims, Indian atrocities were experienced and peculiar incidents occurred.

But before we examine the spots reddened in 1813 with blood, let us look away in thought from the eastern height toward the blue line of the winding Alabama. Between us and that not very distant blueish-green wood, in October of 1540, there might have been seen strange looking bands of warrior men loitering and hastening southward. Who and what were they? De Soto, Hernando or Ferdinand De Soto, of Spain, and Tuskaloosa, the Alabama Tuskaloosa, and their followers.

To introduce the few statements which I wish to make concerning the great battle of 1540, allow me to present a few words from some historical writers.

Quackenbos, in his school history, a work used in Alabama, says of De Soto, page 56, "Landing at Tampa Bay with six hundred chosen men clad in complete armor, he marched boldly into the wilderness in search of gold and slaves." On page 57 he says, "In the fall of 1540 the invaders found themselves on the site now occupied by the city of Mobile." And here Quackenbos says that the great battle took place in which twenty-five hundred natives were killed. And this is taught to many of the children of Alabama as true American history.

That De Soto and his men were not in the fall of 1540 where is now the city of Mobile it is needless at present to attempt to show. The question with which I am now concerned is, Was that battle of 1540 in the present limits of Clarke county?

Charles Gayarre says, referring to "two ponderous volumes" in which "the historian relates the thousand incidents of that romantic expedition," "one thousand men of infantry and three hundred and fifty men of cavalry fully equipped were landing in proud array under the command of Hernando De Soto" at Tampa Bay, May 31, 1539.

It is a little singular that from the same authorities, if authorities there are, writers should differ so widely in regard to the number of that invading force. But they differ also in regard to the death of De Soto, Quackenbos stating that he died on the bank of the Mississippi among the Natchez Indians, and that "The surviving Spaniards wandered as far south as the forests and plains of Texas, turned their course north and * * * reached the Mississippi River near the mouth of the Red." Here, he states, they built some boats and went down the river; and T. B. Thorpe asserting that De Soto himself embarked in the "rude brigantines" already constructed further up, and died at the mouth of Red River. Gayarre agrees with Thorpe in representing De Soto's death as taking place at the mouth of Red River, but whether before or after the boats were built he does not say. Is it not possible for historians to reach something more accurate than such conflicting accounts? And shall we, rejecting both these, accept the representation of our own Pickett that De Soto having reached the Mississippi River in May, 1541, returned to the river from his western wanderings in the latter part of May, 1542, below the mouth of the Arkansas River, that engaging in the construction of two brigantines he there died, and that Morcoso with the remaining troops left the river June 1, in order to reach Mexico through the western wilderness, and failing in that returned to the Mississippi in December 1542, fifty miles above where DeSoto died, and building there seven brigantines departed down the river in July, 1543.

Returning to the expedition of DeSoto and the battle of 1540; I give one more quotation. Stephens says, in his Pictorial History of the United States, page 169, "The number of his followers is not definitely stated; Bancroft says, 'they were a numerous body of horsemen, besides infantry, completely armed; a force exceeding in number and equipments the famous expeditions against the empires of Mexico and Peru.'" Now, unless Bancroft had some idea of the actual number of DeSoto's men, how could he know they exceeded in number the followers of Cortes and Pizarro ? And when Stephens says the number is not definitely stated, he means by whom? Surely Pickett states the number very definitely, and so do Quackenbos and Gayarre. And what was Pickett's authority? What was Bancroft's? I raise here two questions the examination of which will comprise all I may take time to say about the events of 1540.

Is there sufficient evidence to authorize the historians of
Clarke to claim that on her soil was fought the great battle of Manbila, October 18, 1540? And further, have we
sufficient evidence that there ever was such a battle? ever
an expedition headed by DeSoto? ever a discovery of the
Mississippi before the days of the explorers from France?
Some examination of the second question is needful in
answering the first.   I crave a little indulgence in re-
peating some foundation principles.   History is written
either by eyewitnesses or by those who get their knowledge from the same as eyewitnesses, at second, third, or
fourth hand.   There may be many removes, but all
common history must go back at last for its authority
to those who stood as actors or eyewitnesses of the events.
An acknowledged, received Gospel history, even, speaks
of the things most surely believed among the early
Christains "even as they delivered them unto to us,
which from the beginning were eyewitnesses."   Now,
whoever proposes to give historic facts out of his own
range of knowledge, or which took place before his own
day, must have as his authority one or many between
himself and the events which he records or transmits.
Stephens refers to Bancroft. Bancroft had between himself and DeSoto one or more.   Going no further in this
line of thought I inquire, who are the eyewitnesses, or
who give us the words of the eyewitnesses in regard to
this Spanish expedition?   Pickett tells us that he procured from England and France three independent accounts of that expedition.   One was written by a
Portuguese, who accompanied DeSoto, a second was
written by Biedma, the commissary of DeSoto, and the
third by a Peruvian Inca, Garcellano De La Vega,
who obtained his knowledge from two journals kept
by some followers of De Soto, and from the lips of a
cavalier who was in the expedition.   Two of these are
original and one is a second hand account, one is Spanish and one is Portuguese testimony, and the third is
Spanish collected and transmitted by a Peruvian Span-
iard or a Spanish Peruvian.   Had Stephens anything
else ? Had Bancroft anything else ? Spanish records
may exist in regard to the expedition when leaving
Spain, when leaving Cuba, when the shattered remnant

returned to Cuba, but of the expedition itself is it not clearly the testimony of these or nothing ? The next question then would be concerning the credibility of these three documents. Are they entitled to our belief ? Are they, like the works of some American historians, colored, overdrawn ? And, if colored, how much? There are particulars in which I think we may detect some Spanish and Peruvian coloring, but as these do not concern my main question I leave them undisturbed, with only the passing remark, that if this La Vega, when his statements were examined and sifted, was good authority for Prescott in regard to the conquest of Peru, he is equally good for us in regard to De Soto. I claim here and now, that there is sufficient testimony, making what allowance we may for coloring, if we believe that De Soto was ever here at all, to believe that he led here a thousand men, and the very definitely stated number of at least two hundred and thirteen horsemen.

While I should like to pursue this question further, I leave it now for the other, the question of locality. Did the battle of Manbila, according to the Spanish account transmitted to us by Pickett, occurring October 18,1540, take place in what is now Clarke county? Can we of Clarke lay full claim to this as one of our recognized, historic events?

That De Soto and his men were at Tallasse on the Tallapoosa September 18, 1540, seems from the account of his expedition to be beyond doubt, and this Tallasse is a locality well established, as on the opposite side of the river the Muscogees built their town of Tookabatchee, preserving the name of Tallasse until their removal in 1836. Remaining at this old Indian town some twenty days, the Spanish invaders crossed the Tallapoosa and marched for some days down the eastern side of the river and came to its bank again, now having become the Alabama, when they crossed to the western side. Pickett refers to Biedma as saying that the forces of De Soto spent two days in crossing this river, and the locality of the crossing is not certainly known. It can only be conjectured. But the invaders were now certainly on the west side of the

Alabama, and judging from the time occupied on the march from Tallasse they must have been near or within the present county of Wilcox. They then marched southward three days, and on the morning of the fourth, October 18, they reached Manbila. And this large Indian town with an eastern and a western gate, was on a beautiful plain by the side of a large river, surely the same river which the Spaniards had crossed some four days before. And on this plain was "a large pool of delicious water fed by many springs." Where could this town have been, then, but in the present county of Clarke? The Spaniards were, as we now know, after they crossed the Alabama, between two quite large rivers, which finally coming together make a yet larger one the Mobile; and without crossing the Tombigbee or recrossing the Alabama, there was no possible advance southward beyond the limits of Clarke county. As the Spanish forces were thus shut in between two rivers, ignorant as they must have been of the geography of the region, we seem to be confined to the conclusion that Manbila was in the present county of Clarke, how-ever ignorant we may be of its precise locality. It was near the river, and from its having an eastern and a western gate it may be inferred that it stood upon a northern bank. Such a bank it is not difficult to find on the winding Alabama. Can the plain, can the springs and the pool of water be found? Wells and water pools may remain in the Orient unchanged for thousands of years; but in this western world, where we talk sometimes about "forests primeval," we cannot expect to find an Indian pool as it existed three hundred years ago. This is a land of change. The large water courses change, and new springs burst forth. But the plain may remain, although now it may be covered with a forest growth. There is not much vegetation in Clarke that is venerable with the growth of three hundred years. Our large pines have been growing something more than two hundred years. Our cypresses and cedars may some of them be older.

Two special localities have been selected as the proba-ble site of the old capital town of Tuskaloosa's dominions. In favor of one of these, the locality adopted by Pickett.

known as Choctaw Bluff, there are mainly some Indian traditions, or, as he says, "representations of aged Indians and Indian countrymen," that there the great battle was fought. Such representations are not to be lightly set aside. But in favor of the other locality, where is found the name Manbila on the map of Clarke, some different considerations are urged. The distance of either locality from Pensacola on the south, from the place where the Spaniards crossed the Alabama on the north, makes very little difference in the comparative claims of each, as they are only about nine miles apart, and from each locality to Pensacola in a straight line it is not more than seventy-five miles. The Peruvian and Portuguese chroniclers of the expedition computed the distance from Manbila to the Bay to be eighty-five miles. In favor of the locality marked Manbila, known also as French's Landing, are these considerations, the springs and streams at the two places being very much alike. (1) Spanish bridle-bits, many arrow heads, and much pottery have been found here. (2) There is here an old burial ground. Bones have been washed out from the bank, and parts of bones and well-preserved teeth have been found. (3) A great many bullets have been found here, at one time more than a peck measure full were found. (4) There is an artificial mound here, called an Indian mound, circular, some forty feet in diameter. These facts I obtained from County Commissioner J. M. Jackson, of Clarke county, a very reliable man, who lived on this spot for some years, and whom I visited in his home at Gainestown three miles southwest of this supposed Manbila.

To review that fierce and terrible battle is not a part of the design of this paper, but only to look for the battle-field and to lay claim to it, in behalf of the county of Clarke, forever, that is, as long as Alabama and American history shall endure.

This being accomplished, let us return to the western slope of the sheltered and beautiful Bassetts Creek Valley. Here is some true Alabama historic ground. Here was the Kimbell-James massacre of September 1, 1813; and here was the heroic defence of Fort Sinque-

field when attacked by Francis and his hundred warriors
on the next day of that same memorable and bloody
year.   And although that massacre was but one of a
thousand less or more of such atrocities committed by
American Indians on frontier white settlers from the
days of the Virginia colonists in 1609 to very recent
times, extending over New England, along the Atlantic
coast, in Kentucky when that was known as the dark
and bloody ground, and in Minnesota and the far West,
even over on the Pacific slope, yet, as one of a thousand, it has connected circumstances which give it in-
dividual interest in Alabama and Southeastern and
American history.   The historic incidents here may
therefore now be briefly reviewed and re-set.*   *   *

It is true that this is but one among many Alabama
historic spots.   I do not propose to claim for it anything
more than its real merit demands.   It is not where was
fought any of "the thirty battles" in that year of both
British and Indian strife.   It is not where any action
was performed to make for men a Thermopylæ or a
Bunker Hill forever.   I know the influence of such
spots.   In August, of 1881, alone in Charlestown, passing up the slope to the tall granite monument on that
hill which is now called Bunker, I met a Massachusetts
boy and talked with him about Warren and the British
of 1775; and perhaps an hour afterwards I took a wist-
ful little girl, a pleasant, winsome, stranger maiden, who
needed an attendant, to the top of that tower among
the throng of visitors, and enjoyed her emotion and de-
light as well as my own as we looked land-
ward and seaward from that great height.   I have walked
on the green sward at Lexington and have read the
names on the monumental stone of those who there fell on
that historic 19th of April. And I have stood where the
Kimbell and James families were massacred, where now
more fitting surroundings could not well be, and on the
site of the stockade fort, and have walked up and down
the long pathway to the Sinquefield spring, and I claim
that here events transpired making this one of the true

---

*As the Kimbell–James massacre has been given in thi:
work, it is omitted here.

historic spots of our land. The prophet Francis, leading a hundred warriors, was not like Weatherford with his thousand, nor like Xerxes with his million. But to the inmates of that stockade it meant death; and death by Indian barbarity, whether to many or to few, is no little thing. And right nobly, on the second day of September, 1813, was the Indian band repulsed. At Fort Mims there had been shameful neglect and recklessness. Here were the vigilant as well as the brave. And although the massacre of the two households was but one among a thousand, some of the incidents were certainly peculiar, and this was the only family massacre within this ellipse of fifty miles by thirty, as Sinquefield was the only one of these river settlement stockades attacked by the Indians after the fall of Fort Mims. Therefore, in Alabama annals, its name must be perpetually preserved. When a September, or still better an October sun, a few hours before nightfall, is shining over this landscape region, then is it a fitting time to go down the western slope, to cross the rippling brook, still shaded as of yore with the native lowland growth, a foliage so rich in its semi-tropical luxuriance, listening for a moment to the flow of the cooling waters over the pebbles, and then going up near the elevation where stood the Creighton home, to look southward into the dark pine grove, where once was the dwelling of the Kimbells. And that sudden onslaught of the Indians there was—or will be when September comes—just seventy years ago. In only thirty years from now, in 1913, will be the first centennial of the events of that memorable year. I do not expect to be here then: but I have an only son who, if he lives, will be then just where I am now in life, not yet past its prime; and he, loving the beautiful, the good, the heroic, the true historic, will be ready to stand in his father's place in whatever may be in Alabama the celebrations of that year.

(Surely in thirty years from now we shall be a nation of Americans. We shall have learned anew what forty-five years ago, in this place I think, Judge Meek so beautifully expressed in his poem, "The Day of Freedom," "To love alike all portions of our land." Dear to me is the favored region where I was born, in the old

Bay State, in that rich valley of wealth and crowded cities ; dear also to me is that milder southern valley where was born that maiden referred to in this paper ;* and very dear to me is the Lake of the Red Cedars where my youth was spent, and where was born that only son: but on every spot of American soil I look with interest as a part of my country, my own native land, on every historic spot I tread with emotion, on every beautiful landscape I look with gratitude and love, a love which, I trust, for all the blessings we so richly share, goes in its fullness up to God.)

I repeat that in thirty years from now there will be for us a centennial year. And as there are very few living, even now, among us who can relate as eye witnesses the events of 1813, and soon there will be not one, what I propose for us of Clarke is: first, that we teach the children of the State that the great Indian battle of 1540, with its disastrous results, was fought, not where is now the city of Mobile, but in that triangular region known as the county of Clarke; and then, that some suitable granite monuments or marble slabs, something less perishable than wood, be placed where they may perpetuate the sad massacre, the brave repulse of September 1st and 2d, 1813, and the spot at Bashi where Colonel McGrew and his brave men fell, so that they may tell to the passing traveller and to the inquiring visitor, when there is no human tongue to speak, here is historic ground; here fell the helpless, and here fought and fell the brave.

And to the members of this Historical Society of Alabama I have only to add, that while we of Clarke do claim the battle-ground of certainly one of the most fierce and bloody and destructive conflicts ever waged with Indians in North America; and also claim to have made with our cordon of stockades and our pioneer soldiers a resolute and successful defense on the "edge of the storm," when Muscogee ferocity threatened the entire destruction of the Alabama River, Tombigbee, and Tensaw settlers; we are well aware that the fierce conflicts of 1813 were fought on other ground; and we

---

*Martha C. Creighton.

trust that your efforts will result in securing and placing in imperishable form the records pertaining both to peace and to conflict, to suffering and to success, which are yet to be obtained in various parts of our great State; and thus you will transmit to the coming generations the worthy deeds of pioneers and faithful toilers through the first hundred years of Alabama American occupancy. Gentlemen of this society, citizens of Alabama, let not the memory of such deeds pass away into forgetfulness. For we are drawing nearer and nearer to the time when worthy human actions, instead of being buried in the dark night of oblivion forever, will be set forth before the intelligent universe in the bright light of an eternal day.

INDEX.

The nature of this work does not seem to require a very full index of the various items that make up each chapter, and the interest of the readers will, probably, be best promoted by following the order of the pages instead of arranging the particulars in alphabetical order.

INDEX.

INDEX.

EDITOR'S NOTES.

1. DeSoto in all likelihood found some Muscogee Indians, but Halbert and Ball probably assume too much in stating that nations such as the Choctaw and Creek existed in 1540. Most evidence indicates that the nations of Indians developed from more fragmented earlier groups.

2. The origin of the Uchees is still a mystery, and some recent theories even link them with Mediterranean or European cultures.

3. Alliances with the southern Indians were always used as part of the Spanish plan of defense. Spanish policy was to keep the Indians, especially the Creeks, strong enough to protect their own land against the Americans but not so strong that they would initiate a conflict. When the United States illegally purchased Louisiana, invaded Mobile, and supported filibustering in East Florida, most Spanish officials considered all of Florida to be under attack and encouraged the Indians to fight the United States. The Spanish in Florida had few supplies themselves, so they were able to furnish the Indians with only meager amounts of powder and shot. See: A. P. Whitaker, *The Spanish American Frontier 1783–1795*, pp. 201–222; Frances Kathryn Harrison, "The Indians as a Means of Spanish Defense of West Florida 1783–1795," unpublished master's thesis, University of Alabama (1950). See also: Mauricio de Zuñiga to Juan Ruiz Apodaca, Apr. 18, 1813, Legajo 1794; Apodaca to the Minister of War, Aug. 6, 1813, Legajo 1856; Minister of War, Aug. 6, 1813, Legajo 1856; Paples de Cuba, Archivo General de Indias, Seville, Spain.

4. British influence among the Creek Indians remained strong long after the Revolutionary War. The basis of the influence was trade with the Bahamas and Jamaica carried on both legally and illegally for some time after 1783. See: J. Leich Wright, Jr., "British Designs on the Old Southwest: Foreign Intrigue on the Florida Frontier 1783–1803," *The Florida Historical Quarterly*, 44 (April, 1966), pp. 265–284.

5. There is no doubt that local British officials aided and encouraged Tecumseh and other Indians who might decide to follow a course of hostility toward the United States. However, until the actual outbreak of war between the United States and England, these officials, both in Canada and the Bahamas, apparently never put into writing any call for an Indian attack.

Any support the British may have given the Indians along such lines was probably given orally by local officials and was unknown in London until after the start of the war. See: Frank L. Cwsley, Jr., "British and Indian Activities in Spanish West Florida during the War of 1812," *The Florida Historical Quarterly*, 46 (October, 1967). See also: W. V. Munnings to Lord Liverpool, Dec. 12, 1811, CO 23, vol. 58; Charles Cameron to Earl Bathurst, Oct. 28, 1813, CO 23, vol. 60; Bathurst to Cameron, Jan. 21, 1814, CO 24, vol. 17, Public Record Office, London, England.

6.　George Colbert and his family were important leaders in the Chickasaw nation. The Colberts were almost white, fairly well educated, and pro-American throughout the war.

7.　As to whether the Choctaws fought DeSoto, there is considerable question whether a group of Muscogees who could be called Choctaws existed at the time of DeSoto. At any rate, Pushmataha was not entirely accurate in this statement because the French used the Choctaws as allies against the English and their Chickasaw allies.

8.　A few Choctaws actually did become hostile, but they were not allowed to rejoin their tribe. A small group of them was killed in the explosion of Negro Fort at Apalachicola in 1816. See also: Duncan L. Clinch to R. Butler, Aug. 2, 1816, in James Grant Forbes, *Sketches Historical and Topographical of the Floridas; Most Particularly of East Florida*, pp. 203–204 (Gainesville, 1964) [reprint of New York 1821 edition].

9.　Not only were the Shawnees unable to win support from this faction of the Choctaws, but the young men of this group eventually served in the American military forces.

10.　John McKee, Choctaw agent, considered Pitchlyn and Folsom two of his most valuable aids.

11.　After Tecumseh made his visit to the South, some Creeks followed him back to Canada, where they were instructed as prophets and where they met with some British officers. One party of Creeks was led by Little Warrior, who was given a letter for the Spanish commander at Pensacola. When Little Warrior returned south in 1812, he brought a number of Shawnees with him. It is not unlikely that Little Warrior's return or the return of some other party of Creeks from Canada was the source of the rumor that there had been another visit by Tecumseh.

12.　Even as late as 1812 some Indians did not seem to be able to decide whether they were Creeks or Seminoles, and certainly there was always good communication between the groups. Therefore, it seems very probable that there were Seminoles at the Tuckabatchee meeting when Tecumseh spoke. However, British influence among both the Lower Creeks and Seminoles came more from the Bahamas than from Canada. See: J. Leitch Wright, Jr., *William Augustus Bowles Director General of the Creek Nation* (Athens, 1967).

13. Big Warrior's early interest in Tecumseh's cause is also confirmed in George Stiggins, "History of the Creek Nation," Manuscript in Georgia, Alabama, and South Carolina Papers, MSS I–V, Lyman Draper Manuscript Collection, State Historical Society of Wisconsin, Madison, Wisconsin.

14. Tecumseh probably received information concerning the comet from British officers at Malden rather than Detroit, and he might have obtained this knowledge at any time, not necessarily immediately before his southern trip. No one could have predicted the earthquake. Probably Tecumseh was lucky.

15. There is, of course, no way of finding exactly what Tecumseh did say, but certainly the Creeks who followed him, especially their prophets, such as Francis, were extremely brutal, murdering whites as well as Creeks who opposed them. See: Stiggins manuscript.

16. There was no reason for Tecumseh not to have used the comet to impress the southern Indians. He is known to have used extensive appeals to the supernatural through his prophets, and he could have easily learned from the British that a comet was due to appear.

17. Although Ball's information concerning Tecumseh seems to be fairly accurate, there are points of difference between his account and the Stiggins manuscript, and since Stiggins' information came from Creek rather than Choctaw sources, it should be the more accurate.

18. According to Stiggins, William Weatherford never intended to join the hostile element of the Creeks, but was forced to support them when the hostiles captured his family and threatened to kill them unless Weatherford became a Red Stick. Stiggins says that Weatherford joined, hoping to escape with his family, but no opportunity arose before the Fort Mims attack. After that he knew that the whites would never accept him.

19. Halbert corresponded extensively with Lyman C. Draper and furnished Draper with numerous accounts of the Indian

activity during the Creek War. See: the Lyman C. Draper Papers in the Wisconsin Historical Society and the Halbert Papers, Alabama Department of Archives and History, Montgomery, Alabama.

20. Ill health had forced Hawkins to curtail his travel during the few months prior to the war, and as a result he was not as well informed as he should have been. He always knew more about the Lower Creeks than the Upper Creeks because his agency was located among the Lower Creeks. He was probably misled by the fact that the Lower Creeks were much less influenced by Tecumseh than were the Upper Creeks.

21. Stiggins estimated that there were from two hundred and eighty to three hundred Indians on this expedition, and John Innerarity, a resident of Pensacola, agreed that there were around three hundred hostile Indians in this party. See: Stiggins manuscript and Elizabeth Howard West, "A Prelude to the Creek War of 1813–1814," *The Florida Historical Quarterly*, 18 (April 1, 1940), pp. 249–266.

22. The correct spelling of the Spanish governor's full name is Don Mattio Gonzales Manrique.

23. According to John Innerarity the Indians received more than a thousand pounds of powder and a supply of lead and other goods. In spite of this large supply of powder the Indians were dissatisfied because the Spanish would not furnish them with any guns or repair the guns they had brought with them. The Spanish responded to the Indian threats by mustering the entire garrison and militia of Pensacola. The Indians were much less hostile after this Spanish show of force.

24. Stiggins claims that only about sixty to a hundred hostiles reached the Burnt Corn area in time to participate in the battle. Of this number only thirteen had any kind of firearms. Panic among the white forces was a result of their belief that there were several hundred Indians in the woods. Accounts of Caller's actions vary. Stiggins seems to think Caller did as well as he could. However, one W. Lipscomb, a participant in the battle, said Caller was the first person to run and thus caused the panic.

25. Caller's command scattered after this fight, and as a result no really accurate count of dead and wounded was ever made. Stiggins, nevertheless, claims that five whites were killed and ten wounded. He also states that only two Indians were killed.

26.   It is strange, considering the other sources available to Halbert and Ball, that they chose to accept Pickett's figure of five hundred and fifty-three people being in Fort Mims at the time of the attack. Pickett's information came from the account of a single survivor, Dr. Thomas G. Holmes, given twenty-five to thirty years after the attack. Halbert and Ball refused to accept Judge Harry Toulmin's account because it was made before the burial party reached the fort and, therefore, they did not consider it accurate. Actually, it is probable that Toulmin's account was taken from the reports of survivors just as Pickett's was. However, since Toulmin's information was received only a few days after the attack and may have come from several eyewitnesses, it ought to be more accurate than that obtained by Pickett. As for the report of the burial detail which Halbert and Ball considered so important, Captain Joseph Kennedy, who buried the dead, claimed to have buried two hundred and forty-seven whites including men, women, and children, and about a hundred Indians. Generals Thomas Flournoy and Ferdinand L. Claiborne, who commanded the area, reported the loss at Fort Mims as around three hundred. Samuel D. Carrick at St. Stephens, who also apparently had information from eyewitnesses, claimed that there were between three hundred and fifty and four hundred people in Fort Mims. Since at least twenty to twenty-five escaped and a fairly large number were taken prisoner by the Indians, Carrick's figure would also be about three hundred killed.

27.   According to the Stiggins report, Weatherford scouted the fort the night before the attack and found the portholes close enough to the ground that they could be seized from outside. Weatherford laid hold to these portholes when the attack came, giving the Indians an advantage. He also no doubt found that the gate would not close.

28.   It is surprising that Halbert and Ball did not use Captain Kennedy's report, in which he claimed to have buried two hundred and forty-seven whites. The report was published in several places including *Niles Weekly Register*, supplement to vol. 8 (1815).

29.   The Creek War, especially in the Mississippi Territory, was a very "personal" war. Many settlers were half-breeds or at least had a close personal knowledge of the Creek Indians. Various Red Stick leaders were well known to, and in some cases were former friends of, the settlers. Because of these relation-

ships, the war had some aspects of a civil war. One special value in the work of Halbert and Ball is that they have preserved the spirit of the war, along with many eyewitness accounts that would have otherwise been lost.

30. The attack on Fort Sinquefield and the Kimbell–James massacre were not major disasters of the nature of the Fort Mims massacre, but the combination of events caused mass panic on the frontier. This alarm tended to keep all the white troops busy guarding frontier stockades and effectively prevented any offensive actions against the Red Sticks. It was especially unfortunate that the American troops could not take offensive action at that time since the hostile Indians were still adding recruits to their cause. Had the whites been able to pursue the Indians, many of those who eventually joined the hostile faction might have remained neutral, and the war might have been ended quickly.

31. Many people blamed General Claiborne for the Fort Mims massacre, which they somehow considered to have been caused by Claiborne's incompetence and his failure to provide enough military support for the forts. Actually this was not true, but Claiborne himself was so concerned about the safety of the forts that he apparently intended to consolidate a number of them. This doubtless accounted for the orders to Colonel Carson. Interestingly enough, because of Claiborne's efforts to guard the forts, he was forced into inactivity, which caused many people on the frontier and elsewhere to accuse him of cowardice.

32. This practice probably accounts for a number of the survivors of Fort Mims, since there were many Negroes there.

33. General Thomas Flournoy, commander of the Seventh Military District (of which Alabama and Mississippi were a part), was an extremely inept leader. During his brief control of the district, he managed to enrage the citizens of Louisiana and disrupt any plans for an adequate offensive against the Indians from the Mississippi Territory. He was apparently unable to get along with anyone.

34. The Choctaws' activities throughout the war showed them to be extremely well disciplined, probably more so than most of the white formations.

35. The significance of the Canoe Fight was that the white men won a clear-cut victory over a greatly superior force of Indians, after a series of Indian triumphs that must have caused many whites to believe that the Indians were invincible. This con-

quest was gained by sheer strength and courage and was fought
in the Indians' own style of warfare. Sam Dale became the much-
needed hero for the whites.

36. Like many another Indian trader, Sam Dale was not
always on the right side of the law. One reason for Dale's living
in the Mississippi Territory at the time of the outbreak of the
Creek War was the fact that Georgia officials wanted to arrest
him for smuggling illegal slaves and coffee into the United States
through Spanish Pensacola. See: the correspondence of the governor of Georgia.

37. Despite rumors throughout 1813 of British disbarkings
at Pensacola, there were no actual landings there until the
summer of 1814. Several English ships did put into Pensacola
during 1813, but none landed troops. The vessel referred to by
Colonel Bowyer was probably a ship commanded by Edward
Handfield, carrying a request for aid from the Creek Indians to
the governor of New Providence. This letter was instrumental
in bringing aid to the Indians in the summer of 1814. See: Charles
Cameron to Earl Bathurst, Oct. 28, 1813. CO 23, vol. 60, Public
Record Office.

38. Josiah Francis promised his followers that if a white man
crossed this line, he would immediately fall dead.

39. As Claiborne's army advanced, the Indians fired a few
rounds at the troops and confidently waited for them to advance
into the barrier and fall dead. The white men passed through
the barrier and did not die, and the faith of those Indians who
had believed in the Prophets' power was badly shaken. Josiah
Francis, although no warrior, had a fairly good escape route
planned by which he and his party managed to escape from the
area. The only real defense of the Holy Ground, other than a few
volleys fired by Francis's men, was made by William Weatherford
and about thirty of his men who had planned to fight from cover
in the style of the white man. From the start they had never
believed in the Prophets' barrier and thus were not panic-stricken
when it failed.

40. Some prejudice against the use of Negroes as warriors
may have existed among the Choctaws and Upper Creeks,
but the Lower Creeks and especially the Seminoles often used
black warriors.

41. Burning enemies at the stake may never have been a
Creek custom, but it was practiced by many of the northern

Indians. According to Stiggins, when the Shawnee Prophets came to the nation, the mobs who followed them did practice burning their enemies at the stake. However, Stiggins did not mention any burnings at the Holy Ground.

42.   The Burnt Corn battle did not cause the the Creek War, since the Indians were already bringing in arms with which to fight a war; however, it no doubt motivated many who were undecided to join the hostiles.

43.   General John Coffee did not spell his name Coffey.

44.   The Battle of Tallussahatchee was the first of Jackson's engagements of total destruction. All the Indian men were killed and the town and crops were completely destroyed. Jackson's concept of fighting the Indians was total war, and his destruction of their food supply was probably as much a cause of the final defeat of the Creeks as any of their battle losses.

45.   The Battle of Autossee was fought in much the same way as the Battle of the Holy Ground, and once again, because of the failure of certain units to reach their assigned position, the Indians were able to escape. It is probable that any one of the battles of Autossee, Holy Ground, and Talladega could have been as decisive as the Battle of the Horseshoe if the white troops had been able to get into their position and prevent the Indians' escape.

46.   Floyd's campaign ended at Calabee largely because his militia troops' term of enlistment had either expired or was about to expire; also, because he was out of food, the militia insisted on returning home. Actually, Floyd garrisoned Fort Hull with regular and militia forces under Colonel Homer Milton. This much of Floyd's gain was held. Milton joined forces with Jackson after the Battle of the Horseshoe.

47.   General Coffee estimated that in addition to the Indians found on the battlefield two hundred fifty to three hundred were killed in the river and their bodies lost. Some Indian accounts indicate that several hundred escaped during the night by floating down river. See: John Coffee to his wife Mary, Apr. 1, 1814, Coffee Papers, Tennessee Historical Society, Nashville, Tennessee; and G. W. Grayson Manuscript of 1917, p. 34, Eloise D. Smock Collection, University of Oklahoma, Norman, Oklahoma.

48.   The Spanish permitted this landing and the use of their facilities because they believed that the Americans would attack

and capture Pensacola any day. In such an event, all aid would be useful.

49. Major Uriah Blue succeeded in killing or capturing a number of hostile Indians in the area around the Escambia, but his supplies were exhausted before he came anywhere near accomplishing the complete destruction of the hostile Creek forces. Blue had to return to Mobile before he was able to come close to Apalachicola, the main British and Indian base on the Gulf Coast. Once his army reached Mobile, Blue and his command were taken under the orders of General James Winchester, who retained the troops in Mobile for its defense. Because of the importance of this British base at Apalachicola, Jackson ordered General John McIntosh of Georgia to detach part of his army to destroy the Indian base. McIntosh ordered a part of his army under Brigadier General David Blackshear to join some friendly Creeks under Benjamin Hawkins and attack and destroy the British base. Before Blackshear could move his troops against the British and Indians, however, his own orders were countermanded by the Governor of Georgia, and it was necessary to abandon the attack on Apalachicola. Thus it was that the war with the British ended with twenty-five hundred to three thousand well-armed, hostile Indians camped around a British-built fort at Apalachicola. In addition to these Indians there were five hundred or more Negroes, former slaves which the British had organized into a regiment of Black Colonial Marines. The whole force was commanded by Major Edward Nicolls of the Royal Marines and Captain George Woodbine, the British Indian Agent.

Because Article Nine of the Treaty of Ghent agreed to return all land lost by Indian allies of the British who were still fighting at the time the treaty was made, these Indians expected to see the Treaty of Fort Jackson nullified and their lands restored to them. The idea that the lands would be returned was supported by Admiral Alexander Cochrane, the senior British officer in North America, and by all of his subordinates. There is no doubt that this British encouragement, along with later visits to Florida by Woodbine and his young aid, Robert C. Ambrister, was a major factor in causing continuing hostility in the area until Jackson invaded Florida in 1818. See: Marquis James, *Andrew Jackson The Border Captain* (Indianapolis, 1933), p. 190; Benjamin Hawkins to Edward Nicolls, Mar. 24, 1815, *Niles Weekly Register*, June 24, 1815, vol. 8, pp. 285–287; Alexander Cochrane to Pultney Malcolm, "Special Indian Instructions," Feb. 17, 1815, WO 1, vol. 143, Public Record Office; Mark F. Boyd, "Events at Prospect Bluff on the Apalachicola River 1808–1818," *The Florida Historical Quarterly*, 14 (October, 1937); James W. Silver, *Edmund Pendleton Gaines Frontier General* (Baton Rouge, 1949).

EDITOR'S BIBLIOGRAPHY.

BOOKS CITED BY HALBERT AND BALL

Adair, James. *The History of the American Indians; Particularly Those Nations Adjoining to the Mississippi, East and West Florida, Georgia, South and North Carolina, and Virginia: Containing an Account of Their Origin, Language, Manners, Religious and Civil Customs, Laws, Form of Government, Punishments, Conduct In War and Domestic Life, Their Habits, Diet, Agriculture, Manufactures, Diseases and Methods of Cure.* London: E. and C. Dilly 1775.

Ball, T. H. *A Glance Into The Great South-East; Or, Clarke County, Alabama, And Its Surroundings From 1540 to 1877.* Tuscaloosa, Ala.: Willo Publishing Co., 1962.

Bancroft, George. *History of the United States of America, from the Discovery of the Continent.* New York: D. Appleton and Co.,1888.

Beach, William Wallace. Editor. *The Indian Miscellany: Containing Papers on the History, Antiquities, Arts, Languages, Religions, Traditions, and Superstitions of the American Aborigines; With Descriptions of their Domestic Life, Manners, Customs, Traits, Amusements, and Exploits: Travels and Adventures in the Indian Country: Incidents of Border Warfare: Missionary Relations, etc.* Albany: J. Munsell, 1877.

Brewer, Willis. *Alabama: Her History, Resources, War Record, and Public Men.* Montgomery: Barrett and Brown, 1872.

Brice, Wallace A. *History of Fort Wayne, from the Earliest Known Accounts of this Point, to the Present Period.* Fort Wayne, Indiana: D. W. Jones and Son, 1868.

Brownell, Charles De Wolf. *The Indian Races of North and South America.* Chicago: Hurlbut, Scranton and Co., 1864.

Claiborne, John Francis Hamtramck. *Life and Times of Gen. Sam Dale, The Mississippi Partisan.* New York: Harper and Brothers, 1860.

———. *Mississippi, as a Province, Territory and State, With Biographical Notices of Eminent Citizens.* Jackson, Miss.: Power and Barksdale, 1880.

Claiborne, Nathaniel Herbert. *Notes on the War in the South; With Biographical Sketches of the Lives of Montgomery, Jackson, Sevier, the Late Gov. Claiborne, and Others.* Richmond: William Ramsay, 1819.

Dawson, Moses. *A Historical Narrative of the Civil and Military Services of Major-General William H. Harrison, and a Vindication of his Character and Conduct as a Statesman, a Citizen, and a Soldier.* Cincinnati: M. Dawson, 1824.

Drake, Benjamin, *Life of Teumseh, and His Brother the Prophet: with a Historical Sketch of the Shawnoe |sic| Indians* Cincinnati: E. Morga and Company, 1841.

Drake, Francis S. *Indian History for Young Folks.* New York: Harper and Brothers, 1885.

Drake, Samuel G. *The Aboriginal Races of North America; Comprising Biographical Sketches of Eminent Individuals, and an Historical Account of the Different Tribes, from the First Discovery of the Continent to the Present Period.* Philadelphia: C. Desilver, 1860.

———. *Early History of Georgia, Embracing the Embassy of Sir Alexander Cuming to the Country of the Cherokees, in the Year 1730.* Boston: D. Clapp and Son, 1872.

———. *Indian Captivities; or Life in the Wigwam; Being True Narratives of Captives Who Have Been Carried Away by the Indians, from Frontier Settlements of the U. S. from the Earliest Period to the Present Time.* Auburn (state not given): Derby and Miller, 1850.

———. *The Old Indian Chronicle; Being a Collection of Exceeding Rare Tracts Written and Published in the Time of King Philip's War, by Persons Residing in the Country; to which are Now Added Marginal Notes and Chronicles of the Indians from the Discovery of America to the Present Time.* Boston: Antiquarian Institute, 1836.

Eaton, John Henry. *The Life of Andrew Jackson, Major-General in the Service of the United States: Comprising a History of the War in the South, from the Commencement of the Creek Campaign to the Termination of Hositilities Before New Orleans.* Philadelphia: S. F. Bradford, 1824.

Eggleston, George Cary. *Red Eagle and the Wars with the Creek Indians of Alabama.* New York: Dodd, Mead Company, 1878.

Frost, John. *The American Generals, from the Founding of the Republic to the Present-Time, Comprising Lives of the Great Commanders, and Other Distinguished Officers Who Have Acted in the*

Service of the United States: And Embracing a Complete Military History of the Country. Philadelphia: J. W. Bradley, 1848.

Gatschet, Albert Samuel. *A Migration Legend of the Creek Indians, With a Linguistic, Historic, and Ethnolographic Introduction.* 2 vols. Philadelphia: D. G. Brinton, 1884–88.

Gayarré, Charles. *History of Louisiana.* 4 vols. New York: William D. Widdon Publishers, 1866.

Goodrich, De Witt C. *An Illustrated History of the State of Indiana: Being a Full and Authentic Civil and Political History of the State from its First Exploration down to 1875.* Indianapolis: R. W. Peal and Co., 1875.

Goodwin, Philo A. *Biography of Andrew Jackson, President of the United States.* New York: R. H. Towner, 1833.

Hatch, William Stanley. *A Chapter of the History of the War of 1812 in the Northwest.* Cincinnati: Miami Printing and Publishing Company, 1872.

Irelan, John Robert. *The Republic; or, A History of the United States of America in the Administrations, from the Monarchic Colonial Days to the Present Times.* Chicago: Fairbanks and Palmer Publishing Co., 1886.

Jenkins, John Stillwell. *The Generals of the Last War With Great Britain.* Buffalo: G. H. Derby, 1849.

Latrobe, Charles Joseph. *The Rambler in North America.* New York: Harper Brothers, 1835.

Lossing, Benson John. *The Pictorial Field-Book of the War of 1812; or, Illustrations, by Pen and Pencil, of the History, Biography, Scenery, Relics, and Traditions of the Last War for American Independence.* New York: Harper and Brothers, 1868.

McAfee, Robert B. *History of the Late War In the Western Country.* Bowling Green, Ohio: 1919. Reprint from 1816 version Historical Publications Company.

McKenney, Thomas Loraine and James Hall. *The Indian Tribes of North America, with Biographical Sketches and Anecdotes of the Principal Chiefs.* Edinburgh: J. Grant, 1933–34.

Martyn, William Carlos. *The Pilgrim Fathers of New England: A History.* New York: (no publisher listed). 1867.

Milfort, Le Clerc. *Memoir ou Coup-D'oeil Rapide Sur Mes Differéns Voyages et Mon Séjour Dans La Nation Crěk.* Paris: Del'Impr. de Giguetet Michaud, 1802.

Moore, William V. *Indian Wars of the United States from the*

Discovery to the Present Time. Philadelphia: (no publisher listed), 1850.

Morgan, Lewis H. *A Study of the Houses of the American Aborigines; with Suggestions for the Exploration of the Ruins in New Mexico, Arizona, the Valley of the San Juan, and in Yucatan and Central America, Under the Auspicies of the Archaeological Institute.* Cambridge: Archaeological Institute of America Annual Report of the Executive Committee, 1880.

――――. *Houses and House-Life of the American Aborigines.* Washington: Government Printing Office, 1881.

Parton, James. *Life of Andrew Jackson.* 3 vols. Boston: Houghton, Mifflin and Co., 1887-88.

Pickett, Albert James. *History of Alabama, and Incidentally of Georgia and Mississippi, from the Earliest Period.* Charleston: Walker and James, 1851.

Prescott, William Hickling. *History of the Conquest of Peru, with a Preliminary View of the Civilization of the Incas.* New York: Harper Brothers, 1848.

Ramsay, David. *History of the United States, From Their First Settlement as English Colonies, in 1607 to the Year 1808, or the Thirty-third of Their Sovereignty and Independence.* 3 vols. Philadelphia: M. Carey and Son, 1818.

Schoolcraft, Henry Rowe. *The American Indians.* Rochester: Wanzer, Foot and Co., 1851.

――――. *Archives of Aboriginal Knowledge.* Philadelphia: J. B. Lippincott and Co., 1860.

――――. *History of the Indian Tribes of the United States: Their Present Condition and Prospects, and a Sketch of Their Ancient Status.* Philadelphia; J. B. Lippincott and Co., 1857.

Snelling, William Joseph. *A Brief and Impartial History of the Life and Actions of Andrew Jackson.* Boston: Stimpson and Clapp, 1831.

Stoddard, William Osborn. *Andrew Jackson and Martin Van Buren.* New York: F. A. Stokes, 1887.

Trumbull, Benjamin. *A Compendium of the Indian Wars in New England, More Particularly Such as the Colony of Connecticut Have Been Concerned and Active in, New Haven, August 25, anno 1767.* Hartford: F. B. Hartranft, 1924 (reprint). First edition Hartranft and Frederick Berg, 1868.

Tuttle, Charles Richard. *History of the Border Wars of Two Centuries, Embracing a Narrative of the Wars with the Indians from 1750 to 1874.* Chicago: C. A. Wall and Co., 1874.

Venable, William Henry. *A School History of the United States.* Cincinnati: Wilson, Hinkle and Co., 1872.

Waldo, Samuel Putnam. *Memoirs of Andrew Jackson, Major General in the Army of the United States; and Commander In Chief of the Division of the South.* Hartford: S. Andrus, 1819.

PUBLISHED DOCUMENTS

Bassett, John S., ed. *Correspondence of Andrew Jackson.* 6 vols. Washington: Carnegie Institution, 1926–27.

Carter, Clarence E., ed. *The Territory of Mississippi 1809–1817* vol. 6, 1938. *The Territorial Papers of the United States.* Washington: Government Printing Office, 1934—.

Lowrie, Walter, *et al.*, ed. *The American State Papers, Documents, Legislative, and Executive of the Congress of the United States.* 39 vols. Washington: Government Printing Office, 1832–61.

Rowland Dunbar, ed. *Official Letter Books of W.C.C. Claiborne, 1801–1816.* 6 vols. Jackson, Mississippi: State Department of Archives and History, 1917.

MORE RECENT BOOKS DEALING
WITH THE CREEK WAR

Abernethy, Thomas P. *The South in the New Nation, 1789–1819.* Baton Rouge: Louisiana State University Press, 1961.

Adams, Henry. *The War of 1812.* Washington: Infantry Journal Press, 1944.

Bassett, John S. *The Life of Andrew Jackson.* 2 vols. Garden City: Doubleday, Page and Co., 1911.

Beirne, Francis F. *The War of 1812.* New York: E. P. Dutton and Co, Inc., 1949.

Brown, John P. *Old Frontiers; the Story of the Cherokee Indians from the Earliest Times to the Date of Their Removal West, 1838.* Kingsport: Southern Publishers Inc., 1938.

Brown, Wilbert S. *The Amphibious Campaign For West Florida and Louisiana, 1814–1815.* University, Ala.: University of Alabama Press, 1969.

Buell, Augustus C. *A History of Andrew Jackson.* 2 vols. New York: Charles Scribner's Sons, 1904.

Caughey, John W. *Mcgillivray of the Creeks.* Norman: University of Oklahoma Press, 1959.

Coles, Harry L. *The War of 1812.* Chicago: University of Chicago Press, 1965.

Cotterill, Robert S. *The Southern Indians; The Story of the Civilized Tribes Before Removal.* Norman: University of Oklahoma Press, 1954.

Cox, Isaac Joslin. *The West Florida Controversy, 1789–1813 A Study in American Diplomacy.* Gloucester, Mass.: Peter Smith, 1967.

James, Marquis. *Andrew Jackson the Border Captain.* Indianapolis: Bobbs-Merrill Company, 1933.

Johnson, Gerald W. *Andrew Jackson, An Epic in Homespun.* New York: Milton Balch and Co., 1927.

Leckie, Robert. *The Wars of America.* New York: Harper and Row, 1968.

Patrick, Rembert W. *Florida Fiasco.* Athens: University of Georgia Press, 1954.

Pound, Merritt B. *Benjamin Hawkins, Indian Agent.* Athens: University of Georgia Press, 1951.

Pratt, JuliuM W. *Expansionists of 1812.* Gloucester, Mass. Peter Smith, 1957.

Silver, James W. *Edmund Pendleton Gaines Frontier General.* Baton Rouge: Louisiana State University Press, 1949.

Starkey, Marion L. *The Cherokee Nation.* New York: A. A. Knopf, 1946.

Whitaker, Arthur P. *The Spanish American Frontier; 1783–1795.* New York: Houghton Mifflin Co, 1927.

Woodward, Grace S. *The Cherokees.* Norman: University of Oklahoma Press, 1963.

Wright, J. Leitch, Jr. *William Augustus Bowles Director General of the Creek Nation.* Athens: University of Georgia Press, 1967.

ARTICLES DEALING WITH THE CREEK WAR

Boyd, Mark F. "Events at Prospect Bluff on the Apalachicola River, 1808–1818," *The Florida Historical Quarterly*, 14 (October, 1937), pp. 55–96.

Doster, James F. "Letters Relating to the Tragedy of Fort Mims: August–September, 1813," *The Alabama Review*, 14 (October, 1961), pp. 269–285.

Holland, James W. "Andrew Jackson and the Creek War: Victory at the Horseshoe," *The Alabama Review*, 21 (October, 1968), pp. 243–275.

McAlister, L. N. "Pensacola During the Second Spanish Period," *The Florida Historical Quarterly*, 32 (January–April, 1959), pp. 281–327.

Mahon, John K. "British Strategy and Southern Indians: War of 1812," *The Florida Historical Quarterly*, 44 (April, 1966), pp. 285–302.

Owsley, Frank L., Jr. "British and Indian Activities in Spanish West Florida During the War of 1812," *The Florida Historical Quarterly*, 46 (October, 1967), pp. 111–123.

————. "Jackson's Capture of Pensacola," *The Alabama Review*, 19 (July, 1966), pp. 175–185.

Stephen, Walter W. "Andrew Jackson's Forgotten Army," *The Alabama Review*, 12 (April, 1959), pp. 126–131.

West, Elizabeth H. "A Prelude to the Creek War of 1813–1814," *The Florida Historical Quarterly*, 18 (April, 1940), pp. 247–266.

Wright, J. Leitch, Jr. "A Note on the First Seminole War as seen by the Indians, Negroes, and Their British Advisers," *The Journal of Southern History*, 34 (November, 1968), pp. 565–575.

————. "British Designs on the Old Southwest: Foreign Intrigue on the Florida Frontier, 1783–1803," *The Florida Historical Quarterly*, 44 (April, 1966), pp. 265–284.

OFFICIAL MANUSCRIPT SOURCES

Archivo General de Indias, Seville, Spain.
1.   Papeles Procedentes de Cuba, Legajo 1794–1795, 1856.
British Public Record Office, London, England.
1.   Admiralty Office 1 vols. 505–509.
2.   Admiralty Office 50, vols. 87, 122.
3.   Colonial Office 23, vols. 58–61.
4.   Colonial Office 24, vol. 17.
5.   Foreign Office 5, vols. 139–140.
6.   Foreign Office 72, vols. 180, 219.

7. War Office 1, vols. 141–144.
8. War Office 6, vol. 2.

Georgia Department of Archives and History, Atlanta, Georgia.
1. Governor's Letterbook, Nov. 28, 1809–May 18, 1814.
2. Executive Minutes, Oct. 4, 1812–Apr. 20, 1814, Governor David Bridie Mitchell, and Peter Early.
3. Georgia Military Affairs, vol. 3.

Mississippi Department of Archives and History, Jackson, Mississippi.
1. Executive Journal of David Holmes, Governor of the Mississippi Territory, 1810–1814.

National Archives, Washington, D. C.
Record Group 107
1. Letters Sent, Military Affairs, vols. 7–8.
2. Letters to the Secretary of War.
3. Letters sent by the Secretary of War, Indian Affairs, 1800–1824.
4. Letters sent to the President by the Secretary of War, 1800–1863, vol. 1.

UNOFFICIAL MANUSCRIPT COLLECTIONS

Alabama Department of Archives and History, Montgomery, Alabama.
1. Manuscript Section
   A. The John Coffee Papers.
   B. The Henry S. Halbert Papers.
   C. The A. B. Meek Manuscript "History of Alabama."
   D. The Albert J. Pickett Papers.
2. Military Section, Books 205 and 207. Typed copies of letters relating to the Creek War.

Florida Historical Society, University of South Florida, Tampa, Florida.
1. The Cruzat Papers.
2. The Greenslade Papers.

Georgia Department of Archives, Atlanta, Georgia.
1. The collected letters of Benjamin Hawkins (typed copies from originals located here and in other archives).
2. Copies of letters written during the War of 1812–14 by General John Floyd to his daughter Mary Hazzard Floyd,

presented to the General Floyd Chapter, National Society of the Daughters of 1812 by Laura E. Blackshear (a copy in this archives).

3. Creek Letters (a collection of typed copies).
4. The John Floyd Papers.
5. The Benjamin Hawkins Papers.

Library of Congress, Washington, D. C.

1. The Andrew Jackson Papers.
2. The Benjamin Hawkins Papers.

Mississippi Departmen. of Archives and History, Jackson Mississippi.

1. The J. F. H. Claiborne Collection, "Letters relating to the Indian Wars, 1812–1816," Letterbook "F."

Mobile Public Library, Mobile, Alabama.

1. The John Forbes Papers.

National Library of Scotland, Edinburgh, Scotland.

1. The Papers of Admiral Alexander Forrester Inglis Cochrane (portion dealing with Indians is designated MS 2328).

National Maritime Museum, Greenwich, England.

1. The Codrington Collection, designated Cod/7.

State Historical Society of Wisconsin, Madison, Wisconsin.

1. The Lyman Draper Manuscript Collection.
   A. The Georgia, Alabama, and South Carolina Papers, series V, vol. 1.
   B. The Tecumseh Papers, series YY, vols. 1–13.

Tennessee Historical Society, Nashville, Tennessee.

1. The John Coffee Papers.
2. The Emil Hurja Collection.
3. The Andrew Jackson Papers.
4. Miscellaneous files (contain many letters on the Creek War).
5. The John Read Manuscript, "Life of Andrew Jackson."

Tennessee State Library, Nashville, Tennessee.

1. The Joseph Carson Papers.
2. The Andrew Jackson Papers.

University of Georgia, Athens, Georgia.

1. The Telamon Cuyler Collection.

University of Oklahoma, Norman, Oklahoma.

1. The Eloise D. Smock Collection.

EDITOR'S INDEX.